D0233274

Bold Man of the Sea

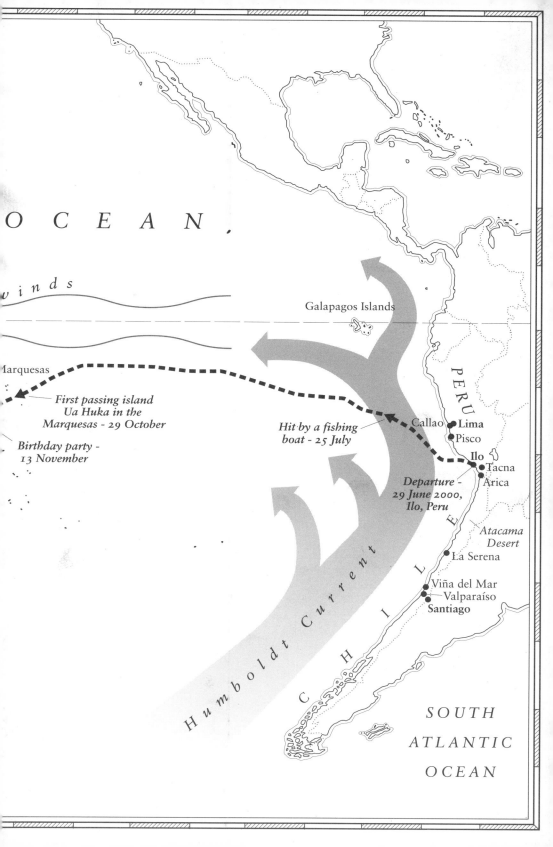

OCEAN

winds

Galapagos Islands

Marquesas

First passing island
Ua Huka in the
Marquesas - 29 October

Birthday party -
13 November

PERU

Callao • Lima
• Pisco

Hit by a fishing
boat - 25 July

Ilo
• Tacna
Arica

Departure -
29 June 2000,
Ilo, Peru

Atacama
Desert
• La Serena

Viña del Mar
• Valparaíso
Santiago

Humboldt Current

C H I L E

SOUTH

ATLANTIC

OCEAN

Jim Shekhdar
with Edward Griffiths

Bold Man of the Sea

My Epic Journey

To Kate

Live Your Dreams

Best Wishes

Hodder & Stoughton

Copyright © 2001 by Jim Shekhdar

First published in Great Britain in 2001
by Hodder and Stoughton
A division of Hodder Headline

The right of Jim Shekhdar to be identified as the Author of
the Work has been asserted by him in accordance with the
Copyright, Designs and Patents Act 1988.

2 4 6 8 10 9 7 5 3 1

All rights reserved. No part of this publication may be
reproduced, stored in a retrieval system, or transmitted,
in any form or by any means without the prior written
permission of the publisher, nor be otherwise circulated
in any form of binding or cover other than that in which
it is published and without a similar condition being
imposed on the subsequent purchaser.

A CIP catalogue record for this title
is available from the British Library

ISBN 0 340 82170 1

Typeset in Monotype Sabon by
Rowland Phototypesetting Ltd,
Bury St Edmunds, Suffolk
Printed and bound in Great Britain by
Clays Ltd, St Ives plc

Hodder and Stoughton
A division of Hodder Headline
338 Euston Road
London NW1 3BH

This book is dedicated to Doris Shekhdar, my mother, who sacrificed whatever was necessary for her children; to Sybil Riley, my mother-in-law, a determined woman in her own right; and to Nariman Shekhdar, my father, in the hope that he feels his faith in me has finally been rewarded.

'Whatever you can do, or dream you can, begin it.
Boldness has genius, power and magic in it.
Begin it now.'

Goethe

Contents

List of Illustrations

Section 1

1. Restless, impatient, looking for the next challenge . . .
2. Building the boat
   Susan Hampshire launches our boat at the Ruislip Lido
   Uxbridge Gazette
3. Early sea trials with David Jackson
   My consignment of pre-cooked meals
4. Charging up the coast of Peru
   Passing through customs at the Chile-Peru border
5. The press conference at Ilo
   Setting off from Ilo, during the festival of St Peter and
   St Paul *Paul Visscher*
6. One of the sharks that repeatedly battered my boat
   My home-made harpoon
   A yellow-fin tuna landing on the deck
7. A ship passing too close for comfort
   The natural beauty of a classic Pacific sunset
8. I just managed to skip past the west coast of Ua Pou

Section 2

9. Happy Birthday to me!
10. At work beside the hatch leading to the cabin
    PA Photos
    Wear and tear: a broken oar *Geoff Pettingill*
    Small boat, big ocean . . .

*All photographs from author's collection unless otherwise
credited.*

Acknowledgements

At first glance, ocean rowing might appear to be the ultimate individual activity. It ought to follow that a list of acknowledgements should be short.

The reality is somewhat different, and this list is long. I have no doubt it should be even longer and, at the outset, I apologise to all those people who helped the 'team' effort but whose names do not appear here.

First and foremost, I thank my wife Jane and my daughters, Anna and Sarah: first, for their love and support; second, for possessing the power to prevent me embarking upon this voyage, but declining to use that power and therefore making the voyage possible; and third, for meeting me on the beach in Australia and creating the most emotional moment of my life.

I thank other members of my family who assisted me along the way: my sister Jan and her husband, Ken, and my nephew Sacha, who even asked the United States Coastguard to keep an eye out for his uncle.

William Butler Yeats wrote that you should judge people by their friends; well, I am extremely proud to be judged by an outstanding group of friends and sponsors who seemed to care and, in that caring, encouraged me towards my destination: David and Jo Jackson, Paul and Maggie Sivey, Nigel and Laura Clutterbuck, Andy Lench, Roger Marwood, Iain Hutchison, Sue and Bruce Degnan, Keith Knowles, Paul Sumpner, Tim Harris, Steve Morris, Rob Malos, Ian Williams, Andy Salomonson, Nigel Rutter, Sinisha Cipkalo, Jozsef Bartuszek and Rajesh Patel.

Companies that these people represent, and who were generous enough to part-sponsor my expedition, include: Le Shark,

BHS, Mobil, Bordeaux Wine Investments, C-Maps, Globecom, Mobilecom Europe, Johnston, G-Push, Bartex 2000, Expedition Foods, Yacht Parts, Callipygian, Degnan Utility Services and Axis Health Clubs.

I am also enormously grateful to members of the AJS Management team in Slovakia who suffered the consequences of my irritation and impatience prior to my departure, most notably Renata Prokova, Martin Catlos, Zuzana Izakova, Renata Pokorna and Erna Dohnalikova; Daniel Strasser, webmaster extraordinaire; and also Yveta Absolonova in the Czech Republic.

As the fifth chapter of this book relates, there are many, many people in Chile and Peru who voluntarily offered their services to me with a charm and a degree of generosity that I found totally humbling. These people include: Pat Waggaman and Paul Visscher, whose names, in truth, should really appear in lights across the cover of this book; in Chile, Giovanni Villaroel, Victor Figueroa, Ximena Montes de Oca, Colleen Baldwin and Carmen Gironás; in Peru, Horty Visscher, Bruno and Jackie Rodriguez, Hugo and Karina Navarrete, Wilfredo and Maria Jose Contreras, Cesar and Magali Aza, Angel and Yolanda Rodriguez, Roberto and Sonia Diaz, Jorge and Mariana Guerrero, Luis and Lily Garcia, Luis and Patricia Gonzalez, Armando and Mariela Vidal, Erick and Ursula Salazar, Weymar Contreras, Carlos Alegria, Jorge Guerrero (senior), Armando Vidal, Corinne Flores Cesar Ulfe, Mayor Ernesto Herrera, Lucho Gonzalez, Pepe Cerdena, Jose Enchandia, Jorge Pesaressi, Cristina Visscher, the Peruvian Navy and Trasub SRL, Paul Visscher's company.

I fear they will never read this book, but I should also like to thank Big Fish and her school of yellow-fin tuna who kept me company for so long.

At the opposite end of my voyage, in Australia, I would like to thank the following people and organisations for confirming the reputations of their country's outstanding hospitality, warmth and enthusiasm: Ken Brown, the Australian Coastguard,

Acknowledgements

Queensland Weather Bureau, Channel Seven, Channel Nine and Channel Ten, Peter Doherty, Alan Gordon and ANL, Tony Barker and P&O Ports, Allan Spurling, Andrew Monks and the Royal Queensland Yacht Squadron, Stewart Bell and Belco Trailers, and the Straddie Islanders, particularly Geoff and Julie Pettingill, and Tony Jennings.

Since the completion of the voyage, I am grateful to many people who have assisted me in facing a new, and at times equally daunting, challenge. Alon Schulman, of World Famous, and Sophie Hicks, of Ed Victor Ltd, have been, and continue to be, tremendously supportive. I am also indebted to Eddie Kohn and Maurice Selwyn.

And, lastly, it would not have been possible to produce this account of my voyage without the various writing, editing and proofing skills of Edward Griffiths, Roland Philipps and the outstanding staff at Hodder & Stoughton in London, and Barbara Ahuja, a long-lost friend from Canada.

In the end, far from being an individual exercise, this adventure turned out to be a team effort and I am grateful to every member of that team.

Jim Shekhdar
August 2001
Northwood

Foreword

'The wild blue yonder' has been a call rooted in the restless movements of man and his/her forefathers for thousands of generations. It is a summons not only to and beyond the horizon, but to find a place where we can express our own individuality for a time, to find peace, adventure and perhaps a home. All of us hear this summons to some degree, and we have unique reactions to it.

This call is paradoxical, and it is heard by everyone – to travel to and beyond the horizon – yet it calls each to his or her own horizon of individuality. An immense range of answers is found, reflecting the varied magnificence of human expression. For some boxed in by the demands of workaday and family life, their individuality may be expressed in the design of their home, or in an auto with the chrome tailfins of the moment; for Jim Shekhdar it was a 274-day solo crossing of the Pacific.

Jim's experiences in fighting his way clear to set off are typical of many of us: he was overweight, hemmed in by the demands of business and family, yet beginning to see light at the end of his career and financial tunnels, and finding a need in the spirit for more. Jim broke through the barriers of the land and off on the voyage towards the horizon. There he found the beauty and the spontaneity, the fear and the boredom, of a life closer to its origins. He made friends with fishes, found fear in sharks and tankers, thought much of life and gloried in his quest. Physically he finished the voyage in much better shape than he began it; he also found a rhythm of nature at sea – and transformed the sea into a home – over and beyond the horizon of daily life.

It seems a great pity to settle for a differently coloured plastic case on a mobile phone as the expression of one's spirit and individuality. May Jim's voyage inspire you in your own life, as you hear and continue to hear the call of the wild blue yonder – whatever it may represent for you, you can make it happen.

Pat Waggaman
August 2001
Concon, Chile

Thomas Ennalls (Pat) Waggaman is a Cape Horner, a business-man, an American based in Chile and one of those people whose selfless commitment enabled Jim Shekhdar to complete his voyage; in his own right, a bold man of the sea.

Introduction

Tell someone you are thinking of rowing across the Pacific Ocean and they will tell you about their last holiday in Bognor. Tell somebody that you have actually spent more than nine months rowing alone across the Pacific Ocean and they will stare at you as though you are mad and utter one word.

'Why?'

Why did I want to spend so much time alone? Why did I want to spend so long on a twenty-three-foot rowing boat? Why did I want to put myself in such a potentially dangerous situation? And why, when no major sponsors emerged, was I happy to put £75,000 of my own money into the adventure?

There are many reasons. Since the completion of my trip, one newspaper generously referred to me as 'one of the last great adventurers', but I never saw myself in such exalted terms. I am a businessman from Northwood, in Middlesex, near London, who has always needed an occasional injection of excitement in his life and who wanted to do something extraordinary. This is my story.

Why did I do it?

The first reason is that I wanted to row across the Pacific because nobody had done it before. Passing my fiftieth birthday as just another stressed, overweight entrepreneur, I felt an urge to do something completely new. People tend to live their lives from one meal to the next, from one meeting to the next, earning their money and spending their money. I wanted to break out of that captive cycle and do something nobody else had been able to do before.

I was not motivated by any hunger for glory or publicity.

After spending two frustrating years trying to raise sponsorship, I came to the conclusion that, with the exception of a handful of enthusiastic individuals willing to support me, nobody was very much interested in my plans. No, I wanted to break new ground for my own spirit, my own self-esteem, just for me.

In a sense, it was the most selfish thing I have ever done. I recognise that, but there has always been and there will always be a strong element of selfishness at the core of any major expedition such as this. One has to be totally focused and single-minded, even bloody-minded, to get off the blocks.

There were a couple of uncompleted business projects in Eastern Europe, but I delegated the responsibility to my colleagues because I had decided I was going to row across the Pacific Ocean. There were several outstanding issues in the purchase of a flat for one of my two daughters in Bristol, bridging loans to be fixed and contracts to be signed, but I dropped these on my wife Jane because I had decided I was going to row across the Pacific Ocean.

It did not matter what happened. I was going to row. Nobody was forcing me to take almost a year out of my life; nobody was asking me to spend so much money; nobody needed me to make the voyage. Most people seemed to think it was a pretty silly thing to do. It was my decision, and it is an inescapable fact that my resolve made unreasonable demands on other people. Some of them could not understand then. I sincerely hope they all understand now.

The seed of my strange ambition was sown in 1997, when I rowed across the Atlantic Ocean with my friend, David Jackson. It was towards the end of that sixty-five-day voyage that we discussed what we would do next. David wanted to cycle across the United States of America, and I said I wanted to do something nobody had done before, effectively to walk on virgin snow. That was crucial to me. That was my *raison d'être* and, after some debate, I settled upon the idea of rowing, unsupported and alone, across the Pacific Ocean.

Others had tried: most notably Peter Bird, of Britain, whose tragic loss at sea during his seventh attempt in 1996 prompted the formation of the Ocean Rowing Society; and Frenchman Gerard d'Aboville in 1991. But no one had ever completed the long route across the South Pacific, from continent to continent, without receiving any physical assistance of any kind, without being towed at any stage, without being replenished with supplies, solo.

Andrew Halsey, another Briton, who started a voyage from San Diego in July 1999, spent 266 days on the ocean but was blown in the wrong direction and eventually had to be rescued from his boat, *Brittany Rose*. Joseph Le Guen, a formidable French sailor and rower, launched a bid from New Zealand in February 2000, but suffered infected feet, developed gangrene and also needed to be rescued. His toes were amputated shortly afterwards.

Rowing oceans can seriously damage your health.

Coincidentally, Halsey and Le Guen foundered within three days of each other during the first week of April 2000. If either of them had completed the trip, I don't believe I would have set off from Peru at the end of June. I wanted to be the first man to row, unaided, across the Pacific Ocean. If either Joe or Andrew had succeeded before me, I would have found something else to do.

Perhaps I was being naive, but all my preparation and planning led me to emphatically believe the voyage remained possible. The first 100 miles and the last 100 miles appeared to be the hardest parts, where one would have to battle against winds and currents around coasts, but the enormous middle section of the trip would just happen, with the current and wind carrying me along. I knew it would be tough and I knew it would be exhausting but, as long as I looked after myself and rowed within my limitations, I believed all would be well.

I grew increasingly excited to have found something that not only had not been done before, but that also seemed relatively straightforward. At least, that was what I thought at the time, contemplating the voyage as I sat in the comfort of our dining room at Northwood in Middlesex. It was not until I reached the deep blue yonder that the reality of lashing storms, oil tankers and hurricanes started to permeate my consciousness and enter the equation.

It also occurred to me that a Pacific voyage would give me an opportunity to rediscover the fit and lean body of my youth, and to break the downward spiral brought on by middle age; and I was right. Nine relentless months of regular and rigorous exercise and stable diet transformed the obese, bloated figure that rowed away from Ilo, Peru on 29 June 2000, into the relatively fit and healthy 54-year-old man that emerged from the breaking waves near Brisbane, on 30 March the following year.

At the start of the trip, my gut was actually wider than my chest. When I arrived in Australia, much to my relief, order had been restored. In addition, my psoriasis had disappeared, the pain in my arthritic hip had eased and my blood pressure had been reduced from 180/130 to 120/60. I also had more hair; sadly, mostly on my face rather than my head.

Rowing oceans can cure almost anything.

So why row across the Pacific . . . Because nobody had done it before, because it seemed achievable, because it would make me feel physically young again and, lastly, because I felt I would benefit from effectively stepping out of my life to take mental stock of my professional and personal progress.

I certainly did not fear the prospect of solitude and, for the first two months of fair winds and currents, the sensation of being alone was wonderful. Inevitably there were moments of profound loneliness and, in spite of our regular telephone conversations, I constantly missed my wife and two daughters. My oft-repeated remark that I rowed across the Pacific to 'get away from the wife' was a joke that had started to wear thin by the umpteenth media interview.

Yet I did believe I would enjoy an extended period away from the pains of my working life as a management consultant and engineer, mercifully removed from the bureaucracy, lies and deceit that seem endemic in the corporate world. I yearned for an environment devoid of man-made crises and people-induced stress. On the ocean, nothing is artificial or false. It is pure, unadulterated nature, not always friendly but always honest. The simplicity is compelling.

All the nonsense seemed to be washed away. In my mind, I was able to resolve business situations that had previously seemed fraught and complex. I was able to sit and ponder how to be a better husband, a better father, a better friend. Rowing across an ocean for nine months could be likened to an extended visit to a health farm: everything was cleansed.

I had something to prove, not so much to anyone else as to myself. I was resolved to show that, even at fifty-four, I could still become the first to complete a voyage that no man had accomplished before. I have always believed objectives should be set just out of reach. One can have intermediate goals to give oneself a boost along the way, but the paramount goal must stretch the individual.

This is why I rowed across the Pacific Ocean.

And, lastly, I wanted to do something to make my family proud. I wanted to see the pride and pleasure in their eyes when I reached my destination. That was the image that sustained me through 274 days, more than 10,000 miles, regular disasters and daily mood swings. And it happened.

Approaching five o'clock on the afternoon of Friday, 30 March 2001, on the beach at North Stradbroke Island, four miles from Brisbane, on the east coast of Australia, I felt exactly that pride and pleasure. Amid the tears and surf, in the moment that I was reunited with my wife Jane and our two daughters, Sarah and Anna, I saw precisely why I had rowed across the Pacific Ocean.

I looked into their eyes, and understood everything.

I

The Joy

Is that Australia or is it another cloud on the horizon?

Early on the morning of Friday, 30 March 2001, I stood tall in the middle of the boat, about seven feet above sea level, and peered west hoping to discover that I was within sight of my destination. It looked like land, but I couldn't be certain. In my excitement, I telephoned my family at the Hilton Hotel in Brisbane to tell them I could see the coastline. It was extremely early in the morning, and my daughter was half asleep. She blearily asked if she could call me back.

The day dragged on, the boat edged forward. I felt as though I was being buffeted between complete exhaustion because I had hardly slept in the past forty-eight hours, and unbridled exhilaration because my voyage was almost complete. It felt as if the telephone had been ringing endlessly, and I seemed constantly in conversation with either the media, my family, the coastguard or the weather bureau.

It was nine months and one day since my departure from Peru, and I was now desperate to see my family, drink a cold beer, eat an ice cream and then go home, preferably in that order. Events had started to accelerate towards the end, assuming their own momentum. I breathed deep and slow, striving to control the powerful surges of adrenalin that pumped through my body.

By half past three in the afternoon, I gazed west again. At last, there was no doubt in my mind at all. I was close enough to see the beach. My spirits soared. Within moments, I could see it was also an empty beach. My heart sank at the thought that I had travelled more than 10,000 miles and would now land alone.

Where was Jane? Where were my girls?

I swooped into the cabin and switched on the VHF radio, frantically trying different frequencies. I tried Channel 16, the default channel for anyone in a boat. There was nobody there. I switched to Channel 6, the channel monitored by search and rescue teams.

'This is *Le Shark*. Can anybody read me? Over. Is anyone there?'

Silence.

'This is *Le Shark*. Can anybody read me? Hello? Hello?'

The sky had been full of helicopters for the past three days, carrying television crews filming the final stages of my voyage; various members of the family or others who had flown out from England to meet me. But now there was nothing. I was about to land, and there was nobody. Five minutes passed like five days until, at last, I saw the Channel Seven helicopter rise above the sand dunes to the south. I tried the radio again, and the pilot responded.

'Everyone's a couple of miles south, down the beach, mate,' he told me, 'but we've told them that we would fly back to the beach in a straight line from where we find you, so we'll get them in the right place. No worries.'

'Oh,' I said. 'Thank you very much.'

There had been a misunderstanding and it had been entirely my fault. In my continual state of excitement, or perhaps exhaustion, I had misread my loyal and trusty C-Map electronic chart, giving the coastguard the precise position of my plotter cursor (a target landing site set several hours earlier), rather than the boat. It was a foolish mistake, but all was well, and I was able to laugh out loud at another crisis resolved.

I stood and looked towards 'Straddie' again.

Back in 1995, we had visited this exact section of the Queensland coast during a family holiday that was designed to show the girls a few life skills before they headed out into the world on their own. I wanted them to see Australia, the only country that I have visited where I had been sorely tempted to settle. We stayed in a backpacker's hostel on 'Straddie' and loved the place. Back then, none of us could have imagined the scene that would unfold on this same stretch of coast six years later.

There was still nobody to be seen on the beach. I sat down in the boat that had been my home for nine months and would be for barely an hour longer. My head was spinning. I was excited to finish, but I was also apprehensive about the nature and scale of the reception that lay ahead on dry land.

After being alone for so long, the prospect of finding myself among people again appeared daunting. In a perfect world, I wanted to reach the shore, give a few media interviews and then escape to somewhere quiet, beautiful and private with my family. I knew that was what Jane would have liked, but I also knew that, if the explosive blast of media attention during the past few days was any guide, the reality was going to be substantially more frenetic.

Before and during the voyage, most people had seemed to reckon I was some kind of mad Englishman who would not only never reach Australia but who would in fact be lucky to leave the Pacific on his feet rather than in a body bag.

However, now that I was nearing my destination, everything changed and I was being persistently pursued for radio and television interviews. I always tried to be co-operative, but the purpose of my voyage had never been to win publicity and attention. The experience of being blanked so often had convinced me that what was happening now was totally out of reach. Conversely, now that it was becoming a fact of my daily life, my instinct was to shy away from the microphones, maybe even to keep rowing, to stay on the water, to hang around with my friendly fish.

Such thoughts did not last long. In reality, I did not see my future as some kind of latter-day aquatic Tarzan. Within moments, the prospect of being reunited with my wife and girls flooded my senses, and I looked towards the shore once again.

At last, there were signs of activity. I was gobsmacked to see more than thirty four-wheel drive vehicles parked on the beach, three helicopters buzzing in the sky and a huddled crowd of not less than six hundred people.

The challenge of safely negotiating the last mile of the voyage had concerned me for several days. My solid, heavy boat had been constructed to be stable in the ocean and was far removed from the lighter, more manoeuvrable craft generally used to operate in surf and breaking seas.

A couple of days earlier, in urgent need of local knowledge, I became indebted to the Channel Seven television reporter who provided me with the telephone number of Ken Brown, a lively character known to all and sundry as 'Brownie', who hosts a daily thirty-minute radio show called *Coastwatch*. If anyone would know the safest way and place to get ashore in this part of Queensland, it would be Brownie.

With his skilful assistance, it eventually became evident that I was heading for North Stradbroke Island, prompting a debate on the boat whether this stretch of coast would count as part of Australia. The alternatives were to navigate a path between North and South Stradbroke Island, or to reach the mainland through the gap between North Stradbroke Island and Moreton Island. Brownie's advice was that neither option was easily navigable, and that I should land at North Straddie.

Some weeks earlier when it looked like I might come ashore on Fraser Island I had instigated a debate via the telephone and Internet as to whether a gap of less than one mile between an island and the mainland constituted a mainland finish. The conclusion had been that it did. On North Straddie, the gap was less than 200 yards, definitely not sufficient to invalidate completing my stated objective. Needless to say there was no dissent from any who entered the debate, including Brownie whose response was: 'Get to Straddie, mate, and you have reached Australia.'

He continued: 'But, Jim, there is going to be a very powerful cross-break as you come in, so I would strongly recommend that you put the sea anchor out the back to give yourself a chance of arriving right side up.'

I knew he was absolutely right. If *Le Shark* was to survive the surf, it would need the additional stabilising force of the underwater parachute that drags 150 yards behind the boat. His advice made perfect sense.

And yet, and yet . . . I wanted to finish the voyage in style and, in my view, that meant catching the crest of a breaking wave and surfing right to the beach. That would be thrilling and spectacular, but also risky. I faced a choice between the dull security of the sea anchor and daring to ride a wave. After travelling for so long and so far, to me that seemed no choice at all.

My initial intention had been to complete the voyage looking every inch the seafaring gentleman, dressed in a blazer and trousers, and I had packed clothes precisely for this purpose. However, now that I was going to arrive on a beach in what appeared likely to be an uncontrolled manner, the formal attire would be out of context and pointless, so I dressed in a T-shirt and shorts.

I even dispensed with the safety harness because, if the boat did capsize, I would much rather be thrown clear than be tied to the craft and run the risk of being trapped beneath the hull.

As the end approached, two surf life-savers appeared alongside my boat in a rubber duck. Brownie had arranged for them to travel up from Southport and be on hand just in case anything went wrong. I was pleased to see them but, in my general state of excitement, I left them in no doubt that they must not come within fifty yards of me unless I was clearly unconscious.

I had set out to cross the Pacific alone and unaided, and I was determined to do nothing less, even in the last 200 yards of the trip.

As I approached the breaking waves, the telephone rang again. It was the producer from GMTV, the ITV breakfast show in

England, and they wanted to conduct a live interview. I said that would be fine but they would have to be quick. With one hand holding the telephone, and the other trying to control the rudder, I answered questions for a few frantic minutes. 'I am about to be very happy or to be drowned,' I told the television audience, burying my nerves in bravado. 'I am not sure which. There is a fifteen-foot cross-breaking surf running at the moment, and this boat has never seen anything like it before.'

It was twenty to seven in the morning at home, and I don't know how it must have sounded to people waking up but I had to cut short the interview, saying: 'I must go. Waves are breaking around me. I have to go.' With that, I put down the telephone, switched off all power from the battery, battened down the hatch and braced myself for one last duel with the Pacific Ocean. As the sea growled and rumbled beneath me, I knew it was going to be sink or swim.

The first breaking wave turned the boat through forty-five degrees; the second crashed into the side and tipped us to an angle fractionally less than ninety degrees. It was clear the awesome Pacific was not finished with me yet. A third huge wave thudded into the boat with such force that, for the first time in crossing both the Atlantic and Pacific oceans, I was thrown into the water.

As I fell, the top of my inside right leg was hurled against the safety strap running down one side of the boat; the effect of this was to squeeze all the fat around my thigh down towards the knee. The harsh pain only started when I reached shore, but the bruising lasted and a strange lump of flesh remains.

My understanding of what happened next is based on what I have seen on the news footage filmed from helicopters above. At the time, it felt as though I had been hurled into a giant, ruthless washing machine.

I emerged from the froth twelve seconds after being thrown overboard and found myself more than thirty yards from the boat. My instinct was to swim back to *Le Shark* and, somehow,

I managed to clamber aboard again. I had just regained my seat and was wildly pulling on the starboard oar to bring the stern into position when another huge breaking wave finally capsized the boat. Yet again the safety strap ripped down the top of my right leg, and I was hurled into a boiling sea. For nine months, we had managed to keep the ocean beneath us; now the boat and I were at the mercy of the elements, to be tossed and turned.

Yet the tide, quite literally, was moving in our direction. The boat managed to right itself, precisely as it was designed to do; I surfaced again and, yard by yard, we were both carried towards the shore.

I was at no stage particularly worried by these developments, although several people on the beach did become alarmed when they saw an empty boat. My anxious sister, Jan, was one of those urging somebody to get in the water and rescue me, but there was no problem. I was swimming comfortably not far away and was certainly, at that point, concealed by the swell.

At that stage in fact, my major concern was to avoid being slammed against the boat by another breaker. I was driven pre-cariously close to the hull at one stage, but fortunately the boat was more buoyant than it was before and the wave carrying me also moved the boat further on towards our shared destination.

The concluding stages of our voyage may not have been elegant, but they provided some spectacular images on television news bulletins around the world, and I was able to swim the last 200 yards to shore in relative safety.

I may have been exhausted through lack of sleep, and my damaged right leg was beginning to falter, but I was soon over-whelmed by an amazing sense of uninhibited happiness when I saw my daughters, Sarah and Anna, splashing into the sea. Each stroke took me closer to the end, closer to them.

Soaked to the skin, smiling broadly through my long, white and drenched beard, I was finally amongst them. That moment when I held the girls for the first time in ten months, one under each arm, all of us standing waist-deep in the sea, remains as perhaps the most emotional experience of my life. My finishing line had turned out to be the welcoming arms of my daughters on a magnificent Australian beach. What more could I have wanted? Every valve and tap in my usually reliable emotional plumbing seemed to burst under the pressure.

'Don't touch the boat! Whatever you do, don't touch the boat,' I shouted, mindful that my goal had been to cross the Pacific Ocean without assistance, all the way from Peru to Australia without any physical assistance. I was not in any kind of race. I was not competing under any agreed regulations. I just wanted to finish, completely unaided

Arm in arm, we waded towards the beach. I appeared to stumble at one point, and insisted at the time that I had stepped in a hole in the sand. In reality, my right leg had started to scream with pain. Exhausted and exhilarated, I was also in agony, but nothing could wipe the smile from my face.

I searched for Jane. She had been taking photographs from the beach but now joined us in the water. We held each other and kissed. We were together as a family again, secure and successful. I have never known such high elation, never known such a surge of relief and satisfaction.

When I lifted my head beyond my immediate family, I was truly astonished to see the number of people who had gathered to welcome me. Representatives from most Australian, British and international media organisations were present and many local citizens stood by and applauded as I found myself submerged by another sea, now of lights, cameras and microphones.

Jan stood nearby. Eddie Kohn, managing director of Le Shark, one of my largest sponsors, was there. Nigel Rutter, a friend and one of the most talented video makers in the business, had flown to witness my departure in Peru and was now present to witness my arrival in Australia. Kenneth Crutchlow, director of the Ocean Rowing Society, was the other man who had not only sent me on my way in Ilo but had also been on North Stradbroke Island.

The Joy

The sand felt wonderful beneath my feet and someone thrust a can of beer into my hand. It hardly touched the sides as I drank down my first beer in nine months, and my declared second wish was then granted when I was handed an ice cream. This too was devoured.

Even now, I find it hard to recall these scenes without my eyes welling and a lump filling my throat. I consider myself extremely fortunate to have experienced such a remarkable moment of fulfilment and utter vindication.

It was a life-affirming moment of joy, pure twenty-four-carat joy.

2

The First Fifty Years

Several sandwiches short of a picnic; the lift doesn't go to the top floor; stark raving bonkers; not merely alone on the ocean but a loon on the ocean.

Many people reckoned I must be mad.

Those who know me a little better have hopefully grown to recognise that I am not certifiably insane but I admit, I do tend to be unconventional in the sense that, in my eyes, everything is either black or white. I considered whether it was possible to row across the Pacific. I concluded it was, so I did.

Of course, there are perilously thin lines between being self-assured and being inconsiderate, between being self-confident and being arrogant; and there have surely been occasions when I have come down on the wrong side of those lines, but my aim has always been to be straightforward and sincere, to settle on a decision and insistently to follow it through. If it makes sense to me, it does not really matter to me whether people think I am crazy or not.

There is a section in my *curriculum vitae* where I refer to these aspects of my personality under the heading, Annoying Characteristics That May Help: 'Arrogant, confident in his own capabilities, indestructible, well-cushioned, likes himself so should not be lonely.' There is many a true word spoken in jest.

This unconventional nature was possibly the inevitable consequence of an unconventional upbringing. My family name originates from Persia and my father, Nariman Shekhdar, was born in Karachi, then part of India. A strong-willed young man, he left home without the consent of his parents and emigrated to England. Naturalised as soon as possible, he enthusiastically stood to sing 'God Save the King' and brought up his family to be and feel 100 per cent British.

My father trained as an engineer, worked in Germany during the 1930s and, in 1936, married Doris Paget, my mother, who came from York. The young couple had met when they were both working for the English Electric Company and settled in Leamington Spa, Warwickshire. In time, they produced three children: my sister Jan was born in 1940, my brother Bob in 1943 and me in 1946. We were not wealthy by any means; indeed, an old family tale runs that my infant brother once slept in a shoebox. But we were together and we were happy. My first clear memory is of sitting on my sister's bed, eating her chocolate, a rare luxury in those days. Many years later, the vivid recollection of happy times like these would lift my spirits whenever I felt lonely on the Pacific.

It was not long before I began the nomadic trend that would be sustained throughout the first fifty years of my life. I have always enjoyed travelling, meeting new people and experiencing new countries, and I have always enjoyed coming home to England as well. In 1953, when I was seven, my father took a five-year engineering contract with the Tata Iron and Steel Company in India. Our family travelled east by boat and we lived in the town of Jamshedpur.

My brother and I enrolled at the Jesuit High School and we enjoyed a typically colonial life, spending most of our time outdoors and regularly getting involved in scrapes and scraps that could be described as 'adventures'. However, my sister did not particularly enjoy India, at that time still a country where women were treated as second-class citizens. She returned to England after only two years, and went to live with family friends.

The highlight of these years on the subcontinent was a holiday when my mother arranged to take my brother and me to Darjeeling, where we were able to stand on Tiger Hill and look across towards the summit of Mount Everest rising in the distance.

I remember being somewhat underwhelmed by the view. Maybe my eager schoolboy's mind anticipated something far more grand and imposing than what looked like just another mountain on the horizon.

However, we were thrilled when we had the opportunity to meet Sherpa Tenzing, the Tibetan who had famously reached the summit of Everest with Sir Edmund Hillary in 1953. It was wonderful to shake the hand of a man celebrated around the world for being the first to climb the highest mountain on earth. I had read his book avidly, and had taken it with me, and he kindly signed his name inside the front cover. Even at the age of seven, I was enthused by the idea of setting oneself against the great natural challenges.

We returned to England in 1959 and, upon boarding the boat home, were delighted to discover that we had once again booked on the maiden voyage of a brand new P&O liner, just as we had on the way out to India. I enjoyed crossing the broad, blue oceans even at the age of twelve, although at that time I was not to know I would not always be able to do so in such luxury.

And I felt as comfortable in the water as I did on the water. I had actually been taught to swim on the boat travelling to India and then swam regularly in Jamshedpur. When we settled back home in Leamington Spa, I wasted no time in locating and joining the Leamington Swimming Club.

The club was run by Mr and Mrs Jelfs, as I knew them (Bob and Vera to their many friends), and their commitment was extraordinary. I started to train regularly with their son, Bob, swimming every morning before school and often again later in the afternoon. It was not long, however, before Bob and I decided swimming length after length was boring. We began to focus on water polo as a much more interesting, stimulating activity in the pool.

There have been many occasions over the years when I have had cause to thank the entire Jelfs family for their wonderful support, but I was particularly indebted to them all when my mother died suddenly in 1963.

She had travelled to visit my father in Ghana, where he was working on an engineering project, and she returned home with malaria. The diagnosis of her condition was slow in coming and she suffered complications with her kidneys before passing away. I was sixteen years old, and distraught. If I close my eyes and think of my mother now, I see her standing outside the swimming pool ready to buy me fish and chips on the way to catch the bus home from club night. She supported me in every way possible, helped me realise my potential and never hesitated to sacrifice herself for the family.

My father rushed home for the funeral, but could not break his contract in Ghana and he returned to Africa to finish his work there soon afterwards. My sister Jan courageously accepted the maternal role, staying as acting parent for as long as necessary. However, in 1967, when I had settled into college, she travelled to live with our Uncle Harold and Auntie Rachel in Edmonton, Canada.

It was further agreed that I would spend extended periods living with the Jelfs family. Nobody could have asked for a more loving and supportive environment from their natural parents, let alone from friends who had agreed to look after us during a time of such searing sadness.

In grief, I focused my energies on water polo, and started to thrive in this demanding, ruthless and intensely physical sport. Young and skinny compared to most of the other players, I trained extremely hard and learned to capitalise on my instinctive quickness and mobility by playing a fast, agile, mobile kind of game. When the 'thugs' did threaten to catch me, I was usually protected by my coach, Bob Jelfs Snr. Bob Jnr also came to my aid: he was bigger and stronger than me and, by the age of seventeen, had been appointed captain of the Great Britain under-eighteen team. We lived for the game.

One afternoon, I had decided to watch a trial match for the

Great Britain water polo squad and, when one of the teams was short, I was offered the opportunity to join the game. Several established players looked after me and, out of the blue, I was selected to play for the Great Britain senior team. I was only eighteen, and had not yet represented either the national under-eighteen or under-twenty-one sides.

I would eventually play my last international match for Great Britain almost twenty years later, in my late thirties, nearing the end of a long, eventful career.

Water polo was, and remains, beyond the very highest level, a completely amateur game. People play because they enjoy the sport. There is no other reason. And, for many years, water polo provided me with a consistent source of fun and an incentive to remain dedicated and physically fit. I was extremely fortunate to be a member of both the Leamington and London Polytechnic Clubs.

At Leamington, it was generally accepted that we play hard in and out of the pool. We loved travelling around the country to play away fixtures, and we invariably abided by our defining club rule that Leamington teams never leave a pub while it is open, a 'tradition' that was scrupulously observed by Mr Jelfs, who, in these early days, held everything together as our trainer, coach and driver.

We were far from the most powerful club in the country but, during the late 1960s and early 1970s, we started to develop a proud reputation, first winning a national title at junior level and then, three years later, against all the odds, managing to win the national championship. These were happy days. As a young man, I was gaining confidence and self-respect. A few of us went on to represent the county, playing in a Warwickshire team that enjoyed sustained success and claimed five national titles during the next decade.

Naturally, the greatest honour was to represent either the England or the Great Britain team but, as the years passed, I found myself growing increasingly frustrated by what seemed to be the inadequate and complacent administration of water polo in this country. The consequence of this malaise was the chronic underachievement of our national sides in the pool.

The paramount aim for the British team should be to qualify for a place in the summer Olympic Games and, in my view, there have been very few periods during the past three decades when we have lacked the natural ability to achieve this goal. The incredible dedication of the players has earned several impressive results, but we have consistently failed to reach the Olympics because the sport is hamstrung by a negative, pessimistic mentality.

In essence, the establishment has always tended to regard a narrow loss as a satisfactory achievement. Through the mid to late 1960s, we never believed we stood a chance of beating countries like Holland, West Germany, the Soviet Union or any major team from Eastern Europe. We went into the pool believing we would lose, and, sure enough, we did lose, often by a large margin.

This overwhelmingly defeatist tone clashed with my fiercely competitive nature and, to say the very least, my relationship with water polo officialdom in Great Britain became turbulent. While so many administrators seemed to accept failure, and simply enjoyed the cocktail party, I raged against their lack of ambition and drive, their lack of vision and determination to succeed.

Perhaps inevitably and certainly unwillingly, I found myself being cast as the *enfant terrible* of British water polo and, always preceded by my reputation, I was twice sentenced to a life ban from the sport.

The first disciplinary action arose when I insisted upon claiming my travel expenses after competing at my first Home International tournament in Scotland in 1970. My second ban, many years later, was perhaps more clear-cut. Towards the end of an extremely close local derby, I was ordered out of the pool for a third and final time. I had done nothing wrong, and shared my view with the referee who, it seemed to me, had been unashamedly blowing in favour of the opposition.

Enraged (although I would not claim that as a mitigating factor since I was serenely aware of my actions), I walked around the edge of the pool until I reached the referee, lifted him off his feet and dropped him in the water. It was a wonderfully satisfying moment, but the second life ban followed soon afterwards.

In both cases, the authorities' resolve to punish me faded with time and both life bans were eventually set aside.

Wherever I settled during my engineering and management career, it was never long before I located the nearest water polo club and offered my services. I represented Sydney University in the early 1970s and then played for New South Wales in an inter-state tournament that also served as the trial for the Australian team to compete at the 1972 Olympic Games in Munich.

I had been excited to learn there was no formal regulation precluding me from selection in the Australian squad. However, opposition started to develop and, despite my status as a permanent resident, the authorities eventually decided I had not spent enough time living in Australia. I was disappointed.

Nonetheless, I continued to enjoy playing for a talented Sydney University team that claimed the national championship. Eight years later, while working in New Zealand, I was part of another eager 'wannawin' team called Maranui, able to contribute experience, know-how and, by then, weight to a young and willing side on the way to another national title. That achievement earned Maranui an invitation to the annual 'Jim Birt' tournament in Brisbane.

Even now, I continue to play water polo whenever I get the opportunity. In fact, I played in a friendly water polo match barely ten weeks after completing my voyage across the Pacific. At the age of fifty-four, I have definitely lost some speed but the game is still as stimulating as it was forty years ago.

And I still have one powerful ambition in the sport. I often think how I would enjoy nothing more than to play a role in helping the British water polo team to realise its true potential.

There was no shortage of dreams in my head as I approached the end of five happy years at the Leamington College for Boys in 1965, but the strongest ambition was to quench my genetic thirst for excitement and thrills by joining the Royal Air Force to fly Lightnings, one of only two aircraft around at the time that were capable of flying straight up into the sky.

I passed the tests and was offered a special five-year commission, but the rules stipulated the offer had to be accepted within twenty-four hours or it would revert to the standard seven-year RAF commission. Part of me still wishes I had accepted that career path but, when push came to shove, I declined.

Like many of his generation, my father steadfastly believed young people should complete the best possible education. He urged me to go to university instead, and I know he was very pleased when I agreed to study civil engineering at Queen Mary College, part of the University of London.

Student life suited me very well. After three years in halls and various bedsits, I shared a remarkably Spartan house with friends Nigel Clutterbuck and Paul Sivey, lived hard, worked as much as necessary and played sport whenever possible.

Aside from the water polo, I had enjoyed tennis and rugby at school, and I started playing open side flanker for what was a respectably strong Queen Mary College team. Alan Old and John Anglin starred, and players like Colin Barker and Nigel Buckley could have walked into most top club sides.

My rugby career took me through many happy days and roughly the same number of blurred nights to the South Warwickshire team. When I was living in Australia, I seized opportunities to play for Byron Bay, New South Wales Far North Coast and New South Wales Country. The rugby was fine, but the cooked chucks and the beer in the bar afterwards were unforgettable.

I also found plenty of time to ski and play squash. I just love games. The tactics and planning, the training and the execution: every element thrills me. I'm competitive by nature and have always relished every contest . . . so long as I am taking part and not restricted to watching from the grandstand.

Oddly, I have never enjoyed being a spectator and have never supported any particular football club, not even as a boy. Rugby internationals, particularly those involving England, are a notable exception to this rule, and I have passed many exhilarated Saturdays in the grandstand at Twickenham.

More recently, I have started to enjoy watching club ice hockey in Eastern Europe. Surely a first cousin to water polo, it is a tremendously fast-moving sport that requires terrific speed of thought and movement, and yet remains physically challenging. I first watched a top-class ice hockey match during the 1970s when I was visiting my sister in Montreal. It took my breath away.

Even so, the prospect of watching other people sweat still seems far less appealing than any opportunity to sweat for myself.

This passion for sport was indirectly responsible when I failed my exams at the end of my first year at university, and directly responsible when I skipped my second-year exams because they clashed with an Olympic qualifying event involving the Great Britain water polo team. The net result of the disruptions was that I required five years to complete my three-year degree.

My housemates experienced similar difficulties, taking between four and six years to qualify, but we all got there in the end and I prepared myself for what turned out to be the nomadic life of a contract civil engineer.

I joined Costain Construction in 1970 and enjoyed working with the team building the M4 motorway heading west from London, but an exciting opportunity arose the following year that seemed too good to miss.

My girlfriend at the time qualified for the offer whereby skilled

Britons who were prepared to emigrate to Australia could buy their boat ticket to Sydney for a token price of £10. In scanning the engineering jobs section of the newspapers, I had seen that the New South Wales government was seeking to fill engineering posts in their Public Works Department. I was young, eager to travel and see the world. So I applied for the job and, before long, we were going.

Sydney immediately struck me as a vibrant and exciting city. I started working initially in the Public Works' design office and latterly with computer and physical modelling at the hydraulics research Lab in Manly. Australians appeared open and friendly, uncomplicated and enthusiastic.

My search for a water polo club took me to the annual general meeting of the New South Wales Water Polo Association and, after falling into conversation with one of the officials, it seemed I would play for Cronulla, one of the top teams in the Sydney league. Then, as we were leaving the function, I was introduced to the delegate from the university club, named Peter Montgomery.

'Jim, where do you work?' he asked.

'Milson's Point,' I replied.

'You travelling by train?'

I nodded, and was gone.

Soon after eight o'clock the following morning, I arrived at Milson's Point station to find Peter standing on the platform, waiting for me. He said he did not want to be a nuisance but there had not been time to talk the previous night and he really thought I should play for the university. It was impossible to reject such unashamed enthusiasm and I happily joined his club.

This type of determination has become Peter's trademark: he played in the Australian water polo team that finished third at the 1976 Olympic Games in Montreal and was singled out as one of the unsung heroes in the organisation after Sydney had hosted the best Olympic Games ever in 2000. He now serves as a vice-president of the Australian National Olympic Committee.

I had hoped to complete my trip across the Pacific to coincide with Peter's fiftieth birthday party on 15 December 2000, but I was unavoidably delayed.

In due course, my employers offered me what I can only describe as an opportunity made in heaven. In fact, the position was based in Byron Bay, a place of such staggering natural beauty that it probably comes as close to Heaven as anywhere on this planet. My new title of 'Relieving Engineer at the Lismore Office' did not sound too hot but the practical reality of my daily existence was to live and work on 200 miles of truly spectacular coastline.

Byron Bay was special, completely unspoiled by man, populated by long-established locals and transient beach bums and bunnies. Indeed, through all my travels, this was the only place outside England where I clearly recall sitting back and contemplating that I could happily settle and remain.

For better or for worse, that was not my nature. There have been times in my life when I wish I could have just relaxed and enjoyed myself, and this period at Byron Bay was probably one such time, but there is something within me that drives me on to the next challenge, the next project. I don't see this as a special strength or a particular weakness. It's just who I am.

So when the telephone rang and I was invited to sort out a road-building problem in Papua New Guinea, it really did not matter how happy I was feeling in Byron Bay. The next challenge started to occupy my thoughts and, before long, I was on my way, daring to throw the dice all over again.

Papua New Guinea was certainly different. The islands were still classified as an Australian Trust Territory in 1971 and the authorities had set about the task of establishing a basic infrastructure, including a road network, to drive economic growth and create wealth. Local people were largely untouched by progress: the women went bare-chested, wearing traditional pull-pulls (grass skirts), while most of the men wore nothing but what they called 'arse grass', large leaves back and front tucked into the belt. It was not unusual to spot other strange items hanging from a man's belt, usually smoked, shrunken human heads. These were apparently prized as valuable status symbols.

The job was to complete construction of a road through the mountains, a project so dogged by difficulties and delays that funding officials from the World Bank appeared to have concluded it was impossible to build on such steep, weathered shale. By throwing away the textbook and relying on the knowledge and experience of the workforce, we put the road back together. I really enjoyed the buzz of addressing an 'impossible' project, and getting it done.

In PNG, we worked hard and we played hard, overcoming the prohibition of card games and restricted access to alcohol (the authorities feared a corruptive effect on local inhabitants) by assembling for evenings of illicit poker at the most private and discreet venue in our neighbourhood, the local prison.

We were young and free, living hard and wild in what remained a primitive environment. The nearest hospital to our prime site was a fifty-mile trek through dense bush terrain, but this plain knowledge did not prevent us from challenging each other to attempt daring and frankly dangerous feats.

One happy evening, someone said nobody could get from Mount Hagen to the top of Mount Willem and back inside twenty-four hours. I asked him how sure he was. He said he felt about '$100-certain'. I told him he had a bet, found a local guide in jail halfway up the mountain, paid his bail and completed the roundtrip with forty-five minutes to spare. I happily collected the wager, and enjoyed signing my name in the visitors' book that is kept in the tin box at the summit of Mount Willem.

Papua New Guinea was sometimes dangerous and never boring, from off-road driving to panning for gold in the Sepik river, but, as soon as the road was complete, I didn't waste much time in returning to London to start looking for the next contract, the next adventure.

Before long, I responded to an advertisement placed by a

company that had recently been appointed managing contractor to upgrade seven airports in Zaire, central Africa. The national airline had purchased a new fleet of Boeing 737s and now needed somewhere to land them. Working in Africa would be a new experience for me, so I applied for the position of project manager; and, after an immersion course in French, packed my bags for Kisangani.

President Mobutu's Zaire proved to be the most unpleasant place I have ever visited. The working environment was relentlessly poisoned by officials who resented foreigners and felt entitled to be bluntly aggressive and fundamentally dishonest. It was exhausting work: client representatives usually liked to discuss issues between 02.00 and 04.00 at the only nightclub in town, but I still needed to be available to the British subcontractors during the day.

Yet we focused on delivery and, armed with a golden pass signed by the late and unlamented Mobutu himself, I was able not only to travel anywhere but also to dissuade fraught soldiers from pointing their guns at me. The first airport was finished inside nine months, at which point I withdrew.

There were brighter moments in Zaire. My stay happened to coincide with the momentous Muhammad Ali vs. George Foreman world championship bout in Kinshasa as well as Blashford-Snell's historic first navigation of the River Congo from its source. Both the so-called 'Rumble in the Jungle' and the completion of a successful expedition prompted excessive, excellent parties.

On the day of my return to London, my connecting flight from Kisangani to Kinshasa was delayed and it seemed as if I would miss the jumbo jet bound for Heathrow; but one final, departing swish of my 'golden pass' persuaded air traffic control to stop the Boeing 747 as it taxied to the runway. In appropriately surreal circumstances, I casually boarded the plane and was gone.

I spent the next three years at home, being challenged and

stimulated in the design office of Sir Brian Colquhoun, but I felt almost imprisoned by the office regimen and routine, and longed to be back working in the field. My eyes moved towards the appointments column once again, searching for another adventure in another part of the world. So far as I could see, that was life.

Pacific Consultants International were Japanese construction consultants who had never employed a Westerner . . . until early 1977 when they hired me to assist in the building of an ambitious shopping centre and apartment complex in Sharjah, one of the United Arab Emirates. The mandate was to work with a local building company, essentially transforming it into a contractor of international quality during the course of the project. I am not certain we were successful, but the complex still stands today, complete with its then spectacular 'space frame' covering the central courtyard, although its lustre has faded in comparison to the more modern and glamorous creations in steel and glass.

I generally enjoyed this exposure to the Japanese culture and initially shared a flat with two senior architects from Tokyo, one of whom was a seventh Dan Karate expert. His training programme involved catching Arabian flies in flight, hurling them towards the ground and stamping on them. I watched his antics with interest, but my cynical view of martial arts was neatly reflected in the film *Raiders of the Lost Ark* when an elaborately kicking and chopping karate king is confronted by the character played by Harrison Ford, who casually takes out a revolver, shoots the black belt in the chest and moves on.

As the shopping centre took shape, however, my thoughts kept drifting to a girl named Jane Riley, whom I had stumbled across at a party in London eighteen months earlier. We had started seeing each other, and she had attended each of three leaving parties held for me at a pub near Sir Brian Colquhoun's office. Jane had visited me in the Emirates and it was during one of my trips home that I eventually plucked up the courage to ask her if she would marry me.

She agreed and we were duly married in the Wren Chapel at the Chelsea Hospital on 13 August 1977, and were especially honoured when two lines of Chelsea Pensioners, resplendent in red, provided a guard of honour. Jane's father, George Riley, had served as the chaplain at the hospital until his sudden death when she was two years old. The dispensation was granted in his memory.

Sybil Riley, Jane's mother, was left to bring up her two children alone in Cambridge. I have always admired her as a strong-hearted, resolute woman and, more often than not, she had seemed to fathom my restless nature. I am pleased to say my mother-in-law has been a source of inspiration, as well as the occasional joke.

I had taken great care in planning what I hoped would be the honeymoon to top all honeymoons, an overland trip by Land Rover from London back to Sharjah, where the shopping centre needed to be completed. Mileage schedules, hotel bookings, opportunities to enjoy staggering sights and scenery: everything was in order; everything had been meticulously arranged.

However, Jane's passport was stolen in Soho just hours after our wedding reception and the process of securing a replacement UK passport and new visas delayed our departure by ten days. A gently paced holiday was thus transformed into a mad dash across Europe to get back to work in time.

We reviewed the schedule and opted to drive for thirty-six hours, then stop for twenty-four hours, then start driving again. Some nights we slept in the most luxurious hotels, other nights we slept in the Land Rover. Jane gamely accepted the imperfect situation and, while I concede our honeymoon may not have been the most romantic of all time, it was certainly eventful.

One day, we got lost in the desert; the next day, we were driving through the palm-tree-lined streets of Beirut during a lull in the fighting. Through ups and downs, we managed to reach Sharjah with our marriage intact.

Within a few months, the shopping centre was finished and

Jane was pregnant (as were most of her squash team); so we returned to London, eager that our first child should be born in England. In the meantime, I accepted a short-term contract with a French/Lebanese engineering firm to establish their operations in Saudi Arabia. Constantly travelling between Paris, Cambridge and Riyadh was not ideal, and I was aware of the danger that I would be caught overseas when our child was born, but I needed to earn.

Anna, our daughter, eventually arrived on 28 May 1979. At the earliest sign of activity, I had rushed to catch a flight from Saudi Arabia to Heathrow and was speeding away from the airport when a couple of policemen flagged me down.

'Do you realise what speed you were doing, sir?'

'I am sorry, but my wife is about to give birth.'

'I see, sir,' the policeman replied. 'Well, I think we had better do our best to make sure you get there in time. Just follow us.'

With that, he hurried to his car and proceeded to give me a police escort directly to the hospital in Cambridge, just like in the films. Maybe I am getting old, but they don't seem to make policemen like that nowadays. To my enduring regret, I arrived two hours after her birth, but mother and child were both healthy and I was elated.

In any case, despite the flashing lights and sirens, I was late for the delivery, which was disappointing, although one compensation was that Anna had been thoroughly cleaned and wrapped by the time I first saw her. I only really appreciated this user-friendly benefit two years later when our second daughter, Sarah, was delivered and I was asked to leave the room before I fainted.

Family birthdays have always been important to me. Aside from Anna's arrival and Jane's birthday on 21 March 2001 when I was drifting somewhere on the Pacific Ocean, I have not missed one party.

Anna was only three months old when our family was on the road once again. I accepted a position as construction manager with Fletcher Construction, the biggest civil engineering company in New Zealand, trusting life on the eastern side of the Tasman Sea would prove as agreeable as it had been on the west.

Our Kiwi adventure did not start well. We landed at Wellington airport in the middle of a downpour and the immigration officer asked us why on earth we were arriving at a time when everyone else was leaving. These ominous words reverberated in Jane's ears as she battled through a deep New Zealand winter, coping with a small, hyperactive baby while we were living in a motel.

I probably had a much easier time at work, where we completed a series of sewerage and earthworks contracts. However, the general shortage of exciting engineering projects in New Zealand left me feeling demotivated and jaded; after eighteen months in the land of the long white cloud, we decided to return home. There was a second factor. Jane was pregnant again, and, on 22 April 1981, back in Cambridge, we celebrated the birth of our daughter, Sarah.

The responsibility of fatherhood had begun to weigh on my shoulders and I accepted the days of wandering around the globe had passed, at least until the girls were old enough to look after themselves. So, having resolved to remain in the UK for the foreseeable future, my initial instinct was to look for a challenging position somewhere in the British engineering industry.

I contacted Paul Sivey, my old friend from university. We had joined Costain Construction together in 1970 and he had since risen to the dizzy heights of project manager in the team constructing the Thames Barrier. I arranged to visit Paul at the site and found a wonderfully exciting engineering challenge. However, I was dismayed to discover how much management time was spent dealing with labour issues, negotiating with unions, trying to coax half a day's work for a double payday. It seemed ridiculous.

The gloomy prospect of a place at the bargaining table, coupled with the reality that, while they may be highly respected in other parts of the world, British engineers were still inexplicably held in low esteem by their own compatriots (and paid low salaries to match), led me to conclude that the time was ripe for me to take my career in a completely new direction.

Walking through the City of London after another depressing job interview, I happened to pass by a computer shop. My interest in emerging information technology had started in Sydney, and I eagerly tracked the latest advances in the fast-emerging microcomputer industry. I looked around, started talking to the shop owner and soon became involved in his growing computer company.

Computing was evidently the place to be and, within months, I opted to take the plunge and launch my own company. My big idea was to use the brand-new technology to establish a car-sharing network in and around London. It had been calculated that just a 10 per cent decrease in the number of single-occupancy car journeys during peak periods would relieve the paralysing traffic jams that regularly blocked the main arteries.

Carshare, as I christened the company, not only seemed to be a sure-fire money-spinner, but easing congestion and pollution was going to be good for the planet and the economy. I worked like a dog for six months, believing completely in the product.

In the event, the business failed. We were unlucky to publicise our service on the day when the media was preoccupied by the collapse of Freddie Laker's airline, and our misfortune was compounded a week later when, on the very day that we officially went 'on-line', a national rail strike prompted several local radio stations to launch similar car-sharing services for free.

Circumstances conspired to undermine a sound concept. Roads became even more congested as the strike continued and, contrary to logic, many people simply switched off from the whole idea of travelling by road. Thus, Carshare achieved the dubious distinction of becoming one of the first and probably the fastest failure of the new business start-up guarantee schemes launched by the Department of Trade and Industry.

It was disappointing for everyone, but I suppose it could have been worse. Jane narrowly escaped being arrested for soliciting at King's Cross station when she was distributing promotional flyers to commuters, in spite of the fact that she was also pushing a double buggy with two infant daughters at the time. The enquiring policeman was perhaps not the most alert in the Met.

We were struggling financially. The outlook was bleak. I wanted to sign on the dole, but Jane was adamant she would return to work as a medical physicist, and she accepted a position at the Royal Free Hospital near our flat in Hampstead. Her transfer to Mount Vernon Hospital in Middlesex two years later instigated the move to our current home in quiet, leafy Northwood.

With Jane working, I tried my hand at being a 'house-husband'. My lifelong allergy to vacuum cleaners and washing-up did not augur well, but I was adept at nappy changing and began to appreciate the time spent with my two young daughters. Each morning, I used to put the two of them in the front basket of a butcher's bike and we would set off on our errands.

Months passed, but there was a strong element of inevitability surrounding my eventual decision to get back into computing and, as a 35-year-old in need of stability and security, to do so with a top company. My instinct was to steer away from the suit and tie of corporate life, but there was no option.

I secured a post in the brand new microcomputer division of Rank Xerox, but it was not long before I accepted what seemed a more exciting opportunity, working as a sales executive with Epson, the innovative and dynamic company that, at this time, was launching the world's first portable computer.

Within four years, I had been promoted to the position of National Sales Director and the company's turnover in the United Kingdom had increased from £50,000 to a healthy £12 million. All seemed well, and I appeared set for an expanded role as sales and marketing director.

However, the company made other plans and it was decided

I would not be given the marketing portfolio. My response was immediate.

I resigned.

Jane was horrified that I should walk away from a highly paid position in a leading company within a fast-growing industry. She simply could not appreciate my deep disenchantment with the snide backstabbing and insincere grovelling of corporate life in Britain. It may have been stable, and it may have been lucrative, but that was not the way I wanted to live my life. There had to be something more exciting, something more worthwhile. Mercifully, there was.

One quiet afternoon, I happened to be reading the Appointments section of *The Sunday Times* when I saw an advertisement seeking engineers to join Operation Safe Haven, an American-led initiative to rescue destitute Kurds in the mountains of northern Iraq and effectively to rehabilitate their villages, which had been decimated by Saddam's bombing and poison gas.

I applied, and was accepted. Ten years had passed since I last worked as an engineer, but I relished the specific challenge assigned to me: to identify and restore water supplies to these ruined areas. The operation was being conducted under the auspices of the Coalition Forces, but the no-nonsense Americans took charge and got the job done.

When it became evident that heavy mining had made walking or driving to these villages impossible, I was not only provided with outstanding maps but was also given access to travel around in a Blackhawk helicopter. This was the way to work. I enjoyed the practical, dynamic, vigorous and upbeat approach. For three months, I believe we made a huge difference to many broken lives.

Then, the United Nations arrived and the emphasis immediately changed from actually helping people to pussyfooting around politics. Our entire team was evacuated because it was suggested that our continued presence would offend, or perhaps provoke, Saddam Hussein, the great dictator.

It was disappointing to leave in the face of such spineless officialdom but, invigorated by the experience in Iraq, I returned home with the intention of driving forward a computer consultancy. However, I was soon distracted.

The European Union was funding a project in Bulgaria where ultrasound equipment was going to be deployed around the country to help address the horrendous peri-natal infant mortality rate. It was thought that the high rate of malformed foetuses was a consequence of the catastrophic accident at the Chernobyl nuclear power plant in Russia. This is not scientifically proven. I was intrigued. I had been referred to the German consultants who required a replacement project manager and I applied for the job.

They studied my career history and requested further clarification of any specific experience in the health sector. I responded somewhat lamely that I had helped to establish several field hospitals in northern Iraq. The Minister of Health in Bulgaria obviously saw the job as a mainly logistical challenge, and I was appointed.

My responsibilities were to ensure the correct equipment was purchased at the best price, and to oversee its proper installation. The project was completed, and I was rewarded not only by a sense of having made a difference, but also by assuming the title of 'honorary obstetrician'.

Somewhat to my surprise, I had enjoyed working with the European Union where a small, dedicated, bright group of people belied the organisation's overall image of inefficiency, complacency and corruption. There are, amid the reams of red tape and bureaucracy, a few decent people doing a decent job.

I was also invigorated by the post-liberation glow that seemed to emanate from Eastern Europe during the early 1990s, as millions of people held such high hopes that democracy would somehow improve their lives.

After assisting with further EU-funded projects in the region, I decided to launch my own management consultancy business in Eastern Europe, aiming to capitalise on a reputation for efficiency and honesty, working closely with the EU and with the governments of these emerging nations.

We initially consulted in the area of informatics for the National Customs organisations in various countries (import duties represented a valuable source of income), and offered a similar service to a series of national statistics offices (the authorities needed to know who, how many and where before resources could be allocated). Within months, we diversified into health and social welfare, labour market restructuring and preparation for accession.

The business has grown during the past decade, but the nature of the EU funding and activity in Eastern Europe has changed dramatically. Naive idealism has been replaced by blatant corruption. Effective support programmes now resemble bureaucratic nightmares in which money is churned around to fill the wallets of greedy businessman and dishonest politicians. Unfortunately the burden of proof means most corrupt people continue to get away with it.

Such an assessment may seem harsh, but it arises from the experience of a company still seeking honest work. In my early days representing the Commission on Tender Evaluations, I refused to approve a clearly corrupt contract and, as a result, was blackballed from that country by the people who were responsible for the funding, but more interested in 'fulfilment'.

It is doubly disappointing that so much of the corruption is imported. Too many Western companies competing for contracts have not hesitated to exploit the relative poverty of local decision-makers. The result has been the creation of a business environment where such conduct is deemed acceptable.

Notwithstanding these frustrations, I have been privileged to work in fifteen different countries throughout Eastern Europe during the past decade, and have met many dedicated and unselfish people intent on forging a better future for themselves, for their families and for their country.

The management consultancy has provided, and will continue to provide, an effective and honest service. From a personal point of view, its success has enabled my own family to move beyond the financial pressures of the 1980s and reach a reasonable level of stability and security . . . In many ways, it enabled me to look beyond the usual parameters for injections of excitement.

My father died in 1993. He had continued to work as an engineer after my mother's death, taking commissions all around the world, but he finally retired in England. As the years passed, I started to assume the old man and I shared very little in common. When I was sixteen, he had been extremely unhappy when I decided to get myself a motorbike, insisting it was far too dangerous. He didn't actually stop me but, like any teenager, I was quick to grumble about old-fashioned intransigence. I thought my father just didn't understand, but the sadness was that it was I who didn't understand him. Several years later, I happened to be sorting through some of his personal possessions when I found a faded photograph of my father as a young man riding a motorbike while doing a headstand on the saddle. It was astonishing. I couldn't believe my eyes. He was clearly enjoying himself, fooling around with his friends.

I finally realised that, after all, my determined father was an adventurer at heart. It was in his genes. We did share something in common.

The circumstances of my father's death were unsatisfactory at the time, and they have unsettled me ever since. He had been reluctant to go into hospital to ease a trapped nerve in his back, but I thought his quality of life would improve and insisted he should go ahead with the operation. Even on the very day that he was admitted to hospital, he told me that something did not feel right, but again I repeated my conviction and managed to change his mind.

In the event, he suffered a thrombosis in bed, and died. I suspect he may have been short-tempered with the nurses and they overlooked the need to keep him moving but, to some extent, I have always blamed myself. In some ways, he was ready to go; however, I am not sure whether I was ready for him to go.

Life grinds on. Some things you casually leave along the way, other things you carry with you. Everything seems fine, if you keep moving.

On 13 November 1996, my long-suffering wife organised an exceptional fiftieth birthday party for me. Amid fine food and wine, friends and family assembled in one place, and I reflected upon fifty eventful years during which I had travelled extensively, enjoyed success in a wide diversity of fields and eventually secured a decent standard of living for my immediate family.

Yet I was not satisfied.

There had to be something more.

I raged against growing old. I was terrified by the prospect of maintaining my business in Eastern Europe, gradually winding down and eventually retiring to look after our garden at home in Northwood. I was consumed by a conviction that I still had so much to prove to myself, so much still to do.

Ease off the accelerator at fifty? No way. I wanted to push harder, do more, travel faster, further . . . anything to provide an injection of excitement. In fact, even as I celebrated my birthday in November 1996, I had already started laying plans for a powerful boost to my spirits, to my self-esteem, to my being.

To adapt the words of Winston Churchill, I wanted turning fifty to be not the beginning of the end of my life, maybe just the end of the beginning.

Somewhere, far away, the oceans of the world were calling.

3
Baptism in the Atlantic

The first steps are the hardest, so the saying goes.

Mr AJS is approaching his fiftieth birthday with some vague notion that he wants to do something exciting and extraordinary. He has always had a natural affinity with water and aquatic activity. That may be a clue. He starts to lie awake at night, wondering where to start, where to take his first steps.

It is almost the time of the year when he makes his annual pilgrimage to the Boat Show in London. He thinks he may as well go. At the very least, he will see his friend, who runs sailing holidays and will once again have his own stand situated close to the beer tent. 'I'll go,' he says . . .

So I went. I bought my ticket at the gate and started to wander around and between the gleaming stands and expositions, like a shopper with a wallet full of enthusiasm but no clear idea of what he wants to buy. I wanted to meet people in this world, and somehow hoped to find a spark of inspiration. After an hour or so, I noticed a signboard indicating Chay Blyth would give a talk about his imminent Global Challenge. That sounded interesting, a place to start.

Blyth is a consummate professional, not only on the ocean but also in his business activities, and his presentation affirmed my belief that sailing around the world could quench my thirst for adventure, but I would sail single-handed, not as a virtual tourist on one of his fleet of expensive racing yachts. It sounded fun. Looking for more information, I decided to hang around after his talk and took the opportunity of approaching this widely admired sailor.

'Excuse me, Mr Blyth.'

He was standing alone, but turned around as though interrupted.

'Yes?'

I continued: 'I am thinking of sailing around the world, solo. Is there anything special you think I should bear in mind?'

'Buy my book,' he replied tersely, before turning away and joining a group of people who looked as if they could prove more rewarding customers than me, an anonymous management consultant with a fuzzy ambition. Maybe I caught him at a bad moment. Maybe a hundred people tell him the same thing. Whatever the case, I was disappointed to get the cold shoulder, but not downhearted as I left the Boat Show. The seed in the back of my mind was starting to germinate. I was making progress.

I reverted to the challenge of building my business in Eastern Europe but, not long afterwards, happened to notice a newspaper article reporting how Blyth and his organisation were planning the first ever rowing race across the Atlantic Ocean. Crews of two would row identical, specially designed boats from Tenerife to Barbados. The seed was sprouting green shoots.

Rowing across the Atlantic Ocean . . . I loved the idea. Without giving any calm consideration to the practicality of the challenge, I impulsively contacted the organisers and asked if it was possible to enter the race.

The response was succinct: 'Sorry, we're full.'

'OK,' I countered. 'Don't you have some kind of standby list?'

'Yes, we do. Your name, please.'

That seemed to be that. I replaced the telephone and switched back into reality. There was a problem with a contract in Hungary, and we were planning the family holiday of a lifetime to Australia. As I addressed the concerns of daily life, the concept of rowing across an ocean seemed to drift away on the wind. Four months of normal existence passed gently by until, on just another Tuesday afternoon, I answered just another telephone call.

'Mr Shekhdar?'

'Speaking.'

'This is the Challenge Business. A place has become available on our Atlantic Rowing Race. Are you still interested?'

The proposition was relatively straightforward: in return for an entry form, I would have to send a £150 cheque and give a dual commitment that I would buy their official kit to build the boat and pay a full entrance fee later. The considered and sensible response would have been to say that I would study precisely what was required to complete the race, in terms of time, physical fitness and money, and that I would get back to them as soon as possible.

But there was nothing considered or sensible about my powerful desire to do something exciting and extraordinary. This was something within me. I could probably have thought of a thousand reasons why I should not dream of rowing across the Atlantic Ocean, but I was not in the least interested in any of them. I wanted to do it. That was all I knew. I wanted to do it.

'Of course,' I replied. 'I'll send the cheque tomorrow.'

It was October 1995, just over a year before my fiftieth birthday and just over two years before the scheduled departure of the inaugural Atlantic Rowing Race. My name was on the list. There would be life beyond fifty, after all.

By this stage, after eighteen years of marriage, my wife Jane had developed an expression that she tends to wear whenever I start to regale her with details of my latest big idea. Furrowing her brow and tilting her head, she would gaze at me with a gentle sigh, as if to say: 'Yes, Jim, what now?'

I outlined how I would persuade one of the national newspapers to run a readers' competition, in which first prize would be the opportunity to be my partner in the Atlantic Rowing Race, and how I would find a sponsor on the back of all that publicity, and how I would court corporate Britain for additional support. Looking back, I suppose I might have sounded as serious as a breathless boy explaining how he wanted to be an astronaut and travel to the moon.

'Yes, dear, all right. Now what would you like for supper?'

By April 1996, only eighteen months before the start of the race, Jane's doubtful approach appeared to be wholly justified. I had been relentlessly busy at work, rushing to and fro across Eastern Europe, and had made absolutely no progress in finding either a sponsor or a partner for the race across the Atlantic. The idea still appealed, but it was starting to look like a pipe dream.

It was time for Fate, whatever he, she or it might be, to step forward again and inject some urgency and action into the process.

'Hello, Mr Shekhdar?'

'Yes?'

'This is Teresa at the Challenge Business, project manager for the Atlantic Rowing Race, and I am calling to find out if you are still looking for a partner.'

'Er, yes, I am.'

'All right,' she continued. 'It's just that I have been contacted by a young man who is a good rower – in fact, he assisted us in testing the prototype of the boat that we will be using in this race. His partner has withdrawn, and he asked if I would help him find someone who might be available. Would you mind if I gave him your name and telephone numbers?'

'No, of course not. Thank you very much.'

I was contacted three days later by a 27-year-old fireman from Plymouth who introduced himself as David Jackson. His voice was firm and I immediately appreciated his straightforward manner. With a minimum of fuss, he explained he was talking to three people who had shown an interest in joining him for the race across the Atlantic. It transpired there was someone in Scotland who said they would have no problem in raising the estimated £45,000 required to fund the trip, but had not rowed much before; there was a competent rower who said he would be keen to assist in finding a sponsor; and then there was me.

In response, I told David that I was an overweight business-man who had decided to do something exciting. I said I had played sport at a reasonable level and that, all things being equal, I would probably be in a position to help with the funding. We were only speaking on the telephone, but we seemed to get along and we agreed to meet in person as soon as possible.

Our first attempt at joint planning did not augur well.

The meeting was fixed for 10.30 on a Wednesday morning at, in our own carefully phrased words, 'the first service station after the junction of the M4 and the M5'. Neither of us could remember our Leigh Delameres from our Gordanos, so this seemed to be the clearest possible arrangement.

There would have been no problem if we had both been travelling in the same direction. However, David was driving north from Plymouth and I was rushing west from London, with the result that I ended up at Gordano on the M5 and he was looking for me at Leigh Delamere on the M4. At this time before mobile phones were common, we only resolved the confusion once I had phoned David's home and spoken to Jo, his girlfriend, who had spoken to him etc.

Sarah, my daughter, was around, so I invited her along. She is not shy to voice an opinion and can be a sound judge of character. A second opinion on my general impression of this prospective partner was going to be welcome. Perhaps I had grown suspicious in my old age, or maybe I had spent too much time in the corporate sewer, but the world is packed with people who turn out to be not quite what they appear and I was deter-mined to get this decision absolutely right.

It was almost noon when, at last, Sarah and I walked into the self-service restaurant of the Leigh Delamere service station on the M4. I looked around and saw a tall young man looking in our direction. He waved towards us and we walked over to join him. Mr Jackson, we presumed.

This was a strange meeting in many ways. There were no cast-iron issues to debate because the paramount questions that we both needed to answer were whether we liked the other guy, whether we thought we could work with the other guy, whether we could share a small boat with the other guy.

As we sipped at our coffee, it soon became clear that we were different in many, many ways: he was young and fit, I was growing old and fat; he was a keen and talented rower, I had hardly stepped into a rowing boat. He needed to find funding; I was probably in a position to provide funding.

Despite these differences, or perhaps because of them, we seemed to get along pretty well. I sensed we were both competitive people who wanted not only to compete in the Atlantic race, but also to win. Conversation was flowing when, at half past twelve, we needed to be on our way. I had scheduled two hours for the meeting, but the problems in finding each other had left us with only thirty minutes to talk. I needed to rush back down the M4 to catch a flight from Heathrow to Slovakia.

Back in our own car, I told Sarah I trusted him. She agreed. David seemed honest, reliable, straightforward; in short, precisely the sort of person who would help me cross the Atlantic in a rowing boat. I was delighted when David phoned a few days afterwards and said he wanted to join forces.

I have never asked him why he chose me instead of the other candidates. I don't even know if he ever met them. It didn't matter. What did matter was that I had found the person whose resolve and ability to get things done would turn my bold intentions of doing something exciting into full-colour reality. Without David Jackson, I would probably not now be rowing across oceans. It is as simple as that.

Our association developed through the months that followed. David began basic preparations for the race, and I talked to him on the phone. From my point of view, this balance of responsibilities was working out perfectly because I was able to stay focused on my business in Eastern Europe, secure in the

45

knowledge that solid foundations were being laid for my 'fix of excitement'.

We both deposited money in the bank when the time to purchase an official boat kit from the Challenge Business became critically overdue. We both understood that this would be the limit of David's financial burden. From that time onward, in essence, he would provide the labour and expertise in constructing the boat and generally completing the preparations, and I would sign the cheques.

As a fireman working four days on and four days off, David had sufficient spare time to set about the task and he wisely called upon the assistance of his father, Graham, who had served as a navigator in the RAF and had experience of building a seventy-two-foot concrete yacht that sailed twice across the Atlantic. Together in Plymouth, father and son constructed the boat.

In fact, it was Graham Jackson who discovered that the plywood supplied in the Challenge Business boat kit carried the British Standards number of a category deemed suitable for use in 'marine furniture'. Somewhat alarmed, we requested clarification from the organisers. Their response was that the wood was fine and the British Standards classification would soon be amended. Erring on the side of caution, David and Graham soaked every piece of construction material in resin before putting the hull together, just to ensure the physical integrity of our boat, and to make certain everything was waterproof.

The 'marine furniture' saga became something of a standing joke between us and, after we had successfully completed the crossing, we were amused to receive a congratulations card from someone in the Challenge Business office that concluded: 'Not bad for a boat you nearly named *MFI Wardrobe*.'

As the boat took shape, I supplemented my occasional telephone calls by twice travelling to spend a weekend with David and his girlfriend Jo. The nominal purpose of each trip was to see how the boat was taking shape but I was hardly in a position to address David and his father and make proposals about where this should go or how that should be attached. They were the experts, and I had decided never to pretend I was anything other than a novice who was occasionally able to offer a little common sense.

My approach to the entire project may have appeared casual at times but that was only because I had developed such a solid trust in David and Graham to prepare thoroughly and foresee every possible eventuality. If I did seem casual, it was no more than an expression of my confidence in them.

It was during the second of these fleeting visits that David said he thought we should set aside a long weekend and take the boat out for a test row, not only to check it was seaworthy but also to get a feel of the living conditions we would endure on the Atlantic. I agreed and proposed a date when Jane, Anna, Sarah and Munchkin, our faithful family hound, could come along as well. At this stage, I wanted them all to feel involved in my adventure.

The assembled Shekhdars set off from Northwood early on the Friday and we duly arrived in Plymouth in what I reckoned was plenty of time for David and me to prepare the boat and start rowing from Tor Point rowing club around noon, approximately an hour before low tide. This was my first mistake because it was soon clear there was more to do in preparing the boat than we had thought and, despite enthusiastic help from other members of the club, we never looked likely to catch the tide.

There was no option but to delay our departure and, literally, wait until the tide turned. If David was irritated by this course of events, he was kind enough to say nothing at the time. We took our respective families to the rowing club bar. A highly social lunch dragged happily into the afternoon and it was with a lingering backward glance that David and I eventually made our way back down to the jetty. We had set our revised departure time for seven o'clock. There was some serious work to be done.

At that precise moment, I think Jane realised I was serious about rowing across the Atlantic. She had heard so much talk but now, at last, she was seeing some action.

Our basic plan was to row down the River Tamar out to sea, swinging right at the Eddistone lighthouse and rowing on west towards Falmouth. It was hard to say how far we would go. We would see how things went. I sensed David wanted to be realistic, wanted to keep me out of the deep end.

I was not particularly fazed. Some people will call it arrogance, I would call it self-confidence: whatever the words, my nature is to start new projects with the strong conviction that, until proven otherwise, there is nothing I cannot do. I had never rowed in the open sea, but I was eager to try.

As we eased away from Tor Point Rowing Club, the blades of our oars forcing the boat through the gently rippling waters of the Tamar, I felt mildly euphoric. Almost two years after meeting Chay Blyth at the Boat Show, through many ups and downs, I had finally reached the water. Now, I was matching David's proficient stroke, and our boat seemed to surge forward, then ease, surge, then ease, surge and then ease. I savoured the beauty of our motion, as we sped on and reached the open sea.

All seemed well.

All was not well.

Within another ten minutes, I was crouching over the side of the boat, clutching my stomach, bent double as I retched. The unmistakable signs of seasickness brewed in my stomach and rose inexorably with the bile. I did feel embarrassed but there was not much I could do. A small boat's motion affects some people more than others and, unfortunately, on this occasion, it hit me for six.

I was really struggling and David tactfully suggested we change the plan, skip the Eddistone lighthouse and head along the coast towards Falmouth. I was certainly not in any kind of condition to argue with him.

'And, er, David,' I mumbled haltingly, wiping my mouth. 'Would you mind if you take the first shift?' We had already agreed to row in four-hour shifts during the night, one pulling the oars while the other slept.

'Sure,' he replied.

I huddled in the cooking compartment, still feeling rotten, and tried to slumber through the sickness. It was not even nine o'clock in the evening. We had been on the water less than two hours. And I had been reduced to a shivering, whimpering wreck. Ah well, I told myself. This is only a teething problem. Cross the Atlantic? Not a problem.

I was still feeling nauseous when I surfaced three hours later but I insisted on taking the oars. David had been rowing hard into a strong headwind, moving the boat a hard-earned mile, and he deserved a few hours' sleep. Pride spurred me to make a contribution. I glanced at my watch as I put my hands on the oars. It was now past midnight, and the lights of Plymouth were sparkling on our left. Before long, I was starting to sweat and shiver again.

So this was ocean rowing? Retching over and over again, getting up in the middle of a cold and dank night, rowing into a stiff wind? If this was my 'fix of excitement', I would have preferred an injection of morphine.

Trial and error swiftly taught me that I felt marginally less sick if I rowed with my eyes closed, so I persevered and was starting to feel quite pleased with myself as I established a steady rhythm and moved on. Eyes tightly shut, I took the oars back with growing confidence, and pulled through.

'Er, Jim?'

It was David. He had only slept for an hour and was now leaning forward, peering blearily out of the hatch. He seemed a little agitated.

'Don't worry, Dave,' I told him. 'Everything is fine. I'm feeling better.'

'Er, Jim?'

'Don't worry,' I said, eyes clamped closed. 'Get some more sleep.'

He spoke more firmly: 'Er, Jim . . .'

'Yes, David, what's the problem?'

'Jim, why are the lights of Plymouth on our right?'

I opened my eyes and was horrified to discover that, while I had thought I was rising to the challenge and powering the boat west towards Falmouth, I had actually executed a 180-degrees turn and was rowing back eastwards at such a pace that we had already passed the mouth of the Tamar.

There was nothing to say, but there was obviously a lesson to learn: never row without at least occasionally glancing at the compass. On reflection, perhaps we should have burst out laughing, but life isn't always so jovial: I was sick, David was exhausted and the 'about-turn' was deeply disappointing.

In these fraught circumstances, David emerged as the personification of calm and mercy. He suggested we should regain our position west of the Tamar, find a buoy close to the shore and park for the rest of the night. After the trials of six hours at sea, he realised we both needed some sleep.

Even when we woke on the Saturday morning, my partner clearly wanted to salvage the positives, pointing out how we had achieved our primary purpose of proving the boat was seaworthy. For my part, I was still trying to wake up from what I hoped would turn out to have been a bad dream but there was no escape from the humbling reality of my sickness and the U-turn.

Our original plan had been to set off at noon on Friday, spend two nights at sea and return to the rowing club on Sunday evening. In practice, we did not leave until Friday evening and it was only nine o'clock on Saturday morning when we agreed to draw a line beneath proceedings and row back to the club.

David said nothing that could be construed as over-critical, and he kindly resisted the temptation to crack jokes at my expense (at least, for a week or so!), but he would not have been human if he did not start to wonder what on earth he would do if I proved such a liability out on the Atlantic.

I reflected carefully during the long drive home, and concluded there was nothing wrong that could not be solved by seasickness tablets. If I had not felt so ill, I would not have rowed with my eyes shut, and we would have continued in a westerly direction and everything would have been fine. That was my conviction: I still believed I could row oceans, and I wasn't giving up.

My commitment to the project and David remained complete. Two weeks later, I learned the whole truth about his commitment to me.

His original partner suddenly reappeared. This man had first withdrawn from the race because he was newly married and his wife didn't want him to go rowing across the Atlantic. The marriage had now ended, and he was free to reclaim his berth in the boat. He contacted David, wanting to know if there was any chance of regaining his position.

In my view, David was well within his rights to make the choice. Taking into account what had happened during our sea trial, I would have understood his position if he had contacted me and said we should not proceed. Of course, I would have been deeply disappointed, but it was possible to make a case that he was putting himself in danger by rowing with me. I was realistic. The other man was younger and stronger. David had to make his decision.

He acted instantly, firmly explaining to his friend that he had entered into an agreement with me and he had no intention of breaking that agreement. I was touched by his loyalty, and decided the best way of expressing my gratitude to him would be to shape up and start justifying his faith in me.

So we advanced.

Reflecting on these months before the race across the Atlantic, ebbing on through the summer of 1997, I have searched in vain for that moment when I sat down and decided, once and for all, that I would start rowing across oceans. This was not a normal thing for a middle-aged businessman to do. It is all very well to say I wanted an injection of excitement, but there must have been a time when I dealt with the cold realities of the situation and made a firm commitment, both in time and roughly £40,000, to row across the Atlantic.

The fact is, there was no big moment. There was no Big Bang decision. It was not a case of me deciding to start rowing oceans; it was a case of me floating an idea and being propelled by quirks of fate towards the starting line.

If I had not found time to visit the Boat Show, I would not have rowed. If I had not been introduced to David, I would not have rowed. If David had not stood by me as his partner after the sea trial, I would not have rowed.

Day by day, it seemed as though events over which I had no control were gradually transforming my crazy idea into a reality; and, throughout this process, I had no sense of being tremendously bold or brave. When I was given a chance to join forces with David, it seemed the obvious thing to do. When it was time to buy the boat kit, I could hardly have said that was not a good idea. When David had reaffirmed his commitment after the test row, there was no way I could turn to him and say that, after all, I would rather stay at home.

In a sense, lots of small decisions, most of which seemed automatic, had combined to make one big decision: I was going to row.

Equally, there was no shattering moment of dread when I suddenly asked myself what on earth I was getting myself into. In the first place, I was too busy in Eastern Europe to be worried about the Atlantic race. In my experience, worry is something that grows to fill gaps in a schedule. And whenever I did contemplate the looming prospect, maybe while driving or during a flight, I tended to visualise myself preparing for some kind of extreme roller-coaster ride.

Yes, I knew it would be frightening. In fact, I hoped it would be frightening. That was the whole point of going. I wanted to be thrilled. However, I also trusted David's ability to prepare the boat in the same way that I believed any fairground would ensure a ride complied with every safety regulation.

In my mind, I was ready to row.

Being so busy proved a double-edged sword. It may have been beneficial to have no time to worry, but I also found myself with no time to launch any kind of serious fund-raising initiative. Under these circumstances, it seemed far easier to pay the bills from the profits of my business than to scurry around in search of sponsors. In essence, I was backing myself to earn the money more quickly and more efficiently than I would be able to find benefactors.

In fact, far from being preoccupied by the costs, I had maintained from the outset that our voyage could serve as a vehicle to raise funds and awareness for a chosen charity and we decided to support Population Concern, an association working for the right to reproductive health care worldwide.

Out of this relationship, it was arranged that the actress Susan Hampshire, one of the charity's active vice-presidents, would formally 'launch' our boat during a media conference at the Ruislip Lido. Susan proved gracious and dazzling, as she posed for photographs on the bow of our boat. A local fire engine and a class from my daughters' school further enhanced the occasion.

We didn't secure much press coverage, aside from a brief interview for the BBC World Service and a couple of lines in the local newspaper, but everybody enjoyed the day, particularly David and I. The picture of our boat with us at the oars and Susan perched on the bow still stands on my mantelpiece at home. In a world full of affected celebrity, she was wonderfully natural.

D-Day was drawing ever nearer.

The start of the Atlantic Rowing Race was scheduled for 12 October and it had become clear my commitment to oversee a project in Romania would force me to spend most of the last three months before our departure in Bucharest. It was not an ideal situation, not least because it inflicted upon David the complete responsibility for conducting our final preparations for the race.

I spoke to him regularly on the telephone, and resolved that the very least I could do was ensure I was physically prepared for the voyage. One tweak of the fat around my midriff suggested there was plenty of work to be done. Confirmation came in the smirks on the faces of my business colleagues when I told them about my imminent adventure. They didn't believe I could row across the Atlantic. That was fine. Every snigger served as a spur to prove them wrong.

The training would begin. One of my friends in Bucharest told me he knew someone who owned a café overlooking the lake where the Romanian national rowing squad were based. This seemed a fragile contact, but a series of calls were made and I was given permission to use the facilities. A time and date were fixed for my first visit to what seemed to be an elite club.

I duly arrived and was surprised to find a group of enthusiastic members had gathered to greet me. If any of them had expected to find a mighty, strapping hero preparing to cross the ocean, they would certainly have been underwhelmed to discover me sweating through my daily routine.

'Mr Shekhdar, please, we have prepared a boat for you.'

A man, who appeared to be the manager of the club, was shepherding me towards one of the 'skinny' rowing boats seen at top-class rowing events. I took a step backwards. Maybe they had mistaken me for Steve Redgrave.

'No, I'm sorry. I am not skilled enough to row a boat like that,' I told them, knowing that even if I was able to squeeze into the boat (and that was doubtful), it was likely that I would capsize within a few seconds.

'Mr Shekhdar, please.'

I was surrounded by expressions that seemed to chorus: 'We admire what you are doing. We applaud your courage. Please try our boat.'

'Well, all right. Just one lap.'

They pushed me gently away from the jetty and, to my relief, I managed to stay upright as I wobbled through one large circle. On subsequent visits to this beautifully appointed location on the outskirts of Bucharest, I specifically asked to row a basic clinker, the kind of pleasure boat typically rented out to families and hooligans alike on lakes in public parks around Britain. My request was granted.

I hardly missed an early morning row through the twelve weeks that followed, invariably arriving at the club around 06.30, jumping into my boat and working up a respectable sweat as I pounded around the lake for an hour. Tremendously fit athletes often started to arrive just as I was leaving to face a full day's work, and they would occasionally gaze at me in astonishment. I didn't care. Even if I was starting from a low base, I was making solid progress.

David had booked his flight to arrive in Tenerife ten days before the start of the race, and I had promised to join him as soon as possible thereafter. In the event, there were too many issues to resolve in Romania, and I did not arrive in the holiday island until late on 10 October. It was D-day minus one and a bit.

...tner had completed most of the ... almost ready for departure ...seful, revealing a talent for ...ull.

...ith the event organisers regard- ...ment of our entry fee, a sum of ..., we had decided to express our ... officials by looking for a last- ...re the start, we paid in full.

...gether with David's girlfriend, Jo, ...ad joined us in Tenerife to see the ... were too busy with our last-minute ...much of them in relaxed surroundings as we would have liked. The pressure was mounting. In every snapped response and anxious glance lingered the crux issue of our safety.

It is not every family that has to stand on the dock and wave goodbye to their loved ones as they row out into the ocean. Perhaps I was insensitive to the concerns being felt by Jane and my daughters. If this was the case, it was only because safety was genuinely not an issue in my mind.

We had installed the most reliable tracking and safety equipment, and we were rowing a well-designed, essentially unsinkable boat. Further reassurance had been provided when the race organisers arranged two racing yachts to patrol regularly between competitors' boats – although, in practice, we saw the 'escorts' only twice during sixty-five days, on Day 35 and on Day 64, and both times it was we who were offering the support, giving them some spare coffee.

Of course, we were not so irresponsible as to pretend there was no risk at all in what was an inaugural race, but David and I had made a sober assessment of the challenge and jointly concluded the risk was manageable.

At last, it was 12 October. Amid an exhilarating atmosphere around the quay and among the various crew members, no fewer than twenty-seven identical two-man rowing boats moved towards the start line, heading for Barbados.

Within a few hours, each crew was confronted by a crucial decision that would determine whether they would remain in contention to win the race or whether they would be briskly consigned to a chasing pack. There was no particular skill in this choice. The fates were stalking.

Hierro is the smaller of two islands lying to the west of Tenerife. Each of the twenty-seven crews needed to decide whether they would pass by on the northern side or the southern side. Having studied the charts and the weather forecast, David and I opted to take the northern route. Ten other crews appeared to concur with our calculations and the rest headed south. In reality, we were all guessing, throwing the dice. It was six of one, half a dozen of the other.

And the winners were ... all the boats that rowed south because, within the space of thirty-six hours, they were being carried towards the Americas by a powerful current and a fair wind. The rest of us, those who had aimed north, soon found ourselves being battered by a series of brutish storms.

Plain bad luck had effectively ruled us out of contention, and the race had scarcely begun. It would be an understatement to say David and I were severely disappointed. With due humility, we privately reckoned we had a decent chance of actually winning the race. David was a tremendously talented rower and, at the very least, I was a determined and confident competitor. However, these dreams had evaporated and, from Day 2, we were rowing for pride.

Frustration nearly became misery as we spent the next four weeks battling against appalling weather conditions. Time and again, we steeled ourselves for a massive effort, rowed with all our strength and made some progress only then to sit powerless as the wind blew us back to where we had started. We crossed several meridians three or five times, suffering a cruel, merciless kind of *Groundhog Day* existence on the grey, hostile, churning Atlantic Ocean.

Ever the incurable optimist, I found some advantages in adversity: first, I quickly learned anger and frustration are useless emotions on the ocean. Aside from being a waste of energy, they are futile because, however frustrated and angry you feel, you never have any option other than to keep rowing. There is nowhere else to go, no alternative, no getaway. In a sense, it was easy to keep going, because there was absolutely nothing else to do.

Second, in sharing the pain of our luckless start, David and I were able to learn a great deal about each other in a short space of time. Although it was eighteen months since our first meeting in a motorway service station, and despite many telephone calls in the interim, the fact was that, prior to the start of the race, we had not spent more than a total of eight days in each other's company. We soon discovered there is not much room for secrets when two six-foot men are striving to survive and advance within the confines of a twenty-three-foot rowing boat.

Our basic strategy was to divide the days into 90-minute shifts, and the nights into 120-minute shifts, always with one of us sleeping while the other rowed. However, even this structure could not pre-empt light-hearted banter about who was contributing more to the general cause. David would argue he was stronger and fitter but, occasionally, I would row beyond my allotted time just so I would be able to claim that, while he might row faster, it was clearly I who rowed for longer.

We had agreed on the first day that the cabin was too small to accommodate us both at the same time, and the consequence of this decision was that one of us would remain on deck at all times, even through the harshest of storms. So far as we were both concerned, we would rather stay exposed to the driving rain and whipping wind, harnessed and huddled in a TPA (Thermal Protection Apparatus, a reinforced plastic bag with only a gap for the face), than have to lie in the warm cabin, uncomfortably close to each other.

Such raging tempests were torturously unbearable at first. The boat would often be turned to angles of sixty degrees and more but we gradually became used to the experience. Curiously, they became just another part of the routine and we became almost blasé about the advent of another storm.

The weather conditions eventually eased and we started to make decent progress across the ocean, holding a position somewhere near the front of the posse of boats that had headed north from Tenerife. I was starting to enjoy myself, beginning to feel the magically beneficial effects of a stable diet and regular exercise.

Seasickness pills had mercifully prevented a repeat of my performance in the sea trial. When I started to run out of tablets, I managed to wean myself off the drug and became accustomed to the unnatural and constant motion of the rocking boat. My psoriasis eased and I had started to lose what became a total of fifteen kilograms during the voyage. Blisters on my hands and sores on my bum caused discomfort, but these problems either healed themselves or were treated with antiseptic cream.

In general, I felt extremely healthy. The human body remains a wondrous machine so long as the owner does not push it too hard.

Some days did inevitably start to drag and, with one of us rowing and the other leaning against the hatch, we resorted to playing time-consuming games such as the one where one person thinks of a famous character or personality, and the other tries to work out their identity by asking questions. We both became so adept at the process of elimination that, over the course of nine weeks, David succeeded in identifying every character that I selected, and he only managed to defeat me by choosing 'The Unknown Soldier' and 'John Doe'.

Another humdrum day, I unleashed upon my partner a riddle dating back to my days at Queen Mary College in London. As the sea lapped gently against the side of our boat, I asked him if he was lying comfortably, and began: 'Once upon a time a man was walking along a cliff. He was just starting to feel hungry when he saw a café, with a standard A-frame blackboard outside proclaiming in white chalk . . . "Special of the Day: Seagull Soup."

'Intrigued by the offer of this unusual dish, the man entered the café and ordered a bowl. Before long, the waitress placed a bowl of light brown soup on the table before him. The man deeply inhaled its aroma and seemed pleasantly surprised by the aroma. He swallowed a spoonful of soup, turned pale, rushed out of the café without paying his bill and threw himself off the cliff.'

'Why?'

David started asking questions, and I answered them all honestly, but I also told him he would have to work out the solution for himself. He started to grow frustrated after a couple of hours, and changed the subject. However, the next morning, he was asking about Seagull Soup again, and this subject kept turning up in conversation through the weeks that followed.

As one day merged into another, we also experienced one unforgettable occasion of wide-eyed wonder at a wandering whale.

We first noticed the presence of this enormous mammal, coloured grey and black and measuring roughly the same size as our boat, when he swam to within five yards of our oars and yet, inexplicably, we did not feel in any way threatened. The whale seemed somehow friendly and gentle, and spent several hours in our vicinity before finally plunging out of sight, his curiosity apparently satisfied.

The next day, our boat was a picture of calm: David was sitting on the bucket and I was sleeping peacefully in the cabin. All of a sudden, the whale spectacularly emerged from the water, rising vertically within touching distance of David at the front of the boat. His performance had started.

We sat entranced and enamoured for the next fifteen minutes as this amazing creature proceeded to roll and dive, flap his tail and produce sounds very dissimilar to the usual whale song. I was occasionally concerned by the volume of water sent surging across the deck when he executed swallow dives and belly flops right beside the hull but this remarkable animal never once touched the boat.

And then, with a final majestic splash, he was gone from our sight, moving on, and yet indelibly and wonderfully engraved in our memory.

Aside from the games and riddles, and the spellbinding confrontations with nature, there were also inevitable moments of conflict. These sparks usually flew during the middle of a cold, dark night when both of us desperately wanted to lie down and sleep, but one of us had to keep rowing.

We generally divided the night into four two-hour sessions, each rowing and sleeping alternately until we ate breakfast together at dawn. The shift starting at ten o'clock at night was fine, getting up at midnight was almost endurable and the two o'clock call was a wrench, but still possible.

However, there can be few more miserable sounds than the roar of David Jackson's voice at four o'clock in the morning, summoning me from my snug, comfortable sleeping bag to row through the coldest hour before dawn. I must confess to having sometimes feigned a deep, deep sleep; and there were days when the roles were reversed, and he refused to get up within the ten minutes' slumber time we agreed to allow each other.

Ten past four in the morning, quarter past four in the morning: these were the precise times when relations tended to fray at the edges.

'Will you wake up and get out here?'

'Ughhh?'

'Get out here!'

Thankfully, our decision to equip the boat with a satellite telephone gave us both the option of hearing another voice once in a while. I generally spoke to Jane, Anna and Sarah every few days, managing to stay in touch with their lives and to reassure them that I was well and enjoying the trip.

I also spent a considerable amount of time on the telephone to staff at the AJS Management offices in Bratislava. My business didn't stop for the race and, in fact, we managed to win the largest contract in the company's history from the middle of the Atlantic. I was exultant, but started to sense my rowing partner was less enthusiastic about my evident affection for the telephone.

Indeed, David appeared less than devastated when, two weeks before the end of our voyage, the equipment ceased to function. He denies, to this day, that he had anything to do with the broken connection to the antenna.

As we closed in on the finishing line in Barbados, we both

61

turned our thoughts to what we would do next. The disappointment of missing the fair wind at the start of the race had faded in our minds and, for my part, I had enjoyed the voyage much more than I had ever imagined would be possible.

David said he wanted to cycle coast to coast across the United States of America, but I had sampled the thrill of ocean rowing, and I wanted more. There was not a single moment when I considered the Atlantic crossing to be anything other than simply the start of a new chapter in my life. I resolutely wanted to row across another ocean, so why not the largest ocean on our planet.

'The Pacific!' I declared. 'That's what I'll do next.'

My partner raised his eyebrows and smiled.

We eventually reached Barbados after sixty-five days at sea, having taken more than three weeks longer than we had hoped. Nonetheless, our achievement was genuine and real and, taking into account our disastrous start, I was not unhappy to have finished sixteenth out of the twenty-seven boats that started in Tenerife.

I understood how much I owed to David Jackson, for his dedication before the race and his strength out on the ocean, but, privately, I also derived immense satisfaction from the fact that the overweight businessman who had retched so pitiably at the mouth of the Tamar had successfully crossed an ocean. Baptised in the Atlantic, I turned impatiently towards the Pacific.

4
The Planning

It was once written of a prominent international sports administrator that he has fifty new ideas every day, and fifty-one of them are bad. My wife would probably suggest the remark applies equally to me. Rowing solo and unaided across the Pacific Ocean was just an idea, but I was resolved it would not dissolve into my frantic schedule like many others. I wanted to make it happen.

Only weeks after returning home from the Atlantic voyage, I sat down and worked out precisely what would be required to turn this concept into reality. I was aware that it was David Jackson's resolve, rather than mine, that had transformed my Atlantic intentions into a cast-iron achievement. The Pacific trip was going to be altogether different. I was on my own. If there was something to be done, nobody else was going to do it for me.

The first requirement was complete commitment to the project. There is a world of difference between wanting to do something because it might be fun and being resolved to do something because you need to do it. From the outset, I needed to cross the Pacific. It didn't matter how long it took, but I always had this strange sense that, somehow, sometime, I would do it.

In January 1998, many of the Atlantic rowers from the previous year's race gathered for a reunion at the London Boat Show. We assembled in a beer tent and were then ushered across to the Sunseeker stand where the makers of the Atlantic Challenge documentary were showing rushes of their video material. David and I scarcely featured because, like most of those who had entered the race without sponsors, we had declined to pay the £5,000 'feature' fee that is common practice in this type of venture.

Nonetheless, I enjoyed the occasion and fell into conversation with two ladies who had been volunteer crew on the race escort boats. As we talked, I outlined my Pacific intentions and one of these ladies seemed quite enthused by the project. She had sailed in one of the crews in the previous BT Global Challenge, the round-the-world yacht race, and was evidently an organised and capable person. She gave me the impression of knowing people who would seriously consider sponsorship of my trip, and she appeared ideally qualified to help me develop my plans. I was excited. I thought I was making progress.

In fact, I wasn't. We eagerly approached a large insurance company, but they declined the proposal and, by April 1998, the lady's enthusiasm started to ebb. Weeks accelerated into months. I became busy at work in Eastern Europe and at home with my family, and, in what seemed the twinkling of an eye, it was the end of 1998 and my Pacific plan was going nowhere.

Aside from commitment, I also needed money. Even without building a new, lighter boat, I had estimated that the solo voyage across the Pacific would cost something like £95,000. My business was thriving but, at that time, I felt it would be essential to cover most of my costs with sponsorship.

Once I had raised the funds, I would advance to the third stage and begin the logistical and administrative planning of how I was going to move my twenty-three-foot rowing boat first from Plymouth to South America and then from there to the east coast of Australia.

Commitment, then money, then logistics: this was the theory. In practice, I remained inactive as 1999 gathered pace. In my own mind, I was certainly going to row solo across the Pacific. In my own diary, I simply could not find the time to prepare proposals and court sponsors. Weeks sped by.

The project remained at the back of my mind and, every once in a while, I would outline my plans to someone who seemed interested. Early in 1999, I gave an interview to a journalist who wrote a regular column for the IT supplement that appeared in *The Times*. He was interested in me as somebody who had used a computer in extreme circumstances, while rowing across the Atlantic; so, when I had answered his questions, we moved on to ocean rowing and he appeared to become animated when I spoke about my Pacific project.

I suppose I am vulnerable during the early stages of planning an unusual adventure such as crossing the Pacific. Most people tend to react with a glazed expression that suggests they think I am mad, and others don't even listen. So I would become encouraged when anyone heard me out, and then tremendously pleased if they showed even the slightest enthusiasm.

Just like the lady at the Boat Show, this journalist was instantly positive and constructive. He explained how he often spoke to decision-makers at many leading computer and communications companies, and he felt sure he would be able to raise something like £100,000 in sponsorship. As he spoke, I started to smile widely, following every word with round eyes. As a dog seems mesmerised by a bone, so I became enthralled by the prospect of funding.

This was wonderful, exactly what I needed, and wanted, to hear. Within a week, I was gaining momentum, getting back in touch with the second lady I had met at the London Boat Show. She had maritime and business experience and seemed interested by the prospect of working with me as a kind of project manager. Everything was coming together and I arranged for the three of us – the journalist, the new project manager and me – to meet Kenneth Crutchlow, director of the Ocean Rowing Society, at his office in North London, and gently pick his brains about the challenge of rowing, solo and unaided, across the Pacific.

Kenneth was evidently not impressed, and could hardly have been more dismissive of my intentions. He brusquely expressed his view that nobody could row the South Pacific route that I was proposing; and he added that, in any case, the Frenchman

Gerard d'Aboville had already crossed the Pacific alone. Where I had hoped to find encouragement, I was being brushed aside.

I replied that, so far as I was aware, Gerard had not only rowed the short route, across the northern Pacific, but had also been assisted at various stages. My plan was to row solo and unaided, from continent to continent, from shore to shore, with no external support of any kind at any stage.

The temperature of the meeting was plunging way below zero. Kenneth sat and listened, deadpan and blank, making me feel like an overweight, deluded businessman who was now wasting his time. He gave me the impression that he believed I had no chance of crossing the Pacific. We had arrived at his office in high spirits, chattering excitedly together. We left in silence.

Within three weeks of this deeply unconstructive meeting, the prospective project manager e-mailed me to say she could no longer make herself available to work on the project; and the journalist came back to me with news that, after all, he would not be able to assist me in raising funds.

My commitment was being tested. I had spent time and effort on starting preparations for my Pacific project, and had made no progress at all. I was not giving up, but I was starting to feel despondent, at a loss to know how and when I was going to get things moving. The process was stuck at square one.

'Hello, Jim?' It was David Jackson calling. 'How are you?'

'Fine.'

'Are you ready to cross the Pacific yet?'

The candid answer would have been a straight 'No', but I was much too proud to admit the truth to myself let alone anyone else, so I mumbled something about everything being on track.

'Great,' he said. 'I have a proposal for you.'

David proceeded to explain how he and Jo were in the process of buying a dilapidated chalet on the cliff overlooking Whitsands Bay, near Plymouth, and how they needed to raise some capital.

Since we still owned the boat we had used during the Atlantic Rowing Race on a 50/50 basis, he suggested that I buy out his half and use the same boat for the Pacific trip.

The rational response would have been to thank David for the call and tell him that, in fact, my Pacific plans were not progressing at all. I would have added that, even if sponsors did suddenly emerge, I was looking to build a lighter, faster boat. And I would have concluded that, for these two reasons, there was no point in my buying his half of the boat. That was all absolutely true.

However, I am not sure there is much room for rational thought during the planning stages of an ocean rowing expedition. I acted on impulse.

'That sounds like an excellent idea, David,' I enthused.

I offered to buy his half of the boat for £7,000 on condition that, as part of the deal, he agreed to adapt and prepare the boat for the Pacific.

'Done,' he replied.

As I replaced the receiver, I suddenly realised that, whatever happened, I was going to cross the Pacific Ocean. I had bought the boat; I had told David. By these impetuous actions, I had effectively become obliged.

The boat was being stored at the Tor Point Rowing Club, near Plymouth, and David started working on alterations during his spare time. With every day he laboured, it became progressively inconceivable that, having purchased and then refitted the boat, I should subsequently withdraw from the project. There was no turning back. One thing led to another and, without ever sitting down and making a conscious decision, I managed to paint myself into a corner. By February 1999, barring disaster, there was no turning back. The trip was on.

These developments significantly changed the nature of my fund-raising efforts. From being in a position where I was looking for a major sponsor before I committed myself to the voyage, I was now searching ever more desperately for companies to help offset the cost. In resolving to go ahead with the trip whatever happened, I had effectively opted to underwrite the costs.

My approach was bold, but not foolhardy. I had made absolutely certain my essentially selfish decision to pursue the Pacific voyage would not seriously jeopardise our family finances. Even in a worst-case scenario where I had to find just under £100,000 myself, I calculated that I would be able to cope without affecting the lives of Jane, Anna and Sarah. We were far from millionaires, and it would have been reasonably tight, but I had done the sums.

More determined than ever to find sponsors, I set to work on the word processor and started sending proposals requesting support from leading British companies. A brief biography, an outline of the trip, the opportunity for branding on the side of the boat, the potential for publicity during and at the conclusion of the voyage: to me, it added up to an attractive and meaty package. I posted the envelopes, and impatiently waited for the replies to arrive.

'Your proposal sounds intriguing, but . . .'

'Unfortunately, we are not in a position . . .'

'Our budget has already been allocated . . .'

'With regret, recent budgetary restrictions . . .'

Early mornings assumed a new ritual. I would be excited to see the letters arrive, would breathlessly open the envelopes and my spirits would then sink as I read through the standard, ruthless expressions of regret. Every day would start with another barrage of rejections. It was soul-destroying.

I eventually reached the conclusion that British business has been taken over by bean counters devoid of vision, imagination and, much worse, devoid of any spirit of adventure. Their approach reminds me of an old adage coined in the early days of computers: 'Nobody gets sacked for buying IBM.'

They play safe. In horse-racing terms, they are only prepared to invest in the odds-on favourites, the traditional and the familiar. The old Victorian spirit of daring and adventure appears to have evaporated in an all-consuming drive to improve the bottom line. It seems as if every sponsorship proposal needs to be quantified in figures and then justified by precedents.

Nobody is prepared to think big, so nobody wins big. I understood the textbook marketing logic of their decisions and the MBA-speak of their rejections, but I was surprised when one marketing executive told me the weakness in my proposal was that I did not offer any opportunity for corporate hospitality. Yacht races are attractive, he explained, but one man sitting in a rowing boat does not add up to something their major clients really want to watch. I was speechless. There was nothing to say. I was striving to do something nobody had ever done before and I was being graded in terms of corporate hospitality.

Most companies at least took the trouble to say no. Virgin did not bother to respond to my first letter at all. I wrote again, but there was still no reply. I wrote a third time, still no response. Perhaps there was no reason for me to harbour such high expectations of Richard Branson's company, but it was difficult to accept the celebrated adventurer and entrepreneur could not even find the time to tell me he was sorry, but no thanks. Despair boiled over into rage.

My fourth letter was angry, and it finally provoked a reply from the Virgin corporate marketing department in which they explained that rowing was not their sport. They also asked me to stop writing to them. That was all. I had hoped they might offer me cheap air tickets, but there was nothing.

British Airways responded more constructively, explaining that my voyage did not comply with their profile of causes to be sponsored, but they were able to offer me a 50 per cent discount on their full economy-class fare to any destination in the world plus additional savings on unaccompanied baggage. I asked if they could transport my boat to South America. They said it was too big.

In the end, I didn't even fly with BA because 50 per cent of their full economy fare to Santiago, Chile, was still more expensive than the discount ticket I was able to secure from Iberia, the Spanish national airline.

By the middle of 1999, I had to concede my mailshot to corporate Britain had failed. I had spent money on postage and telephone calls, and reaped gross sponsorship revenue of precisely zero. The campaign was designed to solve my financial problems. Instead, the initiative had made them worse.

Undaunted, I broadened my quest for support to family friends, to friends of friends, to fathers of friends of friends, to friends of friends who just happened to know somebody at university, in fact to anybody who was friendly. I did not enjoy this part of the process, and felt almost ashamed when close friends who could least afford to help were the ones who came forward to offer assistance. I never wanted anyone to feel they were in any way obliged.

One old friend suggested I should write to Jim Smith, a wealthy Australian entrepreneur who had run a successful electronics business and embarked upon some unconventional adventures, such as flying hot air balloons backwards from New Zealand to Tasmania. I dispatched my proposal by e-mail, and was amazed to receive a reply from his secretary only two days later. She requested details of the bank account where she could deposit the $2,000 that Mr Smith had told her to send me. Such generosity was typically Australian and, not for the first or last time, I was grateful to have that country as my destination.

I also found encouragement closer to home. Keith Knowles, the CEO of Mobil: Pacific Rim, also happened to be the father of my daughter Anna's closest friend. Back in 1997, he had felt unable to assist us in our Atlantic voyage because it was not his patch, so to speak, but we met again in the bar of the cricket club and, apparently enthused by my Pacific plans, he said he would be happy to put my request for support to Mobil's corporate marketing department in the USA.

However, even with Keith's personal backing, the eventual answer was negative, and part of the internal e-mail chain within

Mobil shed some light on why I was getting such an appalling response from the corporate world.

A senior official had looked at my proposal and responded by pointing out that 'in the 1 per cent chance' that I successfully completed the crossing, the company would not receive much benefit because I would not have used their lubricants. He continued: 'And in the 99 per cent chance that he doesn't make it, we run the risk of being embarrassed if worldwide television happens to capture our logo floating in the wreckage when they pull his body from the water.'

His assessment was brutal but, again, I understood the logic. Keith kindly offered some consolation when he forwarded a cheque for $5,000, the limit of his own discretionary powers. In the final analysis, this single donation proved to be more than twice the size of any other cash sum I received.

The continuing failure of the fund-raising campaign forced me to cut costs wherever possible. I had planned an exploratory trip to Chile to secure necessary permits and visas, and to settle on the most appropriate point of departure. With great regret, I felt obliged to cancel this important exercise.

As 1999 drew to a close, I revised my approach once again. I had started by contacting the major companies directly, and had then sought the assistance of any friends and contacts in finding a 'home-run' sponsor; now, I narrowed the search to finding smaller sponsors able to provide assistance in kind.

The 2000 London Boat Show seemed a sensible place to start and, ever the dumb optimist, I started to walk up and down the aisles, effectively carrying a begging bowl to stand after stand. After three hours of fruitless effort, I retired to lick my wounded ego at the exhibition stand of my old friend, Bob Jelfs, and invited him for a beer.

'Jim, you need to be more focused,' Bob ventured. 'Work out exactly what you need and approach the supplier directly.'

This proved excellent advice and, together, we agreed that navigation and communications items occupied a large part of the total equipment budget. I had already investigated the prices of paper charts of the southern Pacific but, as we sat and talked through various options, I suddenly woke up to the option of using the most recent technology and taking electronic maps.

Within fifteen minutes, I had discovered there was only one company that was capable of providing electronic charts with the required coverage. Before long, I was walking purposefully towards the C-Map stand.

I approached a lady, who quickly told me I needed to speak to a man called Paul Sumpner. 'He's busy at the moment,' she said, gesturing towards a group of people gathered across the way. I waited patiently.

He didn't know me and I didn't know him, but Paul eventually came across and concentrated his attention on me. He listened carefully as I told him of my plans to cross the Pacific and my intention to use electronic maps. His response was positive, constructive and immensely encouraging. 'That's a crazy idea,' he told me, smiling broadly. 'Now what can I do to help?'

Through the next thirty minutes, Paul demonstrated how he could construct a special composite chart that would cover not only the areas of the ocean that I intended to pass through, but also areas where I might find myself if the weather did not prove as co-operative as I hoped. Evidently an expert in his field, he was thorough, utterly professional and completely attentive.

When one of his assistants tried to draw him away to help some other, ostensibly more important customers, he firmly told her he was busy and would only come across when he was finished dealing with me. After so many months of being made to feel insignificant and not worthy of anybody's attention, it felt enormously encouraging to be treated so well by a stranger.

The C-Map charts appeared just the ticket, and Paul then took me to visit the stands of companies offering compatible hardware. Raytheon produced plotters that were reasonably priced, and Paul said he would be able to load all the charts I needed on to two cartridges that could then be sealed inside the plotter, thus providing a secure, waterproof, practical and workable navigation system.

A combination of the C-Map charts operating within a Raytheon RC520 Plotter, a grey plastic unit comprising a screen measuring 5.25" × 4" and supported by a few keys, would serve to provide my exact position at all times, show both the speed and direction of the boat, and moreover give me the capacity to study, plan and plot any part of the route at any stage of the journey, even to find my way through the Great Barrier Reef if necessary.

This small grey box proved not only the most important and useful piece of equipment aboard my boat, but also the most reliable and indestructible. Of the six navigation/communication systems eventually installed, only the plotter and charts remained operational throughout the voyage.

More than any other single item, this plotter enabled me to complete the voyage successfully, and I am keenly aware that I would not have found this system without Paul Sumpner's time and knowledge that afternoon at the London Boat Show. He was also able to offer me a special price.

The kindness of strangers is a powerful phenomenon, at once disarming and humbling. Paul had no clear reason to spend more than an hour solving my problems, and has derived no measurable benefit from doing so. All I am able to offer in return is my enduring gratitude for his generosity.

Three weeks later, the telephone was ringing again.

'Hello, Jim Shekhdar?'

'Speaking.'

'My name is Tim Harris, the world's greatest armchair adventurer.'

Another complete stranger had emerged from out of the blue to offer me valuable advice and an enormous psychological boost. Tim had heard about my Pacific project from a mutual friend and wanted me to consider using his tracking and communications system. We spoke for a while, and arranged to meet at a service station on the M40, midway between London and his home in Birmingham.

We discussed the merits of the traditional system using Argos beacons, and his Orbcomm system, which probably convinced me more than him that his product suited my needs. Tim was not interested in the hard sell. He genuinely wanted to help me make the right choice.

In the end, we settled upon a tracking system that would not only provide my precise position but also give me the capacity to send and receive short text messages via the Internet. My basic strategy was to install a broad armoury of overlapping communications and navigation systems that would cover inevitable breakdowns.

Tim Harris proved an important source of advice in this area and, in my mind, stands alongside Paul Sumpner as generous in offering aid to a stranger, without which I would not have reached my destination. I don't know whether I deserved the freely given assistance of such good Samaritans. I hope so. In any event, their role in this adventure should not be underestimated.

Meanwhile, at Tor Point Rowing Club, near Plymouth, David Jackson had almost completed the refitting of the boat. He had reconstructed the deck area to incorporate eight watertight hatches where I would store food. He also shortened the runner base for the sliding seat and removed four rowlocks, which were used when two of us were rowing during the Atlantic crossing but had now become superfluous. He left only the central pair for me.

The plans were gradually taking shape. I had long since abandoned my admirable resolve that the logistics phase should only start once the funding had been secured, and the two processes had somehow merged together, but I was generally feeling comfortable with my progress.

I had accepted the reality that there would not be any media conference with a smartly dressed marketing manager handing me a large cheque amid the flashing of cameras and smattering of applause. I realised the 'big sponsor' was not going to emerge, and I was satisfied by the compromise solution of chipping away at costs with discounts, donations and value in kind.

My solo voyage quickly became a team effort, only made possible by the amazing commitment of many individuals and small businesses.

Expedition Foods produce excellent vacuum-packed pre-cooked meals, only needing to be warmed in boiling water, and they agreed to supply me at cost price. Steve Morris, CEO of Axis Health Clubs, responded to my proposal with a proposal of his own: he said he would donate either £50 before my departure or £1,000 if I managed to complete the voyage successfully. Rarely lacking confidence, and seeing the £50 as pretty insignificant, I chose the latter option and duly collected the cheque upon my return.

Yacht Parts are chandlers in Plymouth, well known to David Jackson. They provided generous assistance before our Atlantic voyage and once again offered support before the Pacific trip, agreeing to loan me a water maker and a life-raft, both high-cost items, plus various other bits and bobs.

Two friends in Slovakia, Daniel Strasser and Martin Catlos, worked long and hard to establish a presence on the Internet, and the site, to be found under the address 'pacific-challenge-2000.com', provides testimony to their success in designing an attractive site and providing updated information.

Martin held the additional distinction of being the very first private donor to the cause; early on, we conceived a plan to purchase and print high-quality T-shirts and sell them as merchandise through the website. This idea never took flight, but it was Martin who selflessly paid the bill for the initial samples.

The entire staff of AJS Management in Slovakia proved wholly supportive during the months before my departure, even though they all regarded me as an audacious eccentric and wondered if they would ever see me again.

Friends and family rallied around in London, helping with

shopping trips, covering all the bases while we rushed to and fro; and genuine heroes emerged from all kinds of places, even Yellow Pages. Searching for someone to help her with an electronic design project the previous year, my daughter Sarah selected a name out of the service directory, called and was enthusiastically supported in her project by Rob Malos.

And Rob happened to be around when the boat was parked on a trailer in the street outside our house and we were busy packing equipment and food into the hatches and cabin in time for everything to be shipped down to Chile. Amid frenetic activity on all sides, Rob stepped forward to ensure electric and electronic fittings were all sound and interconnected.

These individuals, and many others, took their places in my team. Almost without exception, they were willing to contribute and expect nothing in return. This was our team spirit; every gesture and every kindness was gratefully received.

In April 2000, scarcely three weeks before my scheduled departure from London to Chile, an extraordinary series of events resulted in Le Shark, a leisure-clothing brand, emerging as my naming sponsor.

After months of deliberations, I thought I had reached a final, bold decision to set out across the Pacific without the Argos tracking system. This choice could be likened to a jockey deciding to start the Grand National without stirrups. Argos beacons are sealed units that broadcast the boat's position six times every day via a network of bases and satellites to monitoring bases in the USA which are then routed to France. They had come to be regarded as essential for any serious ocean rower and most record-seeking expeditions.

Since each beacon is powered for three months, I was going to need at least two to cover my Pacific voyage, and, after extended negotiations with the company's representatives in France and the United States, I had successfully negotiated a reasonable price of US$5,000 for three beacons.

However, with my budget stretched to breaking point, I

decided to take the Orbcomm system as a viable communications alternative and to dispense with the Argos beacons altogether. I was running out of money. Something had to give. A nagging voice at the back of my mind insisted I was making a mistake, but I took no notice. Economies were required.

At this crucial moment, the unlikely figure of Kenneth Crutchlow, from the Ocean Rowing Society, emerged with a solution to my dilemma. He telephoned me at home and meticulously related the following saga.

Andrew Halsey, a fellow Briton, had secured Le Shark as the sponsor of his attempt to row from San Diego to Australia, but his voyage had run into problems and, after eight months on the water, he had barely reached the halfway point. Kenneth had taken the responsibility of resupplying him with food and a further three Argos beacons, financed by Le Shark.

However, Andrew abandoned his adventure before Kenneth arrived, and Kenneth was literally left holding the beacons. He explained that Le Shark had already paid for them, and asked if I wanted them.

'Yes, please,' I replied eagerly. 'Thank you very much.' I was aware that it was only Andrew's misfortune that had created the opportunity for me but such opportunities produced by quirks of fate need to be grasped with both hands. I sympathised with his situation, but it was no loss to him for me to make use of the beacons and it would have been foolish not to accept this offer of equipment that would provide peace of mind for my family. The Argos beacons may not have been essential, but they were extremely welcome.

Subsequent discussions with Le Shark, through Kenneth, swiftly produced a sponsorship agreement whereby, in return for the three beacons and air fares and accommodation for the family's trip to Australia in the event of a successful crossing, I undertook to wear branded Le Shark T-shirts and sweatshirts during the voyage and also to display the company logo prominently on the side of the boat.

Days before I set out across the ocean, this agreement evolved to a point where the Le Shark logo would be displayed at the front of the boat, and I would actually rename the boat *Le Shark*. Quite rightly, these surrogate sponsors wanted their share of commercial exposure. The gross cash value of this last-minute deal did not exceed US$10,000.

One glance at the cover of this book is enough to demonstrate how this small investment produced a truly sensational marketing return for Le Shark. Photographs of my arrival at the beach in Australia appeared in newspapers and magazines worldwide, with their logo clearly visible across my chest and dominating most photographs of the boat. Marketing experts tell me the exposure received by Le Shark as a result of my voyage can be valued at several million pounds.

Good luck to them. So far as I am concerned, it is only relevant to judge the deal in the circumstances at the time it was agreed; and the reality is that, at that time, just a few weeks before my departure, I had essentially given up hope of finding any kind of major sponsor at all. The Le Shark deal was a great deal for me for the simple reason that it was the only one on the table.

And at least it gave me a name that I could blazon across my boat, a kind of corporate medal recognising my efforts in the sponsorship campaign. Indeed, the lack of glamorous, multinational logos on my boat had troubled me for some time. I decided to resolve the problem by approaching a signage company in Rickmansworth and arranging for them to reproduce large plastic stickers of the logos of every company who had helped me along the way. They need not have given cash; any kind of assistance qualified for recognition.

In due course, these logos would be placed side by side along the boat, a veritable breastful of medals, with the Le Shark logo taking pride of place. I was attracted by the idea of appearing commercially successful, but I also wanted to show my gratitude to as many 'team' members as possible.

This exercise marked the end of two hugely frustrating years spent trying to secure funding for my voyage. As cynicism set in, still mindful of the reasons given for Mobil's rejection, I conceived a parting shot whereby I would propose to other leading oil companies that I would NOT place their logo on my boat, possibly soon to become flotsam appearing alongside my corpse on the world TV news, if they agreed to pay me the sum of $5,000. It was only an idea. In fact, it would probably have been blackmail. I never sent the letters.

We managed to finish packing the boat with food and equipment just hours before I was due to deliver it to Felixstowe, from where it would be shipped to Chile. I had tried to use the same company that had transported the boat to Tenerife before the Atlantic voyage, but they advised me to use a Liverpool shipping agent, and I was indebted to them for helping me to minimise costs by enabling *Le Shark* to share a forty-foot container with a consignment of motorbikes.

At various stages during the previous six months, I had engaged David Jackson in discussion about the course I was going to follow across the Pacific. I had already decided to take the longer southern route, rowing east to west from South America to Australia, rather than the shorter northern path, travelling west to east from either Japan or China to the coast of California. My reasons for this decision were simple: I felt the southern route represented the greater challenge, the real deal; second, I wanted to finish in Australia.

The pressing question that remained was where in South America I should actually start the crossing. David pored over *Ocean Passages of the World*, and reached the conclusion that setting out from Ecuador would position me to catch the most consistent currents and winds through to Australia.

There was a precedent. An American husband and wife team, Kathleen and Curtis Saville, had successfully rowed from northern Peru to Australia. With the able assistance of Kenneth Crutchlow, I managed to track them down and ask if they could offer me any useful pieces of advice.

Curtis gave a passable impression of Chay Blyth by telling me succinctly to read his book, but Kathleen was more helpful, exchanging e-mails with me, in which she made some useful suggestions about the route and warned me that securing permission to leave South America had proved difficult. I did not know at that stage just how prophetic this caution would become.

David and I pored over the pilot charts. The challenge in finding the ideal starting point was to strike a balance between north and south. If I rowed out to sea too far north, I would put myself at the mercy of the Humboldt Current that surges up the coast of South America before splitting into two. The clear danger was that I would be swept back towards Panama or Mexico. On the other hand, starting too far south would subject me to greater distances, and to colder, rougher seas.

We needed to find a place far enough north to stay warm and safe, and far enough south to minimise the risk of being blown back to shore. We studied the map and our index fingers found their way to Chile. We nodded. That was that. I would start the crossing halfway down Chile, and finish in Australia, ideally in Sydney, the most spectacular of coastal destinations.

Further research into weather patterns and conditions suggested the most advantageous time to start the journey, in terms of winds and currents, would be the last week of March and the first week of April. I immediately realised it would not be possible for me to leave before the first week of June because we planned to celebrate Anna's twenty-first birthday on 28 May. Birthdays are important occasions in our family, and I was certainly not going to miss that party.

So I booked to fly from Heathrow to Santiago on the evening of 30 May. David Jackson had agreed to travel with me and spend eight days in Chile when he would oversee the final preparations of the boat. The plan was that I would then row towards the horizon and he would return to England.

The final countdown to our day of departure had begun.

Restless, impatient, looking for the next challenge…

The boat was built by David Jackson and his father, Graham, at Tor Point; David and I were partners during the Atlantic Rowing Race in 1997.

Graham Jackson passed away in January 2001.

Susan Hampshire launched our boat at the Ruislip Lido.

Early sea trials with David Jackson at Plymouth before the Atlantic Rowing Race. The cabin on the right of the boat was our bedroom.

Preparations... My wife, Jane, and Munchkin, our family dog, pose beside my consignment of pre-cooked meals.

Refused permission to leave from Chile, I hired this vehicle and charged 1,200 miles up the coast to Peru.

It took nine days to pass through customs at the border between Chile and Peru, and I would probably still be there now without the help of Paul Visscher (*left*).

A word before leaving… The press conference at Ilo with Paul Visscher (*on my right*) and the Port Captain, Jorge Guerrero Augustin (*on my left*).

My voyage started as the Peruvian town of Ilo was celebrating the festival of St Peter and St Paul, and I headed out to sea with an enthusiastic escort of local boats.

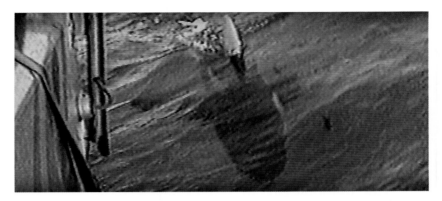

One of the sharks that repeatedly battered my boat. I responded by stabbing them with a homemade harpoon, created from a filleting knife lashed to the end of a broken oar.

Belly flop... One of the yellow-fin tuna, which escorted me for most of my voyage, leaped in pursuit of a flying fish and landed on the deck. I reached for the camera before lifting him back into the ocean.

Get out of my ocean! Passing ships frequently came too close for comfort, probably because I was virtually invisible on their radar.

As hard as the day might have been, I was frequently revived by the natural beauty of a classic Pacific sunset.

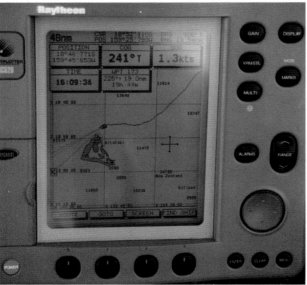

Near miss – my boat seemed drawn towards islands in the South Pacific. As the plotter indicates, I just managed to skip past the northern tip of Ua Pou.

Nothing was going to stop us now, not even a letter from the National Health Service informing me that an appointment had been made for my long-awaited hip operation. I had experienced pain in my right hip for some time, and had been on the waiting list for three years. However, I would not postpone my trip, and I regretfully called the hospital to postpone the precious appointment.

'May I ask why?' the appointments clerk enquired.

'Actually, I am going to row across the Pacific.'

'Oh, I see,' she replied. I am certain she didn't believe me.

As the voyage drew near, Jane and I had taken a conscious decision that we would not discuss my trip with the girls. We sensed both Anna and Sarah had become unsettled during the Atlantic voyage, and this impression was confirmed by their teachers at the time. I had to appreciate not everyone's father disappears to row across an ocean. They never said anything, and they gave no indication of being particularly concerned, but we opted to be cautious.

In fact, while I was crossing the Atlantic, Anna had earned three straight As in her A levels, and Sarah had secured nine As and one B in her GCSEs. Such outstanding performances would tend to suggest both my daughters had come to terms with my occasional urge to do something truly exciting.

The looming reality of my adventure also forced Jane to make a major adjustment in her life. At the start of this book, I noted that crossing the Pacific in a rowing boat was the most selfish thing I have ever done, and it was clearly my wife who was left to suffer most of the consequences. In many ways, Anna and Sarah were able to focus on their exams and their lives at school while my long absence would be most keenly felt at home in Northwood.

I tried to be sympathetic. I am not sure whether I succeeded. How would most wives react if their husbands told them first that they were going to be away from home for as long as six months, then added they would not be earning too much money during that period, then mentioned he had needed to take £75,000 out of the bank to fund the trip and finally concluded by admitting he could not be absolutely certain that he would survive the adventure?

Most wives would simply say no. Jane didn't say no. But she is a highly intelligent, thoughtful lady, and she needed to understand exactly why I wanted to cross the Pacific. As 30 May drew closer, she became ever more desperate in demanding that I provide her with a rational explanation.

'Why are you going?' she would ask, on the brink of tears.

'Because I have to go,' I would reply, instantly aware how inadequate and lame my words would sound, not knowing what else to say.

'Is it me?'

'No, it's not you.'

'Then why?'

'Because I have to go.'

I sought refuge in practical issues, repeating how I had made provision for the family, how we had almost completed the purchase of a flat in Bristol for each of the girls, how all my life insurance policies were in place, how all the insurance companies had affirmed that, because I was of 'sound mind' when I took out the policies, they would have no objections to paying if I died.

Still Jane asked: 'Why?'

Still I replied: 'Because I have to go.'

Eventually, my wife started to understand there actually did not have to be a reason. I had to go because I had to go. There was no entire and unambiguous explanation. I understand it was hard on her, and I will always be indebted to her for supporting me through this trying and uncertain period.

In many respects, it was fortunate that we were able to spend most of May focusing our attention on the celebrations to mark Anna's twenty-first birthday. Everyone was mindful of my plans, but it seemed so much easier to avoid detailed debates about the risks of crossing the Pacific. I was not hiding anything. I was just trying to protect the family from unnecessary worry. Munchkin, the family dog, never mentioned the voyage at all.

Anna had proposed a boat party and, after we had spent a depressing day looking at two terrible options in Bristol, she heard about an ideal set-up on the River Avon in Bath. I was doubtful but perfectly happy to make the booking, sight unseen. We all enjoyed a wonderful birthday celebration for Anna and, although I said nothing, a wonderful send-off for me.

The guests were first collected from a pub in Bristol by a double-decker bus and taken to Bath, where they boarded the boat. Champagne was served on the top deck, dinner and dancing followed below. Towards the end of the party, a group of Anna's friends discreetly approached me and asked permission to throw the birthday girl into the river. I raised no objections.

We celebrated the actual day of her birthday, 28 May, with the traditional tea and cake at home, and I said goodbye to my daughters before they returned to Bristol the following morning. The mood was cheerful and light. They were just going back to university; I was just going to cross the Pacific. That was all. I was often travelling abroad on business. Everyone was strong.

'Bye, Dad.'

'So I will see you in Sydney on 15 December, OK?'

'Sure, Dad.'

I wanted to focus on the next time we would all be together, and the date of 15 December was looming large because that was when Peter Montgomery, my old friend in Sydney, planned to celebrate his fiftieth birthday. I calculated that, all going well, I would complete my voyage around that time; and Jane and I had already agreed the entire family would be reunited in Australia.

My day of departure unfolded as an unavoidably frantic dash, spent trying to ensure nothing was left behind. I had arranged to collect an important piece of electronic equipment on the way to Heathrow and this detour combined with gridlocked rush hour traffic leaving London on the M4 seriously threatened to make David and me late for the Iberia flight to Santiago via Madrid.

We arrived at the check-in counter thirty-five minutes before the flight was scheduled to leave, and I felt embarrassed to discover my sister Jan, Kenneth Crutchlow, and college friend Paul Sivey with his wife, Maggie, had been waiting for almost two hours at the desk to wish me well. However, it was only because of their combined appeals that Iberia had kept the flight open for me.

These last moments were always going to be difficult and, in some ways, I was relieved everything was such a rush because it meant there was no time to become emotional. Even so, I was touched when Paul handed me a cheque from his company and Maggie gave me a teddy bear to keep me company out on the ocean. My daughters had already handed me a soft parrot.

I kissed Jane one last time, turned on my heel and, with David Jackson at my side, began to race through security to the departure gate. At last, after all the corporate rejections and disappointments, the trauma and the trials, I felt genuinely exhilarated to be on my way to South America.

The planning was over.

5

Patience, Patience, Patience

Show me a china shop, and I will be the bull. For as long as I can remember, I have preferred the straightforward, direct approach to problem solving. To be forceful is to be clear, and to be clear is to prevail. This was my conviction, at least until I spent the month of June 2000 in South America.

In trying, trying and trying again to secure official permission to row away from the coast, I learned once and for all that patience is a virtue.

I had imagined I would simply arrive in Chile, collect the boat, run through some final preparations and, within perhaps five days, certainly no longer than a week, be rowing cheerfully towards the western horizon.

I was wrong. In the event, I was repeatedly delayed because my papers were not in order and because top officials did not want to waste their taxpayers' money on having to rescue a crazy Englishman at sea.

In essence, this particular bull suddenly found himself stranded in a shop of diplomacy and bureaucracy, where the full-horn charge tended to wind up in the local jail. Patience, patience, patience was required.

So I learned to listen and oblige, to understand and accept; and, amid the contained frustration of grinding teeth, I eventually prevailed. Newborn patience kept me precariously cool, and a sense of destiny kept me going. Whatever happened, I told myself again and again as obstacle after obstacle appeared in my path, I would get my boat into the water and then across the ocean to Australia. I was an ordinary man being driven to attempt an extraordinary feat by some strange force of destiny.

The first sign of trouble had appeared before I left home but I had been so energised and gung-ho about my imminent adventure that I refused to recognise the severity of the situation. I was determined to be positive. For every problem, there would be a solution. I felt irrepressible and unstoppable. 'I believe I can fly,' *et cetera, et cetera* . . . and yet, I still needed the correct papers.

I made contact with the Chilean Embassy in London two months before my scheduled date of departure, both through the normal channels and also, as a kind of insurance, through a former colleague of my accountant who happened to be married to a high-ranking member of the Chilean diplomatic staff.

My initial aim was to determine precisely what documentation was needed to secure a permit to leave Chile in a rowing boat. My question had provoked the increasingly familiar bewildered, glazed-eye response. In fairness, I suppose this was not the kind of enquiry that crops up every day of the week.

Progress was slow, but I supplied the information as requested and hoped my application for the permit would succeed. However, following a meeting at the embassy, I was informed the authorities in Chile would not be inclined to issue a *zarpe* (permit). Even so, there was no question of abandoning the trip, not least because my boat was already en route to South America. I decided to pursue my case, and there followed further communications by telephone, fax and in person.

Then, on 24 May, six days before I was due to leave England, I received a facsimile message informing me that my application had been sent to Santiago and rejected. The letters following the name of the signatory suggested this decision had been made at the highest level. The tone seemed to give the impression of finality.

I was disappointed, but not wholly surprised, and certainly not bowed. It seemed entirely reasonable to me that the Chilean authorities should be wary of committing public money to the expensive sea rescue of deluded foreigners who believed they would be able to cross the Pacific, but my point was that I was not mad, at least not certifiably, and I would not require help.

Upon further application to the embassy, I was relieved to be told I would be granted an opportunity, when I arrived in Santiago, to put my case to the vice-admiral with responsibility for these matters. Ever optimistic, I backed myself to prove my track record, to demonstrate the viability of the voyage and then to persuade him that I would not need to call upon his rescue services.

This issue was obviously becoming a problem but, as I boarded the flight at Heathrow, I felt confident of finding a solution. I would take one step at a time, addressing each obstacle as it appeared in my path but always making progress, however slowly, towards my destination: this was the plan.

When David Jackson and I walked into the main terminal at Santiago de Chile airport, our primary concern was that local customs officials might express an interest in the large quantity of electronic equipment for the boat that we were carrying as luggage. The nightmarish prospect was that we would have to spend hours explaining the nature of my voyage and, in all probability, would then have to pay a significant sum, in US dollars, as import duty.

In the event, we were extremely fortunate. I had decided to carry all the problematic radios and transmitters, reducing the chance of being discovered by 50 per cent. As we approached the Chilean customs booth, we noticed our queue was being split into two lines on an apparently random basis; some passengers were being rigorously checked, others were being waved through.

I tried to look as uninterested and innocent as possible when I neared the line of uniformed officials, and breathed a sigh of relief when they waved me by. I strolled into the arrivals area. The adventure had started well.

Our next task was to find a public telephone box, work out how to make a call and telephone our only contact person in

Chile, a character who goes by the name of Pat Waggaman, an American, in the boldest, brashest sense of the term. We had been given his details by Tim Harris, the armchair adventurer from Birmingham, who had happened to read in the Orbcomm business magazine how this Waggaman had won a contract to provide tracking and mapping services for the Chilean fishing fleet.

Pat was expecting to hear from us when we arrived in Chile. However, he had made no commitment to assist me in any way. I knew almost nothing about him and had no idea where he lived. In almost every respect, I was making not so much a cold call as a frozen call, just hoping for the best.

'Hello?'

'Yes?'

'May I speak to Pat Waggaman, please?'

'It's him.'

'Hi, it's Jim Shekhdar speaking.'

'Oh, you made it!' he said, sounding surprised.

'Yep.'

'OK, well, get a lift down to the main road, and hop on a bus to Viña. Hold on, you could catch the bus to Valparaíso first. I'm not sure. It shouldn't cost you more than five bucks. Give us a call when you get to Viña.'

'Right, Pat, can we just . . .' The line was whirring in my ear. He had hung up. I suppose he had given me directions, so there was nothing more to say. He had sounded wonderfully unconventional. In any case, I rejoined David and gave him the impression everything was completely under control.

My Atlantic partner had come to Chile under duress because he and Jo, now his wife, had arranged to leave England for New Zealand on 12 June, starting a nine-month job exchange. His time was extremely precious, so I did not want him to suspect he had made his sacrifice to join a wild-goose chase. I told him Pat had given me directions, and we needed to take a short bus ride to the coast.

I was guessing, of course. I hadn't looked at a map of Chile, and had no idea where 'Valparaíso' or 'Viña' was situated in relation to Santiago airport. Oh well, I thought, the fare is only five dollars: it can't be too far.

During the course of the next half-hour, I managed to deduce from several conversations in broken Anglo-Spanish that the only buses to 'Valparaíso' left from the middle of Santiago, and that we would first have to jump on another bus from the airport to the city's main bus centre. Each carrying two heavy suitcases and a box of electronic equipment, with the sun rising on a hot and humid day, we reached the bus centre and clambered aboard a bus to Valparaíso.

'How long does the journey take?' I asked.

'About three hours,' the driver replied.

I glanced at David. Eyebrows raised, David looked at me. I was starting to think my cover was blown, but my good friend said nothing. We were both tired and dirty, and growing increasingly irritated by the discomfort of this trip into the unknown. It was one of those times when close friends look out the window and watch the scenery roll by, because words won't help.

'Hello, Pat?'

I was becoming an authority on public telephone boxes in Chile.

'Oh, you made it!' he replied.

'We're in Valparaíso,' I said, working hard to keep the slightest twinge of frustration out of my voice.

Sweating in the midday sun, I had started to believe Pat was testing me, trying to find out if this British stranger was tough enough to cross the Pacific in a rowing boat, trying to find out whether I was worth helping.

'OK, well, like I said, you need to catch a bus to Viña.'

'Viña?'

'Viña del Mar.'

'OK.'

'Then you must catch a 'collectivo' – that's a taxi – to Concon.

It's not a big place. Call me when you're five minutes away and I'll meet you at the Shell station.'

'Fine.'

Anything he said was fine. I didn't mind. I felt like an unwitting contestant in a new reality TV game show, taking instructions from the host at the end of the telephone and charging around the countryside. This was one game I needed to win. My prize would be his willingness to help me start my trip.

Our suitcases and boxes seemed to weigh more every time we lifted them, but David was staying the course. We arrived in Viña and eventually got into the right area to flag down a taxi heading to Concon. So we collapsed on the back seat, relieved to be nearing the end of this ordeal. It was only twenty hours since we had left London, but it felt more like two weeks.

I was starting to worry. What would happen if Pat didn't like us? Where would we go? We were skating on perilously thin ice. I knew I should have come on a reconnaissance trip to Chile, but there had been no money. I knew I should have prepared the details of my departure more carefully, but there had been no time. In any event, we had put our trust in Pat. We had to make things work. That was all.

The taxi driver kindly used his mobile telephone to call Pat when we were about five miles from Concon, and it was with some trepidation that I looked out of the window, peering through a cloud of dust as we reached the approach to the forecourt of the Shell garage. There was only one other vehicle in sight, parked to one side of the run into the forecourt.

'You must be Jim something-or-other,' declared Pat Waggaman, at first glance every inch the archetype Yank. 'Let's get back to the house.' I didn't mind at all that he couldn't recall my surname. In a matter of thirty seconds, he had shown himself to be friendly, willing to help and in a hurry. I was thrilled and relieved.

When we arrived at his home, he showed David and me to a large bedroom in the visitors' wing where we would sleep, and then took us to an office area, set aside for us with computers and communications equipment. There was also a large double garage where we would be able to store the boat. I could not have imagined more perfect surroundings to prepare for the voyage.

'Make yourselves at home,' Pat drawled, smiling. After our long flight and painstaking trek from the airport, we were soon ready to join Pat for a lunch of home-made soup, tacos, guacamole and fruit. Good company, great food, ideal facilities for work and a bed. We had landed on our feet. By three o'clock, I was resting on my bed, feeling deeply relieved and content. Indeed, with Pat playing the larger-than-life host, I felt as though I had won the game show.

Through the days that followed, David and I grew to know this remarkable man as, first and foremost, a tremendous enthusiast . . . about everything. Nothing seemed boring; every situation seemed exciting. He already had my respect both as a navigator and a man by virtue of having sailed around Cape Horn, an awesome feat, and I liked him from the moment we met. We understood each other.

Pat had left a comfortable, settled lifestyle in the United States to live out his maritime dream in Chile, and he now inspired a team of eight diligent people working from his house, developing systems, programming satellite communicators and using data gathered by Chile's fishing fleet to create detailed charts of the ocean floor. The working space buzzed with that special kind of energy, that shared purpose that tends to distinguish thriving businesses from places where people simply turn up to earn a living. Pat provided the vision, and his fired-up employees eagerly followed his lead.

As we sat and talked through the first evening, I related my plans to cross the Pacific. When I had finished, Pat looked straight at me and said he thought I was completely mad, and that he admired me for that very reason. We also discussed how I should approach the vice-admiral to secure a departure permit.

He dealt with senior members of the Chilean Navy on a regular basis, and seemed ideally placed to help me negotiate the uniformed bureaucracy.

Mindful of my experiences in other parts of the world, my basic instinct to resolve the permit situation was to identify the decision-maker and peel off some US dollars from the wad in my wallet. However, when I intimated as much to one of Pat's employees, a Chilean fishing and IT expert with several old university friends in the navy, he told me quite forcefully that any attempt at bribery would land me in jail very quickly.

'You have to be patient,' he said quietly, prompting me to nod and agree to pursue my case through the proper channels.

Pat made several telephone calls, and a meeting was arranged with a certain Captain Sergio Wall, second in command to Vice-Admiral Jorge Aranciba, the officer who had declined my original application when it was referred to his office by the embassy in London. Aranciba was visiting the south of the country at the time, and we were advised to accelerate the matter by putting our case to Wall, whose report would then be handed to Aranciba.

This seemed a reasonable process, and I was further encouraged when Pat offered to join me in the meeting. His endorsement, since he had sailed from Cape Horn to Arica, would be a major advantage.

Our presentation to Captain Wall, and the operational head of air-sea rescue services, lasted two hours. I wanted to convey an image of supreme confidence and professionalism, explaining that I had already crossed the Atlantic in the same boat, describing the safety equipment and the six communications and navigation systems that had been installed. Time and again, I stressed the Pacific voyage had been rigorously planned and assessed.

The naval officers sat attentive but impassive throughout, their unchanged expressions conveying all the empathy of a brick wall. I started to sense we were making no progress at all, and finally adopted a more direct approach.

'Captain Wall, permit me to be blunt,' I said. 'On the basis of what you have heard this afternoon, are you able to write a favourable report?'

'Your presentation was impressive and you are obviously well prepared. However, the vice-admiral will make the final decision.'

'Yes, I appreciate that. Are there any issues that concern you?'

'The vice-admiral will make a final decision.'

'Well, if you are not persuaded by our arguments, it seems unlikely that he will be persuaded by your report. Would it be possible for us to meet the vice-admiral in person when he returns from the south?'

'The vice-admiral will make a final decision.'

It seemed clear that, even if we had made a good impression in our meeting, we had made no progress at all towards being granted the document we needed and that the meeting would certainly not be the final application. I felt sure that our efforts would be fruitless unless we were able to present our case to the actual decision-maker.

I searched Wall's face for any sign of understanding, any trace of sympathy. There was none. As we left his office, the stiffness of his expression matched the firmness of his handshake. If he had told me one more time the vice-admiral would make a final decision, I might have lost my cool but patience prevailed. 'Thank you,' I muttered.

Pat sensed my despair and, during the drive back to Concon, insisted it was time for his British visitors to discover some local nightlife. A bout of serious clubbing and drinking proved the ideal antidote to depression. With this ebullient American on our side, I concluded, anything was possible.

The pursuit of a *zarpe* had now passed beyond our control and, while we awaited the verdict, there seemed no option but to continue preparing the boat for departure as scheduled. In any event, David could not prolong his stay in Chile, and there was plenty of work to be done.

Due to the efforts of Giovanni Villaroel, one of Pat's employees, we had managed to retrieve the boat from Chilean customs in only three days, and David set to work completing the external fittings, adjusting internal fittings, testing the water tank and double-checking the complex electronic equipment.

For my part, I tried to get the Orbcomm systems to function in receiving and transmitting modes, and I also applied the stickers bearing the logos of my sponsors to the side of the boat. However, much to my embarrassment, I found myself spending much of my time either on the telephone or sending e-mails, desperately trying to settle outstanding issues at home and at work.

The purchase of Anna's flat in Bristol was proving an ordeal for Jane, and I started calling solicitors from the office in Concon, urging them to complete the transaction. When one asked why I was in such a hurry, I told him I was about to row across the Pacific. He sounded quite impressed at the time but, when I met him after my return home, he said he had never believed me. 'I thought you were just making up an elaborate reason,' he said.

In any event, my intention didn't work and, with the help of our very understanding bank manager in Northwood, Jane eventually resolved the issue.

I also dealt with a VAT return that I had overlooked, and managed to sort out a complicated accounting quandary at the office in Bratislava. While I sat indoors with the telephone pressed to my ear, David successfully completed his work and, on 4 June, declared the boat was ready.

All I needed was the *zarpe*. As the days passed since our presentation in Valparaíso, I had allowed my hopes to rise that we might yet be successful, but there was no reprieve. Captain Wall telephoned to say Vice-Admiral Aranciba had reached his final decision: no departure permit would be granted and no further representation would be entertained. What a bummer!

Now what?

Well, I was not going to shrug my shoulders and fly home to England. As anger overwhelmed my resolve to be patient, I decided there was no alternative but to steal away from the coast of Chile under the cover of darkness. Nobody would see me, and nobody would stop me. What else could I do? David would soon be returning home. There was no point hanging around Concon. If I was going to row, I would have to row ... with or without a *zarpe*.

I had started to develop this strategy when Pat called down to say there was a journalist from Santiago on the telephone for me. He had taken an interest in my plans since my arrival in Chile, and wanted to know the latest news. I told him about the final decision.

Strangely, he had anticipated the possibility of a clandestine departure during the night and had in fact already made discreet enquiries through senior naval connections. He said his contacts had been firm and unequivocal, declaring it would be downright dangerous to leave without a permit.

The journalist continued: 'They said they would find you, bring you back to shore, confiscate the boat, charge you and jail you for seventy-seven days.'

'Seventy-seven days?' I said. 'How can they be so precise?'

'Don't you know why?' he asked.

'No.'

'That's how long Pinochet was kept under house arrest in Britain.'

I thought the former President had been detained for longer but, in any case, I had never dreamed that the UK's treatment of Chile's former president would have any bearing on my situation, but the arguments against taking the matter into my own hands and leaving at night were becoming stronger.

First, I accepted the navy's sophisticated tracking and surveillance equipment meant there was a strong chance that they would be able to find even my tiny boat on the vast ocean.

Second, it would have been foolish to risk confiscation of the boat because that would have been the end, sending me home with my tail between my legs.

Third, and most important, it had become clear that any illegal action on my part would have seriously jeopardised the working relationship between the navy and my friend, Pat Waggaman. I owed him better than that.

'What about Peru?'

Pat had asked the question even before the vice-admiral gave his verdict, but I had not given the idea much thought. Now that I was committed to finding a strictly legal solution to this situation, the option of working to secure a departure pass from Chile's northern neighbour seemed attractive.

I had absolutely no idea where to start, and looked to Pat once again. He had become so conjunctive to my entire project that I don't think I would have got past first base without his sturdy, selfless assistance. True to form, he produced the contact details of somebody he knew. This man's name was Paul Visscher and he ran a diving company in the southernmost Peruvian port of Ilo.

E-mails buzzed back and forth and, within three days, Paul contacted us to say that, while nothing was guaranteed, his tentative enquiries suggested the Peruvian authorities would look favourably on my application for a *zarpe* and that a group of his friends were ready and willing to help me. I was encouraged. At last, I was starting to make progress again.

In tandem with Pat and Paul, I made arrangements to hire a four-wheel drive utility vehicle in Viña del Mar in order to tow the boat what I estimated was a distance of 750 miles up the coast to Arica, a Chilean town two miles from the border with Peru. I would then meet Paul at Arica airport, where I would return the 'ute' to the rental company. We would hitch the boat to Paul's vehicle and drive on to Ilo together. This was the plan.

As I prepared to drive north, David Jackson was packing his suitcase and heading back to Santiago, from where he would fly home to England. Yet again, he had proved a tremendous source of support. I wished him luck with his stay in New Zealand; he wished me luck on the Pacific. It seemed somehow inadequate simply to say 'thank you' to someone who had travelled halfway around the world during a frantic period in his life to help me prepare for my trip, but he knows me well enough to realise my gratitude is sincere and lasting.

I had planned to leave Concon early on the Friday morning, allowing two and a half days to drive the 750 miles to Arica, where I had arranged to meet Paul in the airport car park at noon on Sunday. This seemed a reasonable task and, for once, I felt as though events were under control. I woke soon after six on Friday morning, intending to complete one last task – connecting the trailer board to the four-wheel drive – before saying goodbye to Pat and leaving Concon.

Under control? That was optimistic. There had been no trailer wiring in the hired four-wheel drive and, by noon, I was still battling to connect separate wires from the tail lights, brake lights and indicators on the ute to corresponding lights on the trailer. Soon after two o'clock in the afternoon, my electrics seemed in order, but I was tired, so I opted to catch a quick nap before finally hitting the road.

When I woke, I started to hitch the trailer to the ute, but the length of the wiring harness was not much longer than the distance from the trailer board to the rear of the ute, and, in manoeuvring the ute to the trailer hitch, most of the wires were pulled out of their connections. Within another hour or so, I managed to complete the repair job and, at last, was ready to leave.

Pat joined me for a couple of farewell beers. I wanted to say a proper goodbye to this amazing man who had evolved in eight days from just a name and a telephone number in my diary to a friend I could not do without. I shook his hand and thanked him for his hospitality and unstinting assistance.

'Good luck, Jim.'

'Thanks for everything, Pat.'

As I hitched the trailer to the back of the ute I somehow managed to trap the trailing wire under one of the trailer tyres and my Heath-Robinson-style wiring connections were yet again ripped out of their joints. Pat could not help but smile. I was back to square one, and it would be dark in two hours. I took out the toolkit and started working out which wire went where all over again. An hour later, salvation arrived in the form of the electrician in Pat's team.

Victor, the company's electronic wizard, had been working somewhere else during the day but even on a Friday evening, he rallied to the cause and set about the task with his soldering iron. It was past eleven o'clock when he declared himself satisfied and, with only four hours until sunrise, I opted to sleep and leave at six o'clock on the Saturday morning.

True to form, Pat was already up and about by the time I surfaced and he insisted upon driving with me for the first ten miles, just to make certain that I reached the intersection with the Panam Highway safely. When we arrived at the main road, I looked around. It was the middle of nowhere.

'How on earth are you going to get home?' I asked.

'Don't worry,' he replied. 'I'll be OK.'

With that, he was gone.

I received the occasional e-mail from Pat while I was in Peru and a couple more at the end of my voyage, and we have remained in contact, but I am not certain I will ever be able to adequately thank Pat Waggaman for his astonishing generosity and kindness.

The Panam Highway is not quite as grand as its name suggests, but I was making steady progress when I glanced in my wing mirror and noticed something dragging behind the trailer. I pulled over to the hard shoulder and discovered that half of the rear section of the trailer had broken free. This caused the rear member of the trailer, to which the tailboard was attached, to drag behind the car, destroying the trailer board in the process.

A quick test revealed that one red light and one orange light were still working. Since I planned to be driving on the highway for much of the night, this was plainly inadequate and represented a safety risk.

Too bad.

I was already on my way, and by now facing a tight schedule to meet Paul Visscher in Arica airport at noon on Sunday. So I took some all-purpose tape, and coarsely lashed the broken section of the trailer to the rear of the boat. It was not pretty, but it would have to be sufficient. I was moving on.

It had not taken me very long to realise I would not be able to drive any faster than sixty miles per hour. The boat was far too heavy for the vehicle, with the result that the trailer would start to snake alarmingly if I eased on the accelerator and touched seventy. It was going to be a long drive.

In fact, it was going to be even longer than I imagined because, in looking at the map in Pat's house, I had seriously underestimated the distance between Concon and Arica. My rough estimate had been 750 miles, but the reality was now emerging on the road . . . It was nearer 1,200 miles.

Damn. Arica airport at noon on Sunday was starting to seem impossible. I stopped at the next small town with the intention of telephoning Paul and asking if we could meet later in the day. My knowledge of public telephones in Chile led me to believe getting through to a Peruvian number would be tough, but locating a public telephone in rural Chile soon proved even tougher.

When I eventually found a public phone in a café, it turned out to be incapable of making international calls. So I called Pat's office in the hope of getting a message relayed to Paul in Peru. There was no answer. It was Sunday and Pat was out. I was wasting time. My task was now clear: I needed to reach Arica airport, as arranged, by noon on Sunday; and, to have any chance, I would have to drive through the night.

The Panam Highway ploughed on straight and true through

what can only be described as a kind of mud desert terrain, bereft of any distinguishing features except for some strange piles of stones appearing every sixty miles or so on the side of the road. Seen from a distance, these cairns resembled sitting figures wearing sombreros, but this impression diminished as one got nearer and, from alongside, these structures looked disappointingly normal.

Driving deep into Saturday night, I was starting to feel seriously tired and I began to pursue a strategy honed through many years of long-distance driving all over the world: this involved being able to recognise when I felt tired, stopping to sleep for ten or fifteen minutes, then feeling fit enough to drive for another two hours. Following this cycle, I managed to drive safely through till dawn.

Soon after nine on Sunday morning, essentially driving on autopilot, I was magnificently roused when the highway plunged into a spectacular gorge, falling from 14,000 feet to sea level in an eighteen-mile stretch. The crumbly, grey mudstone could never truthfully be described as beautiful, but its harsh rock formations, sheer slopes and hairpin bends created a breathtaking landscape.

The road straightened and flattened into dull monotony soon afterwards and nearing complete exhaustion, I conceded defeat. My decision to stop and sleep for an hour confirmed I would be an hour or so late to meet Paul, but it was obviously better to arrive late than not to arrive at all.

In the event, it was just past two o'clock when I turned into the car park at Arica airport. I was two hours late. Would Paul have waited? If he had returned to Ilo, my desperate dash up the coast would have been in vain. I looked anxiously around the car park. With not the slightest idea of how Paul looked, I was hoping to see a four-wheel drive, or perhaps someone else looking around. Ten minutes passed, but nothing stirred. My spirits were starting to sag again.

Then, somebody walked up to the trailer and started

inspecting my boat. I took a shot in the dark, and mercifully hit the bull's-eye.

'Excuse me, Paul Visscher?' I asked.

The man gashed into a smile. 'You are Jim?'

This turned out to be Hugo Navarrete, from Ilo. He spoke Spanish at speed and, with some effort, I managed to decipher that Paul had gone inside the airport terminal to telephone Pat for news of my progress. Hugo was clearly pleased to see me. I was delighted to see him! This excited exchange in the car park at Arica airport proved to be my first experience of the remarkable warmth and friendship extended to me by so many of the people of Ilo.

Paul eventually emerged from the terminal. We greeted each other, and it soon transpired that Ilo was not just across the border as I had imagined. It was more than 65 miles up the coast from Tacna which in turn was approximately 40 miles from Arica. These two men had sacrificed their weekend with their families to make a 210-mile round-trip to meet me: just another day, just another tremendous act of kindness from total strangers.

I returned my hired vehicle to the rental company, and hitched the trailer to Hugo's four-wheel drive. The tow ball looked too high but three inches clearance between the back of the boat and the ground would have to be enough. We proceeded sedately towards the border where we were to be met on the Peruvian side by a customs agent sent from Tacna to help us through the Peruvian customs.

First, we needed to negotiate my departure from Chile. We drove gently to the customs gate and I duly handed over my papers.

The customs officer looked and frowned. There was a problem. I had been assured in Valparaíso that my documents were in order, but something must have been lost in the translation between Spanish and English because my papers only permitted travel within Chile pending issue of the *zarpe*. It was clear I would need to show releases from both the agent that had imported the boat and Chilean customs before I could leave. Without these, *Le Shark* stayed in Chile.

Paul and Hugo would have been entitled to show some sign of irritation. They had put themselves out to help this stranger, and now his papers were not in order. Yet they both remained cheerful and helpful, and we agreed to seek the clearances with the agents in Arica early on Monday.

In the meantime, they arranged to stay the Sunday night with friends in Tacna, while I prepared to spend my first night aboard the boat . . . not being rocked gently on the Pacific swell but parked fifty yards from the Chilean customs house on the border with Peru. Life was not going exactly to plan!

Monday unfolded miserably: stuck in a cramped office of the agent in Arica, battling relentlessly with the red tape, struggling to contact agents in Santiago who never answered their telephone. Progress was excruciatingly slow, and it soon became clear that nothing would be achieved in one day.

Paul and Hugo seemed almost apologetic as they explained they needed to return to Ilo. Paul had deserted his diving business and Hugo was being called back to work by his increasingly animated father-in-law. I completely understood, and was grateful when Paul said he would be waiting for my call. As soon as the papers were complete, he would return and fetch me.

It was four o'clock on the Wednesday afternoon when the customs agent in Arica finally smiled at me and said my documents were in order. I contacted Paul and, true to his word, he returned early the following morning, this time not with Hugo, but with another enthusiastic friend, Wilfredo Contreras.

I was not at all surprised when the trailer would not connect to Wilfredo's vehicle because the tow ball was too high. Through the past five days, this trailer had never connected to anything without a struggle. My remarkable patience was now starting to fray at the edges. Nothing was easy! In the end, we let air out of Wilfredo's tyres to create two inches clearance between the back of the boat and the ground, and crawled cautiously across the border.

The Peruvian customs house loomed ahead. The agent from Tacna had been dispatched once again to smooth our path, and we strolled into the office to complete what I felt confident would be mere formalities. The official scanned the documents and saw I had described the item on the trailer as a rowing boat. He glanced out the window, and slowly shook his head. He gestured for us to follow him outside. We obeyed, helpless to escape another ordeal.

'What are you going to do with that boat?' he asked me.

I couldn't lie. 'Row across the Pacific Ocean,' I replied.

'Oh, I see. If you are crossing the Pacific, you must have a motor.'

'No, it's a rowing boat.'

'You can't cross the Pacific in a rowing boat.'

'Yes, I can.'

'No, you can't. You must have a motor.'

Money lay at the heart of this progressively comical exchange. Peruvian regulations stipulated no import duty at all on the type of rowing boats you place on the roof of a car, the sum of $1,600 on unpowered boats as large as mine, and a very much higher tax on motor boats, perceived as luxury items.

I was hoping to get through without paying any duty, whereas the customs official eagerly embraced the challenge of finding a motor on board, applying the higher rate and relieving me of several thousand dollars in duty.

'Look at the hull,' I told him, as we prowled around the boat. 'There is no propeller there. That surely proves to you there is no motor.'

He was obviously not convinced and, after perhaps five minutes, gleefully pointed out 'the motor!' It turned out to be only the blades of the wind generator, which he eventually accepted was not a motor. Somewhat crestfallen and evidently disappointed, he slowly retreated to his customs house.

Nothing was going to happen quickly. We were informed the

boat would have to be moved to the inland customs clearance house in Tacna, from where it would only be released when our customs agent had paid the import duty. I was fast reaching the limit of my patience, and I was grateful to Wilfredo for keeping a calm hand on the situation. A former international deep-sea fishing captain, he had taken early retirement and was enjoying a quiet, happy life in Ilo. He understood the process and had friends in the local bank. We eventually cleared the boat within thirty-six hours.

Wilfredo was significantly assisted in the process by Corinne Flores, head of the customs agency, who worked unstintingly in my cause. To my amazement, just as we were leaving the customs yard, Corinne approached me to apologise for the delay. Without her efforts, I would have been stuck there for a week, so I presented her with two bottles of best Chilean wine. In turn, she gave me a kiss on the cheek, a bottle of excellent Peruvian wine and waived all the agency costs.

I was dumbfounded by her kindness. I protested. She insisted. There must have been something in the water. There is no other explanation for the kindness and generosity of the people I was meeting day after day.

Wilfredo even went to the trouble of driving back to Ilo and returning with Hugo's vehicle, which gave us a couple more inches clearance between the back of the trailer and the road. At last, at long last, equipped with impeccable papers, we entered Peru and were soon heading up the coast to Ilo.

From the time I turned into Arica airport until the moment we pulled away from the customs yard in Tacna, I had spent slightly more than nine days trying to move the boat across the border from Chile to Peru. Beyond doubt, patience had been a significant virtue during this unique experience.

And yet, I was moving forward again. The memories of raging frustration and deep despair evaporated like mist in the morning sun, and I looked towards Ilo with excitement, wondering what adventures lay ahead.

Wilfredo drove cautiously. It was almost half past nine at night when we approached the outskirts of Ilo, and he suddenly pulled over to the kerb. My first thought was that more papers were required to enter the town.

'Problem?' I asked, in my best Spanish.

'Relax. No problem.'

The former fishing captain sounded convincing. If he told me to relax and said there was no problem, I was perfectly happy to relax and accept there was no problem. So we continued to sit still, parked on the kerb, stationary, wasting our time, for no apparent reason. No problem. I said nothing.

Eventually, after perhaps fifteen minutes, several cars emerged from the evening gloom with headlights flashing and horns tooting. I assumed the local football side had won an important match, but I was mistaken. Wilfredo started the engine, joined this escort and moved on towards town. I gradually realised, to my astonishment, that this convoy was my welcoming party.

The arrival of an unknown Englishman preparing to row across the Pacific seemed to have provoked implausible levels of excitement in this small town. As our cheering, tooting escort of cars sustained the cacophony, I watched people standing on pavements and waving as we passed by. The last mile of the trip into the centre of Ilo lasted more than fifty minutes, but, even so, I heard people in the convoy complaining that Bruno was driving too fast.

I arrived at the Gran Hotel Ilo, the most comfortable hotel in town, and was again startled to discover the entire establishment seemed to have been put at my disposal. The hotel was managed by Hugo's wife, who greeted me warmly and told me to ask if there was anything at all that I needed.

It was past eleven before I reached the sanctuary of my room. I walked to the window, looked out at the ocean and across towards the centre of town, and concluded that I could search the world and never find a more welcoming and enthusiastic place than this small fishing and copper-smelting town on the coast of Peru.

The core of this remarkable reception was provided by a group of friends who had set their hearts on establishing the Club Nautico Ilo. Paul, Wilfredo, Hugo and others . . . they were all involved along with the head of the local TV station, the MD of the shipping agents and other local luminaries. As a group, they appeared to have decided they would do everything possible, and more, to help this strange Englishman who had appeared in their town.

I am not absolutely sure why. Perhaps they thought my voyage could put their town on the maritime map. Maybe they were just a bunch of decent people who recognised a kindred spirit in need of assistance. Whatever the reason, the fact is that these men and their families took me under their wing with such real compassion that, looking back, I am still amazed and humbled.

It remains fantastic for me to consider that, in a situation where I might so easily have felt so alone, vulnerable and help-less, I should in fact have been so warmly supported and eagerly assisted at every turn.

The Gran Hotel Ilo provided a perfect work environment. The boat was placed in the rear yard, where I was able to repair minor hull damage incurred when one of the roller rubbers split during the desperate drive from Chile, and to apply anti-fouling paint to the areas where the original paint had been scratched away.

I was also given access to the manager's office where I could plug in my computer, use the fax machine and connect to the Internet. Even three weeks after leaving home, issues concerning VAT returns for AJS Management and the mortgage and bridg-ing loan for Anna's flat in Bristol remained unresolved.

Life assumed frantic proportions. Sitting in a coastal town in Peru, I found myself searching for creative solutions within the complex Romanian tax system, then speaking to a building society in Middlesex, then trying to deal with an issue in Hungary, then talking to a surveyor in Bristol. Day by day, taking one task at a time, I began to unravel the endless spaghetti of my life.

And, perhaps more pressing than any of the above, I needed to secure the departure pass. Everyone said the Peruvian officials would be more sympathetic than their southern neighbours, but I was taking nothing for granted. They knew I had been refused permission to leave Chile in my boat, so I needed to treat them with respect and provide a comprehensive, coherent application. It would not be a case of turning up, signing a form and zapping the *zarpe*.

In the end, my formal application for the permit was supported by almost seventy pages of documentation. These included the results of comprehensive physical and mental examinations, the marine surveyor's report on the condition of the boat and a smorgasbord of testimonials and photographs.

Following the proper procedure, this package was lodged with Jorge Guerrero, the port captain of Ilo, a respected and influential man in the town. He had never been less than friendly towards me, but he was obliged to refer the matter to higher authorities in Lima. I subsequently learned that he did so with a clear recommendation that my application be accepted.

Four days passed. Then, one overcast afternoon, I received the news that had seemed so improbable for so long: the authorities had decided to grant me the departure permit. After all the delays and the frustration, after the waiting and despair, I was ready to row. Hello euphoria, my old friend!

The time of the decision could not have been better managed. It enabled me to plan my departure for Friday, 30 June 2000, one of the most important days of the year for the good citizens of Ilo. The feast of St Peter and St Paul, the patron saints of fishermen, is a public holiday in Peru and, every year, Ilo moves into festival mode with street parades and ceremonies.

It soon became clear that the occasion of my departure was

going to be integrated into the day's carefully planned celebrations. I was handed a schedule of official events and asked if I would be able to arrange the start of my voyage to comply with the timetable. I told them I would be honoured. I had never dreamed my adventure would start amid such crowds and fanfare.

Three days before D-day, Cesar Aza, the port superintendent and another of the Club Nautico Ilo group, had helped me operate a giant crane on the jetty used by the local copper company to lower my heavy-laden boat into the water. I had then rowed and been towed by Paul's diving tender around to park the boat at the main town pier, immediately adjacent to the port authority patrol boats. There could not have been a more secure berth.

We had also taken the boat a couple of miles out to sea just to test the water maker and other systems in 'live' conditions, once again with Paul's diving tender providing the escort and most of the propulsion. Ideally I would like to have taken the boat out of the water for a final coating of anti-fouling and to recharge the batteries but there was no time. The date had been set for me to leave on the public holiday, and I did not wish to delay my departure a minute more than necessary. After so many slow weeks of waiting, it seemed odd that I should be leaving in a hurry, but I did not want to disappoint those kind people in Ilo.

My last full day on dry land, 29 June, was frenzied. Cristina Visscher, Paul's sister, had agreed to lead me on a last-minute whirl through the shops of Ilo. We bought some important items, like twine and some more kitchen utensils, we found a cobbler who was able to repair my deck shoes; and I even indulged in the luxury of a proper haircut. I was rushed, but I was ready.

That evening, I hosted a dinner for around twenty people in the dining room at the Gran Hotel Ilo because I wanted to thank most sincerely those friends from this special town who had done so much for me. My voice faltered slightly when I stood to speak, expressing my enduring gratitude to Paul, Hugo, Wilfredo and many others for being so obliging and positive.

It was tremendously encouraging for me to look around the tables, laid out in a square, and see so many excited faces. These people genuinely seemed to believe I would successfully complete my voyage. I don't think I had been particularly good company because I had spent too much of the time feeling grumpy and frustrated, but since the day I arrived in their town I had not stopped telling them I would cross the Pacific. The fact that they had so readily believed me was wonderfully heartening.

Maybe Paul Visscher summed up the occasion most neatly. 'I have never know so many people in this town to work so hard and for so long just to get rid of somebody,' he said. 'Jim, it has been our pleasure.'

Cesar Aza was accompanied to the dinner by his father, president of a civilian support group for navy personnel in the town. I had already arranged for this association to provide me with a fishing boat escort for the first twenty-four hours of the trip, to save me from getting into problems in the unlikely event that I would be blown back to shore by an unfavourable wind; and Mr Aza also brought me a special box of emergency provisions, including twenty one-litre packs of fresh water, and five cans of high-calorie oatcakes. In addition, Wilfredo's father had contributed two woolly hats. Except for the water, these 'emergency provisions' proved to be major contributors to my comfort on the voyage.

This parting gesture was typical of my treatment in Ilo. Such kindness was neither required nor requested, but it was tremendously appreciated. Indeed, the oatcakes sustained me during the latter stages of the trip.

I have remained in contact with Paul and his friends and, at the beginning of August 2001, four months after completing my voyage, my wife Jane and I travelled back to Ilo to report on my experiences and thank them all once again. Following political upheavals and a severe earthquake, there had been changes in

Ilo. The former Mayor and Armando Vidal had been elected as the two congressmen representing Moquegua department, the first time ever that both representatives have come from Ilo. And the port Captain, Jorge Guerrero, had been moved back to Lima to command the submarine base. It was a wonderful surprise to be met on arrival at Lima airport by Jorge and his father.

I was also delighted to discover my dedicated group of friends had secured the use of the jetty they needed for the Club Nautico Ilo. I am sure that my voyage had no significant influence in helping their cause, but I would be thrilled if my efforts spurred their progress in any way.

Having slept soundly during my last night on firm ground, I rose early on a cool, breezy, overcast Friday morning to put several finishing touches to the boat. Inevitably there was far more to be done than I had thought and I missed the first event on the festival schedule, a church service of thanksgiving.

Nobody seemed to mind and I eventually joined the celebrations when the procession wound its way down from the church and approached the main square. According to custom, the statues of St Peter and St Paul had been removed from the church and were being carried aloft at the front of the parade. The atmosphere was infectiously happy and, setting aside some brewing nerves ahead of my imminent departure, I began to relax and enjoy myself in the midst of more than 8,000 grinning, singing and dancing Peruvians.

At the appointed time, I was shepherded away into the boardroom of the port authority building, where I had been invited to attend a private ceremony in the presence of several dignitaries.

Jorge Guerrero opened proceedings with a few words of welcome, and my passport was then stamped by immigration, and my boat papers were approved by customs. Then, the moment for which I had waited so long . . . The port captain emerged from his office and presented me with my official release from the port, my *zarpe*. He then proceeded to remove his submariner captain's badge from his jacket and pin it to my T-shirt.

I had first met this man ten days before and, in a private conversation, when he had first questioned me about my voyage, he told me he believed I would cross the Pacific in my rowing boat and said he would ensure the *zarpe* was granted. I felt unashamedly emotional as he proved as good as his word.

Amid cameras and microphones, we left the port captain's office and headed down the jetty towards my boat. There was one last formality, or perhaps celebration. The Mayor stepped forward beneath a giant banner of the Club Nautico Ilo and, on behalf of the town, he presented me with a commemorative plaque and a letter, which he asked me to hand to the Mayor of the town nearest to the point where I eventually landed. His thoughtful idea was that the two towns connected by my voyage should then participate in a joint celebration. Finally, Bruno Rodriguez, as president of the emerging nautical club, presented me with another commemorative plaque on behalf of my 'exit team', and brought to an end what had been two extremely moving ceremonies.

All that remained was for me to walk twenty yards across to the steps leading down to a waiting tender that would take me out to my boat. However, it took me twenty minutes to make my way through the crowds of excited well-wishers. Amid the backslaps and cheering, I wanted to oblige every thrilled request for a photograph or an autograph, and it was only the intervention of my 'exit team', friends from the nautical club, that enabled me to reach the water.

Meanwhile, the parade had ended in traditional fashion as the two statues of St Peter and St Paul were borne out to sea aboard a fishing boat bedecked with garlands and loose flowers and then thrown into the water. With the harbour full of boats and people gathered at every vantage point on the shore, Ilo seemed bathed in enthusiasm and excitement. In the middle of this remarkably happy and festive scene, I settled on my boat and prepared to start rowing.

There was a slight hiatus while I struggled to untie the boat from the pier and the harbour master's buoys but, eventually, shortly before four o'clock on the afternoon of 30 June 2000, I dipped my oars into the water and started to row. Escorted by a small fleet, including the port captain's patrol boat, I moved out into the open sea, now stretching more than 8,000 miles ahead of me.

By five o'clock, most of the boats and yachts that flanked me out of the harbour were on their way back to Ilo, and I was left with one solitary fishing boat at my side, the escort I had arranged. My journey had started. There was no turning back and, as dusk fell, the lights of Ilo slowly faded into the mist.

I imagined my Peruvian mates reverting to their normal lives, thinking now and then of their English friend somewhere out on the ocean.

As for me, there was work to be done.

Next stop: Australia.

I hoped.

6
The First Week

Ocean rowing is never less than hazardous, but it is generally accepted among the brotherhood of ocean rowers that the first 100 miles and the last 100 miles typically prove the most nerve-racking parts of any voyage.

The early threat is that the boat will be blown back to the shore, forcing an undignified landing and inglorious failure. The dread fear of this horrifying fate occupied my mind for most of the first week at sea following my departure from Ilo. I could scarcely bear to contemplate the nightmare scenario of having to face my Peruvian friends after such a humiliating disaster, let alone the utter misery of flying home to England after such a quick surrender.

And yet, if that was what the fates held in store for me, there was precious little anyone could do to change the situation. When the wind blows to the east, a rowing boat on the ocean will be propelled to the east. Rowing with every ounce of my strength in the opposite direction might make some difference, and putting a sea anchor into the swell might reduce the speed but, in severe conditions, my human efforts would be akin to whistling in the wind.

This is the daily reality of every ocean rower: do what you want, say what you want, plan how you want and train how you want, but you will always remain a tiny, tiny speck at the mercy of a vast and omnipotent ocean. Indeed, nobody can accurately claim they rowed across an ocean. In reality, one strives to cross the ocean in a rowing boat. Human beings can do no more.

With these bleak thoughts in mind, I rowed away from Ilo

and towards the horizon, making decent progress into my first evening at sea. It was shortly after ten o'clock when I crawled into the cabin and, for the first time, fell asleep to the gentle rocking of the restless waves that surrounded me. Just survive the first 100 miles, the first week, I told myself, and you will be fine.

I woke bright and early on the morning of 1 July 2000, opened the hatch to the cabin and reached round to do something that I would do many thousands of times during this voyage: I glanced at the plotter to check my position, and see in what direction and at what speed the boat was moving.

Even on Day 1, the combination of the Raytheon plotter and the C-Map charts appeared every bit as indispensable, informative and sturdy as it looked when Paul Sumpner first described it to me during the London Boat Show. To see my equipment working in practice was profoundly encouraging.

And, on this first morning, the plotter brought good news. We (the boat and I) had already moved a respectable eighteen miles from Ilo and were travelling slightly north of west at 1.6 knots; at that pace, we would cover twenty-six miles in a day, which was below my target of thirty, but we had not yet reached either the consistent and powerful Humboldt Current or the south-east trade winds that, I hoped, would carry us to Australia.

In high spirits, I rubbed my eyes and looked around, surveying the ocean, restless and choppy, a stone-grey reflection of an overcast sky. So this was it. I was finally alone on the Pacific. For more than two years, I had worked to reach this state in this place. It felt strange to have arrived.

My mind drifted around the globe to Jane, sleeping at home in Northwood, and to our daughters in Bristol, and I sensed the old, familiar world was grinding on without me. I had now stepped away from that world. I had made my choice, and the consequence was that I would have to live in a different world, my own world, measuring only six feet wide and twenty-three feet long.

The weather in this new world seemed calm with a fresh easterly breeze, ideal conditions to sweep me away from the coast of Peru, which was just as well because there was no sign of the fishing boat that was supposed to have been my escort during the first twenty-four hours of the voyage. The captain seemed to have lost sight of *Le Shark* during the night and his boat only reappeared, sheepishly, scarcely fifty yards away, at half past nine in the morning.

I was poised to raise the captain on the VHF radio when I thought that, since his English was almost as poor as my Spanish, it would be better to resort to more basic means of communication. So I stood in the middle of my boat and waved madly in his direction, shouting across the waves.

'Good morning! How are you?'

'Jim! OK! No problemo,' he yelled back enthusiastically.

'No problemo,' I replied.

'You want we stay?'

Even at a distance of fifty yards, I sensed these Peruvians were finding the task of watching a small rowing boat less than action-packed and, in a surge of confidence inspired by our healthy progress during the night, I decided there was no longer any need for their presence at my side.

'It's OK,' I bellowed. 'You go! I want to be alone!'

The captain broke out into a peal of laughter, waved farewell, wished me good luck and turned his boat back towards Ilo, towards lives of normality, eating fresh food, sleeping on beds, talking to friends, working hard and paying bills; that was the kind of normality I had deserted. For a moment, I sat perfectly still and wondered what to do. I thought I should row.

Aware that it would be principally the wind and the current that propelled me towards my destination, I had allowed myself to wonder whether the voyage could prove altogether less stressful if I chose to spend more of the cool nights snuggling into my sleeping bag in the cabin, and most of the long, languid days massaging sun cream into my shoulders and enjoying the view.

Unfortunately, ocean rowing is not so simple. It is not a pleasure cruise. The plain, unassailable fact remains that every single stroke of the oar takes the boat more quickly towards the destination than would have been the case if one does not bother to row at all. However hard I tried to convince myself it would be OK to chill out, the unforgiving reality was that I needed to row.

Even if the coast of South America had now dissolved into the haze, the threat of being blown back to shore during these early days remained strong and each stroke would take me further away from catastrophe. On-shore winds could get up at any moment. This was no time for complacency.

So I settled myself into the pliable, comfortable, orthopaedic cushion that I had brought to place on the standard Concept II rowing-machine seat and seized the sixteen-foot oars with purpose and determination. I slowly lowered the blades into the water, and pulled, settling into a steady rhythm.

In, out; in, out; in, out.

Within five minutes, my lower back was starting to ache. Before leaving Ilo, I had developed a daily schedule where I rowed for an hour, took a thirty-minute break, rowed for another hour, then took another thirty-minute break. After only five minutes at the oars, this regime appeared somewhat optimistic.

Hoping the pain would ease, I rowed on: in, out; in, out.

Within ten minutes, I was in severe discomfort, and starting to blame the water. I had not expected the Pacific to be a mill pond, but neither had I anticipated this churning, chopping broth of froth and bubble. Two opposing swells seemed to be creating a kind of double-wobble effect with the boat being rocked not only from side to side but also from end to end. It was almost impossible to establish any kind of decent stroking rhythm. This was no fun at all. I shifted my position in the rowing seat to ease the aching pain in my back.

Breathing deep, I rowed on: in, out; in, out.

Within twenty minutes, my lower left back had become so

sore that I pulled in the oars and stopped altogether. I was in agony. If there had been a pub around the corner, I would have taken a break and nipped in for a couple of pints. On the Pacific Ocean, sadly, there are no pubs around the corner.

I had rowed without difficulty while I was leaving Ilo but, not even half an hour into my first full day at sea, I was in severe trouble. I needed to remain calm and be practical. My first thought was that the pain in my back was related to my problematic left kidney, half of which had been removed when I was twenty-two. Drinking copious amounts of liquid usually resolved the problem; in fact, three or four pints of best bitter had more than once proved an ideal remedy.

However, aside from three bottles of wine to be kept for special occasions, there was no alcohol at all aboard my boat and I had to make do with three litres of freshly desalinated water to wash through my ailing kidneys. So I drank, rested a while, moved gingerly back into position and began to row.

In, out; in, out. The pain seemed to have eased, the sea appeared to have settled and the blades cut into the swell with greater conviction. A quick glance at the plotter told me we were travelling in a west-north-westerly direction at around 2.1 knots. That was fine. I felt encouraged, happy again.

My logbook records it was some time after three o'clock in the afternoon when the pain returned, like some wounded beast that had slunk away and was now retracing its steps to hunt its prey. At first, I tried to ignore the dull, pulsating ache that had now spread from my lower back into my left side. I tried varying the angle at which I was pulling the oars through the water. I experimented with my hand, foot and body positions, tried anything and everything.

Nothing worked completely. Anything that eased the soreness in my side seemed to aggravate a 'locking' sensation in my back, and anything that helped my back seemed to exacerbate the tenderness in my side.

Desperation crept over me. What hope could there be for a

54-year-old businessman striving to cross the Pacific in a rowing boat when he was suffering from back pain that would have prevented him completing a game of squash? A few months earlier, my back had completely seized up during a game and I was left lying on the court, briefly unable to move. I had had to roll onto my side to get back on my feet. What would happen if I 'locked up' on the boat?

I started to blame myself for not being properly prepared for the voyage. I needed to be in a stronger physical condition, should have found more time to spend in the gym. But there had been no more time. There had been so much to do. I wanted to complain, so I looked around but found nobody to listen. Complaining is generally futile even when there are many people within earshot. However, complaining in the middle of the ocean feels uniquely and utterly pointless.

Be practical, I told myself, not emotional; so I reached for the large bag of medical supplies. This array of potions and bandages had been assembled to sooth most ailments but I have always been wary of taking high-street painkillers and, even in a state of near agony, I shied away from the pills.

Instead, I sought relief from the herbal remedy called Devil's Claw, which had been supplied by an old water polo acquaintance who worked for the manufacturer. Albeit with considerably more hope than confidence, I took a full dose. Within a couple of hours, I was able to resume my place in the middle of the boat and, gently, to start rowing again.

With the benefit of hindsight, my first full day at sea seems to have been a perfect microcosm of the entire voyage: I was up and I was down, I was delighted and I was depressed, I was euphoric and I despaired. My mood appeared to soar and plunge like the lightest of feathers borne on the breeze.

In many ways, life would have been much less trying if I had been able to follow Rudyard Kipling's dictum and treat triumph and disaster 'just the same' but equanimity and balance have rarely been my strongest suits.

This first day ended amid a type of calm and serenity that, on *terra firma*, is perhaps only found in the most remote desert or mountain range. As a genuine Pacific sunset gashed gold, orange and purple across the western sky, I sat for twenty minutes or so and watched in awe as a black petrel swooped and dived over gently rolling waves around my boat. At first, I assumed he was searching for his evening meal, but he hung around for such a long time that I began to wonder if, like everyone else, he was not also amazed by the spectacle of someone like me sitting alone on a small boat in the middle of the ocean.

With one last look at the plotter, sending me cheerily to bed with news of westward process at 1.4 knots, I crawled into the cabin and found general chaos. I am not a tidy person by nature, and the morass of items strewn around this tiny, confined space immediately persuaded me to change the habits of a lifetime and ensure that everything was always put away in its place. In a rough sea, anything not safely stowed away or bolted down becomes a missile.

When I awoke on the second morning, I stretched my head around the open hatch to glance at the piece of equipment that, even at this early stage of the trip, had taken a firm grip on my emotions. At times, I would feel like a puppet whose strings were held by the grey box fixed to the wall beside the hatch. If the plotter showed we were moving west, I was happy. If not, I was sad.

Just one glance at the plotter was enough to determine my mood until the next time I looked. It didn't matter if the weather was cold and miserable, so long as the plotter indicated we were moving away from South America and towards Australia, then I would be enthusiastic and bright. By the same token, I might find myself in the midst of extreme beauty, but if the plotter showed we were standing still or, much worse, being blown back east, I would despair.

It was the first thing I did in the morning, and the last thing

I did at night. I would glance at the plotter while I was cooking. I could see the plotter while I was rowing. Before long, I had even settled into a routine whereby I would wake every two hours during the night just to check the readings on the plotter. This grey box soon assumed the status of an old friend, always reliable and always prepared to tell me the truth, irrespective of whether it was good or bad.

The news was generally good through the second day, as we continued to move north-west at a reasonable pace. It was not fantastic, but it was acceptable, and my back appeared to be adjusting to the challenge. Perhaps the Devil's Claw was getting to grips with the problem. The pain certainly eased.

Midway through the afternoon, early morning in England, I telephoned my daughter Sarah in Bristol. I had arranged with Jane and the girls that I would call each of them once every week, and stagger the calls so that I spoke to someone at home every couple of days. I had spoken with Jane on the first day, reassuring her that I was fine, and I looked forward to hearing Sarah's voice.

The line was eerily clear. She sounded as though she could be around the corner rather than on the opposite side of the globe. Through these early days of the voyage, I found it strangely difficult to come to terms with the transient nature of contact between life at home and life on the ocean. I started to look forward to the telephone calls as the highlight of the day, and I would then be consumed by a sense of missing something when I replaced the receiver.

I never stopped missing my family but, with the passing weeks, the regular telephone conversations started to take their place within the daily routine. I may have been alone on the ocean but I never felt alone on the planet.

After another profitable, and relatively painless, period of rowing during the evening, I rested the oars and focused my mind on coming to terms with another activity that would become part of the daily ritual.

Researchers at Leeds University had developed a brand-new energy drink called G-Push, made from glactose and developed to replace energy without leading to overproduction of insulin. I was intrigued by the idea, and the research team seemed keen to use my trip as a trial run for one of their pioneering products. We reached an agreement whereby, in return for complimentary supplies, I would drink G-Push throughout the voyage and would regularly monitor my physical condition.

Thus, I committed myself to the daily ritual of taking a urine sample and measuring my chest, gut and spare tyre thickness. The researchers also wanted me to test my blood, but I was reluctant to puncture my skin on a regular basis and run the risk of infection. They also asked me to weigh myself every week, but this was impossible because the incessant rocking motion spoiled the reading on my bathroom scales.

G-Push is produced in a variety of flavours, and if there was one flavour that I probably would not choose, it would be lemon and lime. Needless to say, Sod's Law took effect and the special consignment sent to me before the boat's departure for Chile was predominantly flavoured lemon and lime.

With no time for anything to be changed, I was stuck on the Pacific with a lemon and lime energy drink. Under normal circumstances, I would have moaned and groaned, and probably taken something else. On the Pacific, as I have said, there is absolutely no point moaning and groaning. There is no alternative but to make do and, before long, I was enjoying lemon and lime.

As the voyage wore on, it seemed clear that the G-Push was effectively replenishing my energy levels during the night and I developed such confidence in this new product that I decided there was no need to supplement my carefully balanced diet with any other kind of vitamin or tonic.

My only frustration with G-Push arose on windy days when any attempt to deliver a spoonful of powder from the tub into a small bottle invariably resulted in the lemon and lime powder being sprinkled over the deck. I spent several furious hours trying, and generally failing, to resolve this problem.

The first two days on the ocean had felt more like two weeks. At that rate, I calculated, the anticipated six-month voyage would last for fifteen years. Perhaps it was this kind of thinking that kept me awake for several hours during my second night on the Pacific. I stared at the cabin ceiling scarcely twenty inches above my head and quietly expressed the hope that time would start to fly.

Lying perfectly still, I found it increasingly difficult to separate fantasy from reality. At one point, I managed to convince myself I could hear either the distant rumble of lorries thundering up and down the Panam highway, or perhaps the sound of large earthmovers working the copper mines. Was that my imagination, or was it for real? I didn't know.

I stirred on the third morning to discover the ocean calmer and quieter than at any stage of the voyage to date. This was welcome because it was easier to row under such conditions; on the other hand, it was even more necessary to row on such days or the boat would scarcely move at all. Still compensating for my back pain, I pulled well within my capabilities but managed to keep the boat moving west at a speed of 0.6 knots. With no wind, it was a decent effort.

Midway through the morning, my stroke was interrupted by a sudden thud. I looked down to see a small black bird lying stunned and still in the middle of the deck. It had collided with the side of the boat and knocked itself out. Even for a bird, this seemed a particularly stupid thing to have done.

An incurable animal lover, I cradled the stricken creature in my hands and laid him, or her, tenderly in a small cardboard box. I was not exactly sure what to do next, but I was resolved the box would not be a coffin. I gave food and water, but he, or she, hardly moved. Every ten minutes or so, like the doting mother of a newborn child, I found myself involuntarily peering into the box just to check that his, or her, tiny feathered breast was moving up and down. At four o'clock, to my surprise and delight, the bird stirred, stood and flew away.

The sustained rowing followed by the bird rescue had kept me busy, with the result that, compared to the first two days, Day 3 rushed by in a blur. The key to passing time was obviously to keep busy.

I was starting to realise my time on the Pacific would be spent ducking and bobbing between two zones, the practical and the psychological.

Inside the practical zone, I would be preoccupied with doing whatever was required to ensure I reached Australia: I would need to row, keep the boat intact, maintain all equipment, stay healthy and generally keep going.

The challenge inside the psychological zone was quite different: it was to deal with total solitude, to rationalise vivid dreams, to reminisce about people and places long since forgotten, to contemplate the past and the future, to dwell upon things I had done and still wanted to do, to think about the person I had been and the person I wanted to become. This could be a tough place.

Even after only three days, it had become clear I would have precious little control over when I moved from one zone to the other. Life was more simple and straightforward in the practical zone, but moments of psychological introspection were inevitable at some stage of every day. Occasionally, I would feel as though I was somehow suspended in both zones at the same time.

In fact, I was beginning to appreciate this was the dual challenge of my voyage: to survive at the practical and at the psychological level. I needed to win both these battles if I was going to reach Australia and win the war.

We had continued to make respectable progress through the third day, in spite of the still conditions, and later in the evening I turned my mind to arranging my sleeping conditions more effectively and comfortably.

There was no problem with the actual bed, comprising two one-inch foam mattresses one placed on top of the other. It felt just as comfortable as our bed at home in Northwood. However, I had not been able to enjoy a decent night's sleep because the rocking of the boat threw me around the cabin. When medium-sized waves frequently tipped the boat to angles of thirty or forty degrees, I would be hurled against one wall and then the other as the hull righted itself.

It is true that I enjoy most games, but being bounced around like a human pinball at two o'clock in the morning is stretching the limit.

On this third night of the voyage, I tried to address the situation by lying in a position where my right arm was braced against the hatch and my left leg was wedged up against a bulkhead. It was not comfortable, but at least my body would now remain relatively stable throughout the night.

As the weeks passed, I became accustomed to this unorthodox sleeping position in the same way that I grew used to a lemon and lime energy drink. Out on the Pacific, where you have no alternatives, it becomes easy to do what you have to do . . . just because there is nothing else to do.

In rearranging my 'bedroom', I also found an appropriate perch for the soft parrot that my daughters had given me as a leaving present. I was battling to find a place for the small teddy bear that Maggie Sivey had given me at Heathrow, so I used a rubber band and tied the bear to the parrot's feet.

This unlikely pair of trapeze artists became my sleeping companions for the duration of the trip. I won't admit to having been so lonely that I entered into lengthy conversations with them, although I won't deny that I did wish them both goodnight on more than one occasion. Towards the end of my adventure, when everything else was sodden, the parrot rose magnificently to the challenge when pressed into emergency service as an impromptu pillow.

With the cabin thus prepared and personalised, I excitedly

looked forward to a sound night's sleep, and all seemed well until approximately 02.20. It is not easy adequately to describe the sensation of being roused from a deep sleep by a violent, cruel surge of ice-cold seawater drenching your bed.

One moment you are warm and dry, the next moment you are soaked and freezing. Imagine how bad it could be, double the distress, treble the misery, and you have some idea how I felt at around 02.25 that morning. For an instant, I lay soaked and sodden, trying to understand what had happened. I felt certain I had closed the hatch before turning in for the night.

In fact, there were two standard positions on the main hatch: the first was 'sealed', implying nothing could pass; the second was 'cracked', which meant the hatch was still closed but a flow of fresh air was able to pass into the cabin. I had looked at the 'cracked' position and firmly concluded that no wave would be able to get up and gush through such a tiny gap into the cabin.

Wrong! A wave had broken across the boat and propelled an astonishing volume of water through the slim crack of the hatch and into my cabin. I dragged the sopping mattresses and sleeping bag outside and hung them out to dry; and, since what could be described as the ultimate cold-water shower had left me wide awake, I decided to start some temperate rowing in the moonlight.

So I had been soaked. So what? This was the reality of life on the ocean. It might have been the first time that I was rudely awoken during the night, but it was certainly not going to be the last. In months to come, I would work endlessly to ensure every hatch and compartment was sealed, and I would frequently stay dry. Yet, sooner or later, one or other rogue wave would crash over my boat, find a crack in my armour and drench me all over again.

I eventually started to realise that, however hard I tried, the concept of being completely waterproof on the Pacific exists only in theory. There is no point getting angry. It is better to accept the fact that, while it is possible to keep some things dry for a while, the ocean always prevails in the end.

Before long, I had learned the etiquette of the ocean: if the Pacific wanted to soak me, he didn't bother to knock. He simply let himself in.

There was no dramatic dawn to herald the fourth day of my voyage. I can verify this because I was sitting on deck when a dark night grudgingly brightened to a grey, overcast morning. 'Typical Ilo weather,' I wrote in my logbook, perhaps unfairly, but I had hardly seen the sun since arriving in Peru. The ongoing lack of sunshine, and the absence of powerful winds, was starting to cause me considerable concern. No sun and no wind equalled no power.

As my means of generating electricity, the solar panel and wind generator lay at the heart of my game plan to cross the Pacific, but the calm weather began to drain the reservoir batteries alarmingly. Such generally unexpected anxieties over power would become a feature of the first few months at sea, prompting me to restrict use of my computer, water maker and telephone.

I sat and stared at the LED indicator for almost thirty minutes during the fourth morning, watching the colours that indicated the state of the batteries ebb from green to yellow to orange and into red; and there was absolutely nothing I could do. The southern Pacific was supposed to be a place of regular sunshine and powerful, prevailing winds, but this was not the case in my corner of this vast, unpredictable ocean.

The problem with the weather was that there was no weather, only miles and miles of dull grey nothingness stretching away to every horizon. As I began to row, keeping the boat moving west, I sensed the start of another day when my moods would ride the roller coaster of delight and despair.

When the weather had depressed me, I raised my eyes to the skies and saw a flock of pelicans flying past, not more than thirty yards from my boat. They might not be the most graceful birds on earth, but they are majestic in flight. In an instant, I ceased worrying about the vagaries of wind and sun, forces that, in any event, lay far, far beyond my realm of influence.

I had been down, but now I was up. I had continued to row through most of the morning, with no back pain, and, appearing as reward for my efforts, I felt a perceptible breeze on my face soon after two o'clock. By mid-afternoon, the boat was heading north-north-west at around 2.2 knots and I was grinning again. Even the battery indicators perked up, showing a charge of half an amp with the regulator LED moving from red back to a yellowish orange.

However, early on the fourth evening, I was brought back down by a first encounter with another vessel, and an early warning that my radar reflector might not measure up even to my low expectations. Its purpose was to ensure that other shipping was aware of my presence, a particularly important task as I passed through the busy shipping lanes running down the west coast of South America. Other ships needed to see me on their radar because it was likely to be too late for them to change direction and avoid a collision by the time they spotted me with the naked eye.

A large fishing boat suddenly appeared perhaps 250 yards away on the port side, moving in a parallel direction to me, going about its business. I looked across and saw somebody standing on the bridge, looking through a large pair of binoculars in my direction. He was evidently intrigued.

I tried to raise a response on the VHF radio, without success. Two minutes later, a thickly accented voice announced itself on the transceiver, asking me if I required any kind of assistance. This was clearly the captain of the fishing boat.

'No, thank you,' I replied. 'I am fine.'

'OK, small ship,' the voice boomed again. 'You're sure?'

'Absolutely sure, thank you.'

As the boat chugged into the gloom, I started to wonder whether they had seen me on their radar. And if they had seen me, why had they passed so close to me? Did their proximity mean they had not noticed me? If I was overreacting to the situation, it was only because I did not want to be run over.

'In any case,' I asked myself out loud, 'this is an enormous ocean. There is more than enough room for everyone who wants to spend some time here, so why does any other vessel have to come anywhere near me?'

Nobody answered.

My last glance at the plotter before heading off to bed suggested the wind and current was starting to push my boat more north than west. I was not overly concerned, but my response graduated to genuine discomfort when I looked at the plotter on the fifth morning, and recognised a new threat.

This portion of the west coast of South America lies at such an angle that boats heading in a north-westerly direction effectively travel parallel to the shore. Thus, while we had progressed a reasonable 104 miles from Ilo, we had generally been drifting too far north and the plotter confirmed that, early on Day 5, we remained only eighteen miles away from the coast. In other words, we remained extremely vulnerable to a sudden change in the wind, and were not yet safely on our way.

I was taken aback. Five days on the ocean seemed an eternity, and it was difficult to accept that normal life existed just beyond the horizon. I wanted to get clear of South America and focus on Australia. Surprise swiftly became resolve, and I settled in seizing the oars with renewed conviction.

In, out; in, out; in, out.

Due west. Left hand. Due west. Left hand.

The bountiful rewards of working hard every day started to appear in the form of lower back muscles that had emerged from the agony of the first day and strengthened to the point where, sitting in the cooking area, I was able painlessly to lean to one side and pick up a knife from the footwell. My daily challenge was to push my body to the limit of its physical potential, but no further. One of the enduring dictums of the voyage was fixed in my mind: 'Know your body or perish.'

Progress was slow but measurable as I rowed throughout the morning. If I started to tire, one sighting of a seagull effectively reminded me of the proximity of land, and stirred me to keep pulling the oars through the swell. Soon after four in the afternoon, the plotter revealed we were now 28.5 miles from the coast. I was getting somewhere, achieving something. I felt better.

The ocean churned restlessly into the evening, producing conditions that, somewhat to my relief, made rowing seem impossible because one stroke would feel like pulling through treacle and the next like pulling through air. In any event the current was carrying us west, so I felt justified in resting.

In the months to come, my technique would become much more compact and efficient, enabling me to row in even tougher conditions, but this was still only the first week of my adventure. I was still learning, finding my way.

The plotter sympathetically sent me to sleep with news that we had made outstanding progress during the day and now stood 152 miles away from Ilo and barely 7,408 miles from Byron Bay, my favourite place on the northern coast of New South Wales. The danger of being hurled back against the coast of South America, so real that morning, had significantly receded.

When we drifted a further fourteen miles west during the night, I decided to call Jane and share the satisfaction of recent successes. I had set myself two major challenges during the first week of the voyage: to get safely away from the coast of South America and to establish a practical daily routine.

I seemed to have been partially successful on both counts, and decided to reward these achievements by slotting 'Johnny Cash's Greatest Hits' into the portable CD player and tapping forward to my personal favourite, 'The Gambler'.

In many respects, I had gambled and survived – so far. Alone on a vast ocean, still swishing and swirling on every side, my voyage was truly under way.

7
Magic Cream and Duck Tape

It took only five days at sea to make me realise that the greatest challenge of my voyage would be to keep two objects in working order.

If I succeeded, I would reach Australia. If either of them broke down, the adventure would end. Both these objects would be regularly battered and bruised by the elements, placed under enormous pressure, tested to the very limits of their physical capacity, ruthlessly examined.

It was my task to maintain them: my boat and my body.

As day flowed smoothly into day, week into week, through nine months existing alone on the ocean, I cared and nurtured, listened intently for signs of stress, eased and compensated, improvised and mended, often worked gently and occasionally rested completely, soothed and soldered.

I survived . . . with duck tape and magic cream.

Through the last days before my departure, my wife Jane frequently asked me what on earth I was going to do with all my time on the ocean. I was clearly going to row, eat and sleep but, from our living room in Northwood, that did seem to leave many, many hours of doing nothing.

'I don't know,' I would reply, somewhat unsatisfactorily. That was the truth. I really didn't know. In the end, I took aboard a pile of books, my laptop computer to play various games, send and receive e-mail and write business plans, and a portable CD player, but I still couldn't be sure this was enough to keep me stimulated and alert during my solitary confinement.

The issue hardly surfaced during my month-long pursuit of a departure permit from the authorities in Chile and Peru, and it had required scarcely five days on the ocean to prove this was not an issue at all.

Through nine months, I remained perpetually busy. There was not one day when I could sit back and afford myself the pleasure of knowing there was nothing to do. There was not one night when I could retire to bed comfortable in the knowledge that every task and chore had been done. There was always something to mend, something to heal, something to dry.

'Maintenance!'

That was the answer to Jane's question.

Maintenance! Keeping body and boat in working order. This would be a task as unending as painting the Sydney Harbour Bridge: when they finish the north end, it's already time to start painting the south end again.

The challenge of looking after my body was, of course, not new. During more than fifty-four years, I had managed to handle the task without too many major alarms. Aside from the removal in 1968 of half a kidney, probably damaged by an underwater kick during a water polo match, I had enjoyed good health, touch wood, through most of these five decades.

I have never smoked but often enjoyed a drink, occasionally in excess, and have always delighted in taking exercise: playing tennis, squash, rugby and water polo in my youth; swimming and walking the dog more recently.

It was true that I had steadily put on weight through most of the 1990s, and I was tipping the bathroom scales at a fraction over 242 pounds, when I rowed out of Ilo on 30 June 2000. Yet, far from being a reason to stay home, the prospect of being able to shed some flab had always appeared one of the most attractive aspects of rowing across the Pacific.

However, I was determined this generally sound state of health should not lull me into any sense of complacency, and I went to considerable trouble and expense to assemble a comprehensive medical kit.

In 1997, sharing similar sentiments ahead of the Atlantic race,

David Jackson and I agreed to spend £800 on a package of medicines, potions and bandages. However, this bundle was hardly used during that trip, so it became the foundation of my medical supplies for the Pacific voyage.

The first supplement was a dose of common sense. In 1997, we set off with a glamorous array of advanced medicines but failed to take enough of the dull, humdrum, absolutely necessary antiseptic substances such as TCP and Savlon that were needed almost every day. I was not going to make the same mistake again. I also calculated how many normal sticking plasters I would possibly need, and then packed double that number.

Second, I asked Dr Peter Skew, my doctor and friend in Northwood, to suggest any items that he thought could be added. Trained as a conventional doctor, he has gained broad experience of alternative medicine, established his own sports clinic and worked extensively with the English National Ballet. Since he knew me and understood the nature of the challenge, he appeared ideally placed to ensure every base was covered.

My daughter Anna, a medical student, then completed the process by preparing a detailed inventory, listing every medicine, what symptoms it was intended to ease and precisely how it should be used.

All said and done, I felt like a floating ambulance. My supplies included no fewer than three levels of drugs to be used if I suffered a heart attack, which all appeared to be of limited use since I had no idea how to tell if I was suffering a heart attack. However, the first two were to be taken by mouth. The third came with a syringe and the instructions that it could be taken orally but was more effective if injected directly into the heart! The required procedure seemed to be something akin to that famous scene in the cult movie, *Pulp Fiction*. I shuddered at the thought that I would have to do that to myself. I packed the syringe, hoping never to see it again.

And I also took a dozen tubes of an analgesic ointment used to soothe aching muscles, the substance known as 'magic cream'.

If anything hurt and could not be seen, I rubbed on the magic cream. All-purpose, all-conquering, magic cream emerged as the hero of my pain-fighting forces.

Even with this armoury at my disposal, my overall strategy was first to know and understand my body as thoroughly as possible. I had to be sensitive to the earliest signs of pain and try to alleviate the stress before it became too serious, particularly since there was such limited opportunity for recovery. Any medicine, even the magic cream, was used as a last resort.

At least, this was the theory before my departure. In practice, I have to say the theory worked reasonably well. Far from suffering any serious injuries or illnesses, I have no doubt that the nine-month voyage across the Pacific significantly improved my general state of health.

My medical report card would read as follows:

Head: frequently bumped when climbing in and out of the cabin, often cut and grazed due to lack of protective hair, once gashed deep enough to be dripping blood over the deck, sporadically burned by pitiless sun if the owner carelessly neglected to wear his floppy hat while rowing.

Teeth: ached in sympathy with my ego when spirits sank, becoming a reliable indicator that owner should cheer up; faithfully brushed every evening because serious dental problems would have been disastrous and, in any case, I hate kissing with smelly breath.

Sinuses and throat: largely untroubled because there are more cold germs flying around the No. 31 bus than around the entire Pacific Ocean; also, I was far too busy to catch cold; according to medical wisdom, most people only suffer flu-like symptoms when they have the time.

Shoulders and chest: similarly singed when the owner rowed without a T-shirt on sunny days, or even when he rowed with a torn shirt, resulting in a scorched red-raw stripe across the back; internally untroubled.

Back: pure agony on the first day, eased during the first week, worked gently for the remainder of the voyage, cast-iron by the end.

Hands: initially wore gloves while rowing on the Atlantic, but eventually discarded them because they succeeded only in changing the positions of the unavoidable blisters; never wore gloves on the Pacific; since hands appeared to be constantly damp and soft, resembling wet paper, blisters generally burst early and disappeared, leaving a small dent in the flesh; thus, blisters caused discomfort but never represented a major problem.

Claws: prolonged bouts of rowing tended to leave fingers locked in the shape of a claw, as if grasping an oar; would wake in the morning and have to press against the wall to transform the claw back into a human hand; strongly denied any common heritage with werewolves etc.

Wrists: generally fine, but once accidentally slammed against hatch of the cabin, most probably fracturing a small bone in the process; treated with a tightly bound crêpe bandage and bravely borne for two weeks.

Bowels: a stable diet, including copious supplies of dried prunes and apricots, ensured I could set my watch by regular activity.

Backside: a combination of an orthopaedic cushion and the Concept II training seat proved successful in avoiding the blisters and boils that caused me problems during the Atlantic row. Even if I was exhausted at the end of a gruelling day at the oars, I was still able to sit comfortably.

Feet: subjects of special care because owner was ever mindful of the ocean rower, Joe le Guen, who had injured his feet and ultimately had ten toes amputated after being rescued; Quayside deck shoes, veterans of the Atlantic crossing, performed magnificently once again, until one was lost in the waves of the dramatic arrival at North Stradbroke Island; one blister on the heel was pampered with Savlon and a new dressing every day.

From head to toe, I not only survived the Pacific crossing, I started to reap tangible benefits of regular exercise and a healthy diet. Aches and pains that had troubled me for years gradually evaporated in the fresh sea air, and sides and hips started to function more smoothly.

I may not have been completely successful in my aim of redis-covering the lean, hard body of my youth, but I certainly rolled back the years, and the flab. The man who emerged from the surf in Australia had lost a total of forty-nine pounds during nine months at sea, and weighed in at a trim, fit and strong one hundred and ninety-three pounds. More importantly, the Pacific left me feeling ten years younger.

Whilst my body needed to be kept healthy during the voyage, it did not necessarily have to be kept impeccably clean. With apologies to any sensitive readers, the plain truth is that I only washed thoroughly three times during the nine-month adventure. I realise this revelation may provoke knowing remarks about the English and their reputed antipathy to soap, but the simple reality of the situation was that it was not necessary for me to wash.

It is clothes that cause smell because they stimulate the pro-duction of body oils and then retain the odour. Since I rarely wore any clothes, my body adapted to its surroundings and didn't smell at all. Those tiny particles of skin that would normally have caused clothing to smell simply fell harmlessly away, and I was left feeling permanently fragrant ... Well, almost.

When there were used T-shirts or shorts to wash, I used a special soap that supposedly cleaned with seawater, but I gradu-ally learned to be content if clothes came out less dirty than when they went in. Since I was not willing to waste precious drinking water on washing clothes, the simplest option was not wear clothes; so, unless I felt cold, I lived in sunglasses and a hat.

In a sense, I was returning to a natural state. It is the modern world's self-perpetuating obsession with deodorants and cleanliness that has in fact taken us away from our inherently clean condition.

Each of my three thorough washes was a memorable occasion. Twice, I made absolutely sure there were no sharks in the vicinity and plucked up the courage to swim for a few minutes alongside the boat. The third time, I stood naked on deck beneath the most dramatic, magnificent downpour, enjoying by some distance the most invigorating shower of my life.

There were other areas of personal hygiene that had to be addressed to ensure my body remained in effective working order.

I grew tired of long, straggly hair after three months at sea, and decided to shave my head completely. However, a couple of days later, my daughter Anna said on the telephone that she would be disappointed if I didn't look like a bearded hermit at the end of the trip. In deference to her, with the exception of some deft trimming around mouth and nostrils, I didn't shave again. It was a clever call. The long white beard and flowing locks did seem to fit the occasion when I eventually appeared on an Australian beach.

A galvanised bucket, fitted onto the lid of a hatch, served as a perfectly adequate lavatory facility, and its specially reinforced wooden seat became prized as the most comfortable berth on the boat. The sewage system can be explained in four brief words: bucket and chuck-it.

My body obviously also needed fuel, and enough food for the trip had been packed in four deep hatches near the bow.

I decided these hatches would be opened as rarely as possible to avoid another potential disaster: contamination of the food supplies by seawater. It was clear that the hatches that were repeatedly opened and closed tended to be the hatches that leaked most. Nothing was ever easy on the ocean but, by adhering to guidelines and not opening hatches, life was tolerable. In the final analysis, the sea managed to ruin only four boxes of rice and quarter of a small birthday cake.

Expedition Foods, based in Cheshire, emerged as a primary supplier, and they generously provided me with a range of meals only needing to be heated in boiling water. This was a process well within my ability, and dishes such as chilli con carne and chicken tikka masala rose to the top of the menu out on the Pacific.

Most of the other provisions were bought on a mammoth shopping trip to Costco, a discount, bulk-buy store in North London to which our neighbour has access. We also made a separate visit to Sainsbury's to stock up with more than 400 of their superb own-brand powdered soups, the leek and potato variety, with croutons, being the ultimate luxury.

My master plan was to consume 6,500 calories per day for six months, the initial estimate of the journey time; this equated to a substantial quantity of food, as required by a large body taking regular, strenuous exercise.

Breakfast would generally be a large bowl of porridge, followed by baked beans with either sausage or bacon. Lunch would be a proper, three-course meal, usually with soup to start, then a pre-cooked Expedition Foods dish served with rice, pasta, noodles or even mashed potato, and finally dessert, most often rice pudding. Dinner would follow a similar pattern to lunch.

Determined never to go hungry, I decided to supplement these regular meals with large supplies of snacks such as pepperoni, muesli, biscuits, nuts and cereals, and these tended to be happily nibbled throughout the day, at hand whenever I was rowing, resting, or reading, always a grab away.

The king of treats during the voyage was my supply of Cadbury's dairy milk chocolate. I took no fewer than 144 one-pound bars and, in the darkest hours of deepest depression, the mere sight of the blue packaging would be enough to raise my spirits. A full bar of chocolate was a special pleasure, although I did not enjoy tremendous success in stopping at half-bars. In some way, somehow, the other half tended to disappear before too long.

An absolute last resort, to be consumed in times of genuine crisis if all the real food had been contaminated, was a large quantity of dehydrated egg and onion. I don't want to dwell on this substance, suffice to say it represented the best possible motivation to keep the hatches sealed.

My thirst was generally quenched by fresh water, from the water maker (of which much more later). I was drinking as much as nine litres per day during the summer months, but I also took eighteen large bottles of Ribena, the blackcurrant cordial, to be enjoyed as a rare indulgence.

When these supplies were gathered at our house in Northwood, prior to being packed in the boat and shipped to Chile, they added up to an awesome, nutritious, tempting, planned, five-foot food mountain. Since I wanted to cross the Pacific alone and unaided, there would be no question of anyone coming to resupply me with provisions. This heap was the lot.

It was not long before a journey time of six months was looking rather optimistic; fortunately it was also becoming clear that 6,500 calories was more than enough to sustain me for one day. As a result, the ratios were painlessly stretched and the food supplies just about lasted until the end. Give or take a bout of reasonably draconian rationing during the last month, I had unwittingly packed almost exactly enough food for nine months.

A succession of three well-designed petrol stoves almost managed to last the distance as well. These neat units, comprising a fuel container and a cooking ring, efficiently warmed the meals and boiled the water until, one by one, they suffered premature death by suffocation, caused when a thin wire in their vaporiser tubes became caked with carbon. Stove No. 3 shuffled off its mortal coil when I was still six weeks from Australia, forcing me to finish the trip on a diet of cold porridge and raw spaghetti.

In terms of utensils, much has subsequently been made of the fact that I forgot to take a can-opener on the boat. People have picked up on this as a successful line on television chat shows where there are fifteen seconds to convey 'eccentricity', but the actual impact of this oversight was minimal.

The mackerel and sardine containers had ring-pulls. The corned beef, ham and pork all had wind-up keys, and it was only the tuna and salmon that required a can-opener, and these containers were easily opened with a pocket knife that Pat Waggaman gave me in Chile. Whisper it to the chat show hosts, but the truth is I never really needed a can-opener at all.

As I worked my way through the meals and snacks, I constantly faced the dilemma of waste disposal. On the one hand, I wanted to leave the ocean pretty much as I found it; on the other hand, it was clearly impractical to store the litter on my already overcrowded boat. With second thoughts and with an element of guilt, I simply hurled the rubbish overboard.

In fact, it is extremely unlikely the amount of non-biodegradable waste that I fed to the waves could have damaged the eco-system of such a gigantic ocean. In 274 days spent on the Pacific, I saw only one small sign of pollution, a 200-yard slick of oil globules floating on the waves.

With a sensitive eye, ample medical supplies and wholesome food, I managed to ensure that not a single day passed during this long and arduous journey when illness or injury left me unable to row my boat.

However, the challenge of keeping my body in working order involved a psychological as well as a physical dimension. Human potential is realised by an optimum fusion of both physical and mental capacity. Keeping my body in sound physical working order was only half the job; it was crucial for my body to be kept psychologically calm, alert and strong as well.

A laptop computer seemed the obvious means of stimulating my brain and, for the first three months after leaving Ilo, I used the technology, writing a couple of embryonic ideas into business plans for life after the Pacific, keeping a log of my six-hourly positions, listening to MP3 music, sending and receiving e-mail, even playing a few games and writing a couple of basic programs. This was the plan.

However, power supplies ran low in the face of an ongoing lack of wind and sunshine during the second three months and I was increasingly forced to conserve remnant power for more essential items such as the plotter, satellite telephone and water-making machine; the laptop computer started to assume the status of a power-draining and awkward luxury.

It became hard to store securely in the cabin and difficult to keep dry on a boat often drenched by crashing waves. In truth, the unit survived remarkably well for the first six months but ultimately proved too delicate and intricate for a rough-and-tough life on the ocean. I was not particularly surprised when 25 per cent of the keys began to malfunction. Chronic dampness and perhaps a few stray drops of water were responsible. It didn't matter. Scarcely two-thirds through the voyage, my computer passed away.

My hand-held Psion 3C unit had already stepped into the breach as a source of electronic entertainment. Powered by easily rechargeable batteries, it could not match the power and functions of the laptop but it did at least feature its own version of Solitaire. This appeared to be a particularly appropriate pastime for someone trying to cross the Pacific, alone and unaided.

As the weeks passed, I assumed the status of what could be described as a Psion Solitaire junkie. It was that bad. On the perfectly realistic assertion that I was playing fifty games per day, I estimate I completed more than 9,000 games during the voyage. Practice tends to make perfect in these activities, and it became rare for me to score less than 1,000 points in a series. That total became my standard target. I would tell myself that I would not start rowing or start cooking until I had secured my 1,000 points.

A more traditional source of mental stimulation was the box of books provided at the last moment before my departure by one of Pat Waggaman's colleagues in Chile. I had been thanking

Colleen Baldwin for all her help when she happened to ask what books I was taking on the trip.

'Books?' I asked.

'Yes, what books are you taking?'

'Damn, I knew I had forgotten something.'

'Look, I once ran a second-hand book shop here. Let me have a look at home and bring you some books tomorrow, all right?'

'No, you really don't have to bother.'

'It would be no problem.'

'Well, that would be extremely kind.'

When Colleen offered me a selection of books the next day, I glanced through the titles, said thank you very much and packed the entire box aboard my boat. She had chosen with care and, in due course, I particularly enjoyed reading *Ra*, the story of Thor Heyerdahl's trip from Africa to the Caribbean on a papyrus boat, and found some interesting stories in Sir Francis Chichester's account of his famous single-handed voyage. She also included adventure books about potholing and mountaineering.

The most challenging book was a transcript of conversations between Joseph Campbell and Bill Moyer on the subject of 'comparative mythology'. I was intrigued and enthused by the parallels drawn between stories related in mythology, the Bible and texts of other religions. Indeed, the subject was so compelling that I read the book several times during the voyage.

In conversation with Colleen, I had also happened to mention how an inability to speak foreign languages was a constant source of embarrassment in my professional life; she responded by including in the box a cassette tape course in Spanish.

I had already packed a French course and a Slovak language course, and resolved I would use the voyage to develop these skills dramatically. At various stages, I would lie in the cabin, conscientiously following instructions from the cassette tapes, tirelessly repeating words and phrases. I was trying my best.

Slovakian proved beyond me. After three weeks of sombre

effort, I had still not grasped the basic principles of the opening lesson. I had done exactly what the tape said, but nothing was sticking. Moving on to the French, I found the cassettes had been waterlogged and ruined. That left the Spanish course, but the tapes meant nothing without a missing textbook.

I reluctantly conceded defeat, resigned to continue blundering through various forms of broken English for the rest of my days.

When the computer had failed, the books had been read and the language courses had overwhelmed me, my ongoing quest for entertainment and mental inspiration began to focus solely on my short-wave radio. From the middle of the voyage through to the end, I grew accustomed to listening to the radio throughout almost every day, with the occasional CD providing some variety.

A simple but effective five-metre aerial, rigged between the light pole at the front to the main hatch bulkhead and on through the cabin, provided a generally acceptable quality of reception on the same Sony radio that I had bought ten years earlier when working with Operation Safe Haven in Iraq.

Radio has often been described as 'The Theatre of the Mind'. Well, I was thrilled to settle in my seat and gawp from the stalls.

The BBC World Service arrived loud and clear through the first four months of the journey and, although I did find the tone occasionally pompous and patronising, the quality of programming was excellent. I looked forward to their discussion programmes more than the music shows, perhaps because I was starting to miss the sound of other people's voices. It didn't really matter what they were talking about. So long as they were coherent and logical, and they invariably were, I was delighted to hear them out.

Book at Bedtime was eagerly awaited and rarely missed, even if the times of broadcast did become increasingly difficult to track as I travelled west from time zone to time zone. The radio stories recalled cheerful memories of times when our family would pile into the car and drive across Europe on an annual pilgrimage to the Alps; Jane would have brought a couple of audio books, and the fourteen-hour journey would speed by as we listened.

Any BBC sports broadcast also cheered my day and, quite by chance, I happened to catch Alan Green's inspirational radio commentary of the coxless fours rowing final at the 2000 Olympic Games in Sydney, the victory that gave Steve Redgrave his amazing fifth Olympic gold medal.

As the British crew crossed the finish line, the commentator bellowed at his listeners to stop what they were doing, stand up and cheer. Well, since I just happened to be rowing somewhere out on the Pacific, as excited as anyone, I was delighted to pull in my oars, get to my feet and oblige.

The neat postscript to this particular episode is that, not long after the completion of my voyage, I was profoundly honoured to receive a message of congratulations from the rightly ennobled Sir Steve Redgrave.

Into October, a broad range of radio stations appeared and evaporated on the short waves. At stages, I listened to English-language broadcasts from Radio Bulgaria, Radio Japan, the Voice of Russia and the Voice of America. The repertory of this Theatre of the Mind evidently knew no bounds.

However, from roughly midway across the Pacific, my regular searches across the dial yielded one solitary station whose signal could be consistently and clearly received on my boat. From November 2000 until January 2001, there was only ever one show in town. It was going to be one long, hot, summer with Radio New Zealand International.

It would be an exaggeration to say I enjoyed every minute listening to RNZI, but I did develop an enduring affection for this station broadcasting out of New Zealand to the far-flung South Pacific Islands. I listened regularly from early in the morning until late at night, and the programme schedule started to weave itself in and out of my routine. The various presenters became nothing less than constant companions, familiar voices in my ear.

Their discussion programmes were rarely less than interesting, and at one stage I even started noting down the dates of broadcasts with the intention of one day asking the station to send me transcripts because I felt they might help me develop certain business opportunities.

And I also passed many cheerful hours gently pulling at the oars while listening to a full season of RNZI cricket commentaries. I had always followed the game from a distance, but my understanding was taken to a different level by the infectious enthusiasm of the partisan commentators as they described New Zealand's home five-day Test series against Zimbabwe, and the limited overs triangular tournament with Pakistan that followed.

However, it was the news bulletins and current affairs shows that truly intrigued me. The New Zealanders seemed so anxious to avoid offending any group that every story was couched in terminology so politically correct, gender correct and everything else correct that it generally ended up saying nothing at all. It was hilarious to hear the presenters tripping over their words as they read scripts trying to sound better than good.

Then, there were the repeats. One outstanding programme, concerning the future of democracy in Fiji, was starting to wear thin when it was broadcast for a fifth time during the period around Christmas and New Year, particularly since the specific issue that the panel were previewing was resolved between the third and fourth time of broadcast. I suppose it was just my misfortune that I happened to be listening all day, every day.

And then there was the air-conditioning breakdown in the studio! What else could have been the problem on the day when everyone present seemed to be suffering from a respiratory problem, swallowing in the middle of each sentence as they read the news; for example: 'And now (gulp), we have the rest of the news (gulp). In London today (gulp), Prime Minister Blair (gulp) . . .'

And I won't easily forget the weather forecasts that moved around the schedule like squalls on the ocean, often without warning, and were sometimes issued in one or other of the local island languages. In fact, sometimes the forecast did not take place at all because, as the presenter explained with endearing honesty, 'The reporter has not telephoned us yet.'

I want to emphasise that, so far as I am concerned, these issues were as freckles on the face of a well-loved friend. In irritating me with their political correctness, and frustrating me with their repeats, RNZI grew to represent an important, reliable spark of stimulation in my daily existence.

In reality, the station is probably run by a group of highly dedicated people working in extremely difficult circumstances within a tight budget; and the truth of the situation is that I would have been lost without them. I understand there is a website that broadcasts RNZI on the Internet, and I suspect there will be a time when I log on and tune in, just for old time's sake.

By the first few days of February 2001, my spirited, unflagging radio had started to pick up a signal from the Australian Broadcasting Corporation, enabling me to listen to yet more upbeat Antipodean cricket commentary from the Test series between Australia and the West Indies. The ABC also brought me into contact with 'Macca', a larger-than-life presenter whose early Sunday morning show was never less than entertaining and who emerged as the first media person to take any continuous interest in my adventure: he interviewed me twice on his show, long before the hordes descended.

Alongside the Psion 3C, the books and the radio, my portable compact disc player represented the fourth apparatus in the mental gym that effectively kept my mind in sound working order. Linked up to my computer speakers, it provided a decent sound system and didn't need much power.

I suppose my CD collection aboard the boat should have been carefully and lovingly reaped from my living room at home; in fact, maybe a dozen CDs were thrown into a box literally as I was leaving the house, yet I still managed to recruit a high-quality group of musical companions.

Johnny Cash and Boxcar Willie provided a classical Country element, and Louis Armstrong, The Beatles, The Rolling Stones and Queen were always welcome. I also took a soppy CD of Naked Pop, a little-known band from America.

And then there was Leonard Cohen, the Canadian singer/songwriter, who initially impressed me with his strong, deep voice and those provocative lyrics that seemed to hint at a rigorous intellect. However, the more I listened to the words, the more I was convinced that he had an inflated view of himself and, from that perspective, the words started to seem pretty shallow and meaningless.

Perhaps the 'Field Commander' did suffer from being played over and over again, inexorably for several days on end. My general inclination to open and close things as rarely as possible, either from laziness or to reduce the risk of damage, extended to the CD player with the result that I would listen to one disc repeatedly until I was absolutely certain I could bear it no longer. Then I would start a complex packing and unpacking process to find the next one.

I might not have been able to learn a foreign language, but at least this routine enabled me to learn the lyrics of some great songs.

My favourite source of music was the compilation tape arranged for me by Anna and Sarah, with each track bringing back memories of some incident or happy occasion in our lives. The experience of sitting back in the middle of the boat, watching a watery Pacific sunset, listening to various pieces of music that had meant so much to our family always raised my spirits.

Words intrigue, but music inspires.

Thus I managed to sustain my body and mind in working order during nine months on the ocean. Maintaining my boat, and all its equipment, proved an altogether more daunting and exhausting task.

My weapons in this continuing struggle to repair fittings, block leaks, adjust, improvise, resurrect and change were two pairs of scissors, two tubes of sealant, two paintbrushes, some fibreglass matting, resin and hardener, a small plastic toolkit including spanners and screwdrivers to fit almost every nut and bolt on the boat, and one fifty-yard roll of multi-purpose black duck tape.

This collection may seem relatively rudimentary and unsophisticated for the size of the task, but one can go a long way with common sense, duck tape and a reliable pair of scissors . . . Across the Pacific, in fact.

Hardly a day passed when there was not something to be repaired, and the despair of discovering a piece of equipment was broken was usually healed by the equal and opposite joy of seeing it mended. Almost every item aboard my boat failed at some time but, with the exceptions of the cooking stoves and the laptop computer, everything was mended.

A full and complete chronicle of my DIY activities would be interminably dull to assemble, and perhaps impossible to read; however, this central theme of my voyage can be adequately reflected in The Miraculous Tale of the Water Maker, a true story of ocean-rowing folk and their water.

Are you sitting comfortably? Now I'll slip into the third person and start. Well, it's easier than reliving these events in the first person.

Once upon a time there was a Water Maker sitting quietly on the shelf of Yacht Parts, a chandlery shop in Plymouth. A tall, broad man was studying the box, reading the instructions and looking anxiously at a price tag that read £2,250. The Water Maker knew he was expensive, but he also knew he was indispensable to all ocean rowers, and he had happened to overhear this man saying he was going to row across the Pacific.

'Look, Jim, I tell you what,' said Andy Salomonson, the owner of the shop. 'You can take it on loan. How about that? Try and bring it back in decent condition.'

'That's very kind of you,' the man replied. 'Thank you.'

The deal was done, and the Water Maker was soon installed aboard a twenty-three-foot boat destined for the voyage of a lifetime. He felt alternately exhilarated and anxious, for he recognised the absolutely crucial role he was being asked to perform within the adventure. Jim, his new owner, would need to drink water, sometimes as much as nine litres per day, and it was going to be the Water Maker's responsibility to suck seawater from a small inlet in the hull and reliably produce fresh, desalinated water.

If he failed, the voyage would end. It was as simple as that. All right, he knew there was always a chance of catching rain-water for drinking, and it might be possible to create some crude kind of still for distillation, but these options were not viable or efficient or any solid form of substitute. The Water Maker needed to be utterly dependable. 'On my list of the "must-works",' Jim whispered softly in his tubes prior to departure, 'you stand at Number One.'

The Water Maker gurgled with pride, and scarcely shed a tear when the large tank beneath the middle section of the boat, intended to store the fresh water once it had been produced, was rendered useless.

This 150-litre tank had been filled in Chile, prior to the initial departure date, but the water had then turned stagnant and brown during the delays at customs and the drive to Peru. Jim tried everything to destroy the algae and bacteria, rinsing repeat-edly, emptying, filling and re-emptying the tank, even flinging in handfuls of water-purifying tablets, but nothing worked.

'Ah well,' sighed the Water Maker, 'he'll have to store the fresh water in large bottles, and now he's going to need me almost every day.'

When the voyage eventually began, the Water Maker rose magnificently to the challenge: sucking the seawater in at the hull, pumping it to the header tank, then running it down through a reverse osmosis filter and out into bottles. Powered by an electric motor, he was accommodated in his own compartment beside the footwell. All was well. 'Another drink, Jim? My pleasure.'

Then, one wild and stormy night, a succession of heaving waves broke across the deck and the Water Maker frantically battled for air as, inch by tantalising inch, his compartment was flooded with seething seawater. Jim had assumed that area was waterproof, but it wasn't. When he woke the next morning, Jim scooped out the water only to find the Water Maker still and lifeless.

Gloom settled on the boat, as Jim hoped against hope that the drying sun would heal and cure. By midday, still nothing stirred. Increasingly worried, Jim began to tamper and twiddle, twist and turn, cajole and coax. He did not pretend to understand everything, but at least he was prepared to persevere, to try something, do anything not to lose his precious Water Maker.

What was that? A splutter? Yes, a splutter! With a cough and a shake, the Water Maker slowly opened his valves and drew water again, a drip at first, then a drop and by evening, fresh water was starting to flow. The machine bounced bravely back to life, determined to pump another day.

Yet this journey, that at first had seemed so serene, suddenly began to feel like an ordeal. Some days were fine, some a little bit harder, as the Water Maker staggered on through August and September, occasionally emitting peculiar noises, never seeming completely happy, fighting on.

It couldn't last and, on 11 November, Armistice Day, the increasingly doddery soldier collapsed again; this time he was only revived when Jim deftly performed a precarious and dangerous operation.

Jim realised the Water Maker's·carbon brushes had seized in their guide slots, and saw the only way of extricating the brushes for cleaning was to pull them out by a perilously thin wire attached at one end. Working under the pressure of knowing that if the wire broke at any time, the brushes would be stuck, the machine would die and his voyage would probably end, Jim managed to extract the brushes, clean them on both sides with an emery cloth, scrape the insides of the slots and spray silicon grease all over.

The Water Maker came round soon afterwards and, amid thrilled celebrations, felt young all over again. The operation had been a complete success, almost a miracle. His motor purred, his pump chugged and sparkling water streamed forth as sweetly as any famous brand from an Alpine spa.

It was not long before tough times returned. On at least five occasions, when power supplies were almost non-existent, Jim was forced to detach the motor and power the Water Maker by hand. There was clearly no alternative, but the machine was not designed for manual operation and it took almost an hour for Jim to lash the filter to a hatch top, run the output tube down into a bottle in the footwell and wedge himself in a gap beside the cooking seat.

With extreme difficulty, he began to work the lever up and down and, in a spirit of solidarity, the Water Maker began to produce water again.

When the batteries recovered, Jim would restore the motor; when the batteries flagged, he would have to detach it again. Restore and detach, over and over again: this was no way to treat a veteran Water Maker. Jim knew as much, saw the peril in manhandling the unit so often, but also recognised there was no alternative. Even without power, he needed to drink.

Progressively worn out and even dispirited, the Water Maker started to grate and grind as it set about its daily chores . . . until, soon after lunch on Saturday, 9 December 2000, the Water Maker suddenly let out a shuddering yelp as one of its rubber O-rings snapped and water spurted from its midriff.

Moments later, all was still and silent. Jim sat motionless in despair, in grief. His heart urged him to plan another miraculous repair, but his head told him to be realistic; he took one look at the snapped O-ring and knew all life had fled.

Two days passed in misery, before Jim tried to attach the broken ends of the O-ring with a sealant. Yet this process amounted to not much more than switching on a life support machine and, although the Water Maker did dribble a drop or two before the O-ring snapped again, it proved futile.

Jim was living through the deepest crisis of his voyage, a period when he could not see how he could finish his adventure, a time when he virtually accepted the reality of failure and considered other options. He could not live without drinking water. The O-ring was broken. The Water Maker was dead. Ergo, he would not be able to reach Australia, alone and unaided. These were the cold facts. There was nothing to be done. He assessed his options.

'I am trying to stay positive,' he told his mini-disc recorder, 'but that is an impossible task. I think this is the beginning of the end.'

In need of a second opinion, he telephoned David Jackson, who was still on his job exchange in New Zealand, and his Atlantic colleague agreed the Water Maker simply would not work without an O-ring and that, somehow, Jim needed to get hold of this spare part as soon as possible.

Jim's mind was racing, searching for solutions. He was 390 miles away from the island of Neui, a remote protectorate of New Zealand. If David could buy an O-ring, or even a new Water Maker altogether, in Auckland, it could surely be flown out in time for him to stop over and collect it in Neui.

'Tonga might be easier,' David ventured.

Jim replied: 'Why not Auckland itself?'

Hold on! If he was going to stop for a day in Auckland, he might as well stop for a week. There would be no material difference. Jim glanced again at his plotter and excitedly calculated it would be possible for him to fly home to London, make a surprise appearance at Christmas lunch in Northwood, rush back to New Zealand and resume his trip to Australia. Jim loved the idea. He had never missed a family Christmas since his daughters were born, and had quietly been dreading the reality of a Yuletide separation.

And yet, yet, he also wanted to keep rowing, to finish the voyage. 'Let me think about it all,' he told David. 'I'll get back to you.'

Nineteen days of excruciating indecision followed. Jim was surviving on his emergency water supplies, trying to catch rainwater, trying to create some kind of petrol-fuelled still to produce drinking water, refusing to give in, hoping against hope that somehow he would be able to keep going . . .

It was just another perfect evening on the Pacific. The sun was sinking spectacularly into a softly swishing, swirling ocean, and Jim sat quietly sipping at a sundowner, not a gin-and-tonic but a lemon-and-lime G-Push energy drink, not from a crystal glass but from a bottle. Absent-mindedly, he played with the plastic cycling bottle he had bought from Halfords in England.

What was that?

He felt three rings at the top of the bottle. What was that? Was it part of a moulded decoration? No, it wasn't! What is that? It's a rubber ring. Yes! It's a rubber ring. I don't believe it. It's an O-ring. It's three O-rings!

Eureka and euphoria were soon followed by a realisation that he would not be able to set about instantly reviving the Water Maker in the fast-gathering darkness, so he retired to bed, tucked the precious rubber rings under his pillow and slept as restlessly as a seven-year-old on Christmas Eve.

Jim rose with the sun soon after six the following morning, laid out his toolkit and started to dismantle the still-motionless Water Maker. Telling himself to be calm and careful, when he wanted to rush the process like a seven-year-old unwrapping his presents on Christmas morning, he slowly placed the Halfords ring into the place where the O-ring had once been. It fitted.

He was breathing slow and hard when he began to pull the

handle. Ten strokes, twenty strokes . . . Nothing was happening. Thirty strokes, forty strokes. At fifty strokes, he was starting to panic. Still nothing. Then, a gasp and a murmur as pressure started to build in the once-moribund pipes of the Water Maker. With a burp and a babble, drops of glistening water started to appear.

'Yes!' Jim's cry of delight reverberated around his corner of the ocean, as the Water Maker gurgled back to life. Beaming broadly, smiling the heartfelt smile of the suddenly reprieved, he filled a tumbler and happily toasted this miracle with the most delicious, sweetest water he will ever drink.

He proceeded to pump four litres of water during the next hour, drinking two in the process. Relief, delight, pleasure, pure joy: these emotions coursed through his body. With a little luck, and a great deal of determination, Jim had survived the most severe logistical crisis of his adventure.

As for the Water Maker, he stuck to his task and eventually ended up on an Australian beach alongside his owner. He never did return to that shelf at the Yacht Parts chandlery shop in Plymouth, as agreed, but was instead allowed to drift into gentle retirement; and he lived happily ever after.

The End.

It is hard to exaggerate the extremes of emotion that I suffered during this saga. I was not simply staring over the precipice of failure when the O-ring snapped. In my mind, I had fallen over. The adventure was over. The bizarre discovery of the rubber rings on the water bottle was lucky, of course, but maybe I earned that good fortune during the nineteen days when I refused to fail. During that period, I had no idea how I was going to find drinking water, but I just couldn't bring myself to concede defeat and abandon the adventure.

Just as the water-making machine survived, so most of the other parts and fittings aboard the boat staggered through to Australia.

With no great technical ability, but with a lot of willpower and a powerful faith that things would work out in the end, with magic cream and duck tape, it was possible to maintain both body and boat in working order.

Just.

8
Mind Games

There are probably thousands of American pyscho-babblers who would diagnose me as severely repressed and suggest I be sent for therapy to a clinic in the middle of the Arizona desert. There again, maybe I'm just British.

Perhaps I am the personification of the 'stiff upper lip'. Show me a murky, wet, overcast sky, and I will tell you the sun will soon come through. Show me a difficulty, and I will look straight past it to focus on something positive. Ask me to express the inner sentiments of my heart, to analyse the details of my child-hood, to assess my relationships, and I will tell you I prefer to think my own thoughts and let others talk of theirs.

Problems?

Bah! Nonsense!

I try not to criticise anyone else for the way they choose to approach life but my choice is to focus on the positive, overlook difficulties, keep busy and move on. For most of the past few centuries, markedly during wartime, this attitude has been regarded worldwide as being quintessentially British.

Prior to my departure for South America, people warned me that I would feel indescribably lonely on the ocean; they said I would shrink at being helpless in the face of the elements; some suggested I would be driven to distraction, not Australia. They said the maintenance challenge, outlined in the previous chapter, would be a picnic compared to the grim, grisly, mental struggle.

I shrugged my shoulders and wondered why. These things would only be problems if I allowed them to become problems.

I was in control. How could they have an impact if I simply, resolutely elected to ignore them?

As I stated at the outset of this book, I have always enjoyed games: card games, board games, sports, almost any kind of game, but I was left cold by the mind games that supposedly awaited me on the Pacific.

I took a firm decision that I would not wallow in sentimentality, that I would not allow myself to be distracted by analysis paralysis, that I would not indulge in any spurious brand of convoluted introspection. I was not remotely fascinated by such froth and, in any event, I was going to be far too busy.

This is not to say I would bottle up every emotion. I recognised the voyage was going to be a succession of highs and lows. Mood swings were unavoidable. My resolution was that I would not dwell interminably on these situations and that I would address the issues as best I could, and move swiftly on.

And, from first to last, I remained supremely confident that I would not lose any mind games, for the simple reason that I could not afford to lose, and therefore I was not going to play any mind games. My task was to cross the Pacific in a rowing boat, and every minute of every day was going to be spent working towards that overriding aim. I believe the modern idiom is 'focus'.

This approach was crucially underpinned by the fact that I am, and always will be, an incurable optimist. I make no apology for this condition. In my eyes, the glass is always half full, never half empty. Every morning, I choose to look to the east and I see the sun rise on another day full of opportunity.

Optimism yields two major dividends. First, you have more fun because most of your days are spent eagerly looking forward to events that you inherently know will turn out well; pessimists spend that same time dreading and fearing the disasters that they inherently believe are going to happen.

Second, even if things do turn out wrong, optimism still enables you to be cheerful because you believe that all will be well in the end. For we optimists, disappointment is never anything more than a temporary blip. If it never rained, who would be able to appreciate sunshine?

Pessimists submit a counter-argument: that fearing the worst means they are never disappointed and are often pleasantly surprised. They claim they are able to lead lives of calm, moderate equilibrium while we are condemned to live on a roller coaster of wild expectations and crushing downers.

Whatever the pros and cons of these contrasting mental states, there is no earthly way I would even have contemplated rowing across the Pacific if I was a pessimist. Ten minutes pondering everything that could possibly go wrong out on the ocean would have been enough to keep me at home.

As an optimist, I believed from the outset that I would be able to complete the voyage to Australia and, even if my faith did waver on a handful of occasions, such as the day when the O-ring burst, these troughs of despair lasted only a few minutes before I shook myself down and moved on again.

Armed with my optimism, I prepared to ignore the two mental dangers that supposedly lurked in the depths of the ocean: plain, downright loneliness and an unsettling terror of being small, insignificant and helpless.

The prospect of being alone did not scare me; on the contrary, the idea of escaping the pressures and stresses of daily life had been one of the factors behind my decision to pursue the voyage in the first place. And, of course, I recognised the practical implications of rowing solo: David Jackson would not be at my side, supportive and encouraging, as he had been on the Atlantic. It would be just me and the boat on a vast ocean. That concept didn't faze me.

For all this bravado, I never tried to persuade myself that I would not miss my family terribly throughout the voyage, and it was this factor that finally persuaded me to install a satellite telephone on the boat.

The issue had weighed on my mind for several months and,

in fact, shortly before leaving England, under extreme budgetary pressure in the absence of any main sponsor, I had taken a firm decision not to install a telephone, thus saving the sum of £4,000, plus the prohibitively high cost of telephone calls.

My logic was that it would be far easier to communicate with Jane, Anna and Sarah by sending and receiving e-mail, via the Orbcomm satellites. I declared this to be my final position.

After a few days in Chile, I was having second thoughts. First, I wasn't able to get the Orbcomm units working as well as I would have liked and I was concerned there was no worthwhile means of testing their reliability. Second, I was becoming increasingly irritated by waiting for people to respond to e-mail. There was still a great deal to be said for the instant exchange of a good, old-fashioned telephone call.

Pat Waggaman provided the name of Edward Cornely and Doug Price, two of his suppliers in the United States, and when they provided very decent quotes for the hardware, and a generous offer for the airtime, I ordered a combined voice and data unit and signed up for the services from Comsat. My first request, of course, had been to receive both the hardware and the airtime free of charge, but at least the Americans came up with a much better deal than anyone in Britain had managed to propose throughout the preceding two years.

I knew that Kenneth Crutchlow, director of the Ocean Rowing Society, was planning to fly out to witness the start of my trip, so I contacted him and ultimately paid for him to make an unscheduled stop in Miami, where he collected the telephone before bringing it to Ilo.

This decision represented an inspired change of heart. With hindsight, knowing that the computer would fail and the Orbcomm units would gobble too much power after a few months, I shudder to think how I would have coped without the telephone. I would have been completely unable to communicate not only with the outside world but, worst of all, with my family in England. That particular mental game may have proved almost impossible to ignore and overlook.

Instead, we swiftly established a firm schedule whereby I would telephone Jane, Anna and Sarah at a fixed time once per week, and I staggered the calls to ensure I spoke to somebody at home at least every few days or so. There were occasions when one of them was held up somewhere or simply forgot but, after a while, everyone settled into a routine and hardly ever missed a call. Even though I was far away, it was comforting for me to realise Jane and the girls were willing to organise their hectic lives around my telephone calls.

'Hello, how are you?'

'Fine, and you?'

'Fine. No problems at all.'

Every call started with confirmation that everyone was all right, and I then invariably took the initiative, perhaps asking whoever I was talking to for details of their daily routines, where they were going, who they would be meeting, what time they needed to be where. If I got one of the girls, I would ask whether they had exams, how their courses were going and the inevitable questions of their success or otherwise with lacrosse, water-skiing, boyfriends, etc. I wanted to know everything.

I am not sure why I needed to know such details, but I wanted to feel that I was still a presence in the family, still a factor in all their lives even if I was rowing across an ocean on the opposite side of the globe. I remained constantly aware of the time difference between my position and London, and regularly tracked my family's movements through the day.

When the conversation turned to my own news, I probably tended to be much less effusive and animated. In the first place, I didn't think Jane or the girls would be particularly interested in the condition of the water maker; second, I wanted to protect them from unnecessary worry and preferred to keep discussion on a hazy and safe 'no problems', 'fine', 'making progress' level.

These regular telephone calls home became eagerly awaited

highlights in my routine, all of which made it harder for me to accept the knowledge that I was going to lose the signal completely for around two months, from the first week of August right through to the first week of October. I knew my capacity to overlook loneliness would be severely tested during this period.

The issue was out of my hands. We were going to move beyond the range of AOR-West (Inmarsat's geo-stationary satellite above the West Atlantic) when we crossed the 95 degrees meridian, and we only expected to regain a signal when we reached the longitude line at 110 degrees. These were plain facts, so there was nothing to be done except inform Jane and the girls they should not expect to hear from me for probably two months or so, and also prepare myself to be enveloped by an eerily complete, deafening silence.

I missed the regular contact from the moment the dialling tone dissolved into the atmosphere: missed the sound of their voices, missed hearing how they cared for me, expressed not in words but in their tone, and missed knowing exactly what they were doing and how they were feeling.

Time and again through the increasingly drawn-out days, I would find my thoughts drifting away to Jane and the girls and, by night, the vivid dreams that had until then focused on times and places in my own life now seemed to focus more specifically on the family. Occasionally, my dreams became nightmares, once depicting my daughter Anna in an appalling car accident.

If some force was trying to engage me in mind games, I resolutely looked the other way. I forgot about the nightmare within moments of waking, settled on some task to keep me busy, crossed off another day and looked forward keenly to the moment when the whirring dialling tone returned.

Days ran into weeks until eventually a month had passed and, even though I knew the signal was only going to return at around the 110 degrees line, I started picking up the receiver from the day we crossed 103 degrees, just to check on progress. No luck, no luck, no luck; suddenly, on 10 October, the reassuring tone

Happy Birthday to me! Celebrating alone, I treated myself to a veritable feast. The starter was a finger dip in the Marmite... What more could I want?

Shekhdar calling. At work beside the hatch leading to the cabin.

Wear and tear: two oars broke during the course of the trip and this one was returned to service as an impromptu harpoon.

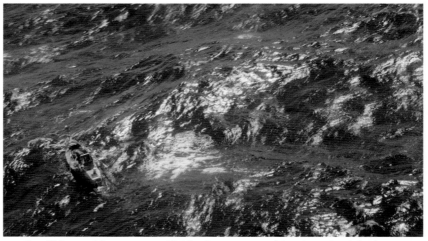

Small boat, big ocean... If I had ever seen this view, I might have started to worry.

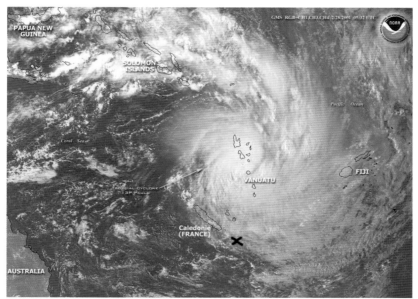

Hurricane Paula terrorised the south Pacific during February 2001, but veered away from me at the last moment, sparing me from disaster. The 'X' marks my position on February 28.

Each morning I found misdirected flying fish had inadvertently landed in the boat. Another one bites the dust...

'It was really no problem.' Summing up the voyage upon arrival at North Stradbroke Island, with my wife, Jane, and my daughters, Anna and Sarah.

Even unconventional arrivals in Australia require presentation of a passport to the customs and AQUIS officials.

Prized possessions aboard the boat: a plaque from Ilo, a family photograph album, the log book, the heirloom watch given to me by Jane and (*far right*) the Peruvian submariner's insignia presented to me by Port Captain Jorge Guerrero, at Ilo.

(*from left*) Sarah, Jane and Anna... the team.

Saying farewell to an old friend... the barnacled boat in Brisbane, with Eddie Kohn, from Le Shark.

Happy memories... My sister commissioned this 1:10 scale model, made by David Jackson, as a souvenir of my voyage across the Pacific.

returned. I dialled our home number, and excitedly let Jane know I was back in the world.

The loss of contact had been unnerving, but the thought that I so nearly had not taken a satellite telephone at all was positively terrifying. Not for the first time on this voyage, I had flirted with disaster, but somehow I had managed to scuttle around the edge of the abyss and hurry on my way.

As the days rolled on by, the unremitting daily routine served as my shield against feeling alone, but three pivotal occasions loomed ahead in the space of six weeks from the middle of November when, I realised, the forces of loneliness would mount almighty assaults on my mind and soul.

These would be the battles to decide the war: my birthday on 13 November, Christmas Day and New Year's Eve. If I was ever going to be overcome by sadness and seclusion, it would be then. However, I would not yield easily and my preparations for the fray began before I left England.

One option had been simply to ignore the occasions, to row through the calendar as if each day was no different to another. This was not possible for the reason that these days meant so much within our family. I could not deny them. I resolved to face them, prepare for them and even try to enjoy them.

So, while packing the boat in Northwood, I enlisted the help of Jane, Anna and Sarah to prepare sealed packages of presents that I planned to open on my birthday, and special meals and wine for me to enjoy on each of the three occasions. Like the resolute baron of a threatened castle in medieval times, I stood behind my carefully prepared defences, my cannons and catapults, and calmly awaited the arrival of the invader.

On the premise that I am English and that my birthday should properly be marked in England, I had resolved to celebrate the day according to Greenwich Mean Time. GMT, or UTC as it is sometimes known today, was the time constant upon which my clock was fixed throughout the voyage. This plan allowed me to start the revelry at the stroke of midnight in London, as

12 November turned into 13 November, which on the Pacific equated to a warm, balmy two o'clock in the afternoon on the Pacific on 12 November.

I sat down in the cooking seat, wished myself a 'Happy Birthday' out loud, and started to open my presents. The first was a plastic whale with a clockwork tail for my bath, the second was a plastic reading book, and the third was a large pair of yellow plastic slippers, all chosen by my daughters who affectionately bore in mind that objects in my cabin tended to be regularly drenched.

There was also a book, *Sophie's World*, which I read in every available moment through the next three days, and an entertaining tape featuring Seinfeld, the American comedian. My present from Jane seemed to be a Tupperware box full of anhydrous salts, but these further concealed two sealed plastic bags. They hid a small box, which, with mounting excitement, I opened to reveal an antique pocket watch inscribed 'Chile to Australia 2000'.

I was taken aback, amazed. It had been her father's watch, an heirloom. To have received this present on a normal birthday at home would have meant a great deal; to receive it alone on the ocean was profoundly emotional. I studied the superb workmanship, and felt a lump rise in my throat.

This incident assumed a strange significance later when, after we returned home from Australia, Jane and I finally found the time to see the film *Castaway*, starring Tom Hanks, on video at home. So many people had told us about a number of striking similarities between the film and my own voyage, from slow days drifting on the vast ocean to trying to avoid being washed onto islands, but we both sat aghast in wonder when the central character received a present that became an important catalyst for his will to survive . . . a pocket watch.

My last present was a family photograph album, compiled with care and attention by Jane and my daughters. It featured photographs of Anna and Sarah as babies and adolescents, and of other family occasions right through to the present day, and there was even a picture of the family dog. I wallowed in this collection of so many happy memories and, if I ever happened to be feeling blue during the remainder of the trip, all I had to do was leaf through this album and I would feel better.

In managing to stretch the process of opening the presents to more than two hours, by studying and appreciating each gift along the way, I felt as though I had successfully repelled the opening charge of loneliness, and I looked forward to the second element of my strategy: the birthday feast.

My starter might not have been notably elegant, and I suspect it will never emerge on the dinner party menus of upper Islington but, from my point of view, there can have been few more mouth-watering delicacies than a deep finger-dip in the Marmite tub. I have always adored the taste, and had packed two one-pound tubs aboard the boat. The day of my birthday seemed an appropriate excuse to allow myself not one but two wallowing scoops with my index finger.

After a new personal favourite, a whole tube of spicy pepperoni, I moved on to the leek and potato soup with croutons. David Jackson had taught me the morale-boosting qualities of Sainsbury's powdered soup during the Atlantic race, and soup is just not half the soup it can be unless it includes croutons. With no fresh bread available at the local corner store, croutons proved the next best thing.

The main course was chicken tikka masala, my favourite of all the dishes produced by Expedition Foods, served with a healthy portion of basmati rice and washed down with a decent half-bottle of red wine cunningly packed away on the boat by Jane, aided and abetted by David Jackson. All this was then followed by rice pudding for dessert and a one-pound bar of chocolate. What more could anyone have wanted? Well, maybe just a little birthday cake . . .

Even that had been arranged. Small but perfectly formed, the cake cannot have measured more than three inches in diameter, but it was generously coated in royal icing and had been supplied complete with a candle and box of matches.

The occasion demanded a song, so I sang out loud.

> Happy Birthday to me!
> Happy Birthday to me!
> Happy Birth-day to Me-ee!
> Happy Birthday to me!'

All sung out, I managed to blow out all the candles with one big huff and cut the cake into equal quarters. One had been contaminated by seawater and was thrown to the fish; another was going to be eaten immediately, another was for Christmas Day, and the fourth would suffice for New Year.

I leaned back in the seat, finished the first half of the bottle of wine and spent the rest of the day reading my book and listening to the tape, completely satisfied. I had to wait until eleven o'clock at night on the Pacific, which would equate to early on a dark and cold winter's morning back home, before it was decent for me to telephone Jane and the girls and thank them for their presents and generosity.

They each sounded close and concerned and, as I replaced the receiver and headed for bed, I did so happy in the knowledge that I had not just survived but positively enjoyed my birthday on the ocean. Since the forces of loneliness had scarcely landed a blow, I sensed the first battle was won.

Christmas Day followed a similar pattern, although my defences were not quite as carefully prepared because, according to my original calculations, I was supposed to have arrived in Australia in time for the planned party with my friend Peter Montgomery on 15 December. Obviously, it had soon become clear the voyage was taking significantly longer than planned, so I had needed to improvise and generate my own festivities.

The Yule celebrations started with a telephone call to my daughters just after one o'clock in the afternoon on Christmas Eve in the Pacific, or just after the stroke of midnight in London, the start of Christmas Day proper, and Anna and Sarah both sounded emphatically healthy and extremely happy. They were leaving a pub, and I could hear the laughter and carousing around them.

All of a sudden, I felt a long, long way from home. 'Cheer up,' I goaded myself. 'They're both healthy and happy. What more can any father wish for his daughters?' Nothing, I supposed. That was all a father had any right to expect, even a father far away rowing across an enormous ocean.

'Remember to open your present!' Sarah said.

'What present?'

'We packed a present for you, just in case you didn't make the party in Australia on 15 December. It was a precaution.'

'Oh, that was kind of you.'

'OK, Dad, have a great Christmas.'

'You too.'

As I replaced the receiver, I sensed loneliness approaching the gates, so I moved on and felt excited about the prospect of, after all, opening an unexpected but welcome Christmas present. I was touched by the thoughtfulness of my girls and started to wonder what this present could be. I desperately hoped it would be something to take my mind off being alone on this important family day; I wanted, perhaps even needed, something to fill the rest of my day.

If it were a book, I decided I would read it straight through until dusk. If it were an audiotape, I was going to listen to it over and over again. I took the present out of the hatch and discovered a fluffy, yellow, singing duck.

The only conceivable home for this annoying yet cheerful creature was alongside the parrot and the bear, perched inside the cabin, and there he sang contentedly (whenever I could bear to switch him on) until his batteries expired on Boxing Day. That left me with one fluffy, yellow, silent duck: much better, still bright and cheerful but significantly less annoying.

Another powdered soup with croutons and another perfect

chicken tikka masala with basmati rice provided the backbone of the Christmas dinner, and my spirits were lifted by the bottle of red wine presented to me by Giovanni Villaroel, who had so kindly helped me retrieve my boat from customs in Chile. It was late at night on the Pacific before it was decent to call Jane at home, early on the first Christmas morning we had spent apart since our wedding.

Once again, I started to feel so far away from everything, but we arranged I would call again when the whole Shekhdar family, except me, had gathered for a traditional Christmas lunch at the house of my sister, Jan.

It was two o'clock in the morning on the Pacific when I made that call, and wished everyone a Happy Christmas. I heard the party was buzzing and yearned to be there as well. Some hours later, I telephoned my brother Bob in the United States, and spoke to my sister-in-law, Branka, and to my nephew, Sacha. They all seemed to be having a great time as well. Bob asked me how I was feeling, and I resolutely assured him that I was perfectly all right.

Was I? I suppose so. Christmas was almost over, and I felt unable to deny that the forces of loneliness had landed a couple of telling blows.

New Year's Eve followed within a few days (as it usually does) and, once again opting to mark the occasion according to GMT, I tried to phone Jane and the girls soon after the stroke of midnight in England. It was several minutes past the hour when I finally raised an answer from Anna on her mobile telephone. She was celebrating with friends in Bristol and had been entering into the spirit of the night.

'Hello, Anna,' I said. 'Happy New Year.'

'Who's that?'

'Who do you think it is?'

'Who is that?' she asked again.

'Guess,' I said.

My daughter proceeded to run through several of her friends' names, and I blankly stated 'no' after each guess. I suppose this is the sort of behaviour that makes 21-year-olds despair of their fathers, but I was slightly put out that she did not recognise my voice, even if I was on the other side of the world. Nonetheless, I was amused by her frustration and it was only the realisation that this prolonged call was costing me money that prompted me to reveal myself.

'Anna, it's your father.'

'Oh, Dad! It's you!' she said, sounding irritated with me.

I should point out that Anna maintains to this day that the line was bad and the extraneous noise made it impossible for her even to hear, let alone recognise my voice. She is my daughter and, of course, I believe her.

Happily, Jane and Sarah experienced no such problems and, forty minutes into 2001, we had all wished each other a very Happy New Year. I had marked the occasion in what was becoming traditional fashion on the ocean, by demolishing another powdered soup with actual croutons, another impeccable chicken tikka masala and my last remaining bottle of fine Chilean red wine.

This formidable combination fortified me against pangs of sadness and, by dawn on 2 January 2001, I was able to conclude with certainty, and some pride, that I had successfully repelled the forces of loneliness on the three dates when I appeared most vulnerable. I will not pretend any of these days were much fun on my own, but I felt as though I had survived the mental test.

If I was not overcome by a sense of being alone on these occasions, then the chances were that loneliness would not be a serious problem at any other stage of the voyage; and so it proved. I sorely missed my family but, except for the sixty-two-day break in signal, I stayed in close contact with them throughout.

The second class of mind games on the ocean dared me to come to terms with the knowledge that, as an object, my boat and I were insignificant and utterly helpless in the face of the Pacific's enormous power.

As human beings, both in our own homes and at work, most of us become beguiled by a sense of our own importance within the wider scheme of things. All such delusions are swiftly, ruthlessly shattered on the ocean. The wind, rain and waves do with you precisely what they will and when they will.

The challenge is to accept the weather conditions with equanimity: to stay calm when you are regularly soaked by waves breaking over the boat; to remain focused when the wind and currents propel you in the wrong direction or, maybe more frustrating, when you are moving forward so slowly that your estimated journey time is measured in years rather than weeks.

As somebody who has spent most of his life being more volatile and direct than most, such serene tranquillity would not come naturally. My relationship with the elements grew to resemble that which exists between an overbearing regime and a resolute, though realistic, human rights activist.

I never liked the elements, because they didn't treat me well through those nine months, but I never lost the sight of the fact that I needed to function within their rules and regulations and that there was never any point fighting them because their inherent power meant they were always going to win.

So I muttered and moaned under my breath, and occasionally despaired when I suffered what I perceived as unjust treatment, but these passing protests were generally irrelevant within my total subordination.

This became my psychological strategy to deal with the apparent conflict between my defiant and forthright personality and the fact of my situation: always accept but never tolerate, always obey but never surrender.

I understood that the natural elements did not remotely care about my personal point of view, as they regularly proved during the voyage, but this fact was not going to prevent me from expressing my views.

My basic attitude towards these natural elements (ocean, winds, currents) was clear and straightforward: if they were propelling me towards Australia, I was happy; if they were not doing that, I was going to be grumpy.

I genuinely did not mind being battered by a storm, slammed against the walls of the cabin as the boat tipped to angles of ninety degrees, compelled to batten down the hatches and remain in my cabin for two days until the weather cleared, so long as we kept heading west at a reasonable speed.

I genuinely did not mind having to wear a woolly hat and sweatshirt during the first part of the voyage because the winter months were so cold and grey off the coast of South America; and I didn't even mind when a wave crept up on me and drenched those clothes, condemning me to week upon week of feeling cold and damp because, at this time, nothing ever dried properly.

And I genuinely did not mind the stultifying, merciless heat of the summer months, when the blistering sun forced me to take shelter in the cabin, to drink up to nine litres of water a day and to row during the night.

All these unpleasant situations were inconvenient and frustrating, but I did not mind so long as we kept heading west. That was all that mattered. My target was to reach Australia and I felt capable of tolerating almost any hardship so long as I was making measurable progress towards that goal.

If we were not heading west . . . then I rumbled.

I rumbled frequently during the first two months of the trip when my initial distance targets of thirty miles per day for the first month and forty-eight miles per day each month thereafter were exposed as being hopelessly optimistic. I felt as though I had been sold a Mediterranean holiday, only to discover the hotel and beach did not remotely resemble the description in the brochure.

The entire concept of crossing the Pacific had seemed attractive because of the supposed strength of the Humboldt and Equatorial Currents, the smooth consistency of the south-east trade winds and the long wavelengths, all moving the boat west. Well, in reality, the Humboldt Current whimpered, the trade winds came and went and the waves invariably proved to be short, messy and unproductive.

Any idea of completing the trip within six months evaporated within a few weeks of leaving Ilo, and my mood soon became as grey as the overcast skies on another windless day. 'I would rather have a storm than this,' I raged. 'This is like trying to fight an opponent who won't get off his stool.'

Calm down, I told myself, calm down; and the winds returned.

And I rumbled again during September and October, when the unfriendly winds were propelling me so far north that I seemed more likely to complete the voyage in Indonesia or Japan than my chosen destination, Australia. Every day, teeth grinding with frustration, I would study the plotter and watch my actual path veer further and further north than the intended route.

Anxious to do something, desperate not to appear helpless, I set the rudder to head me towards port while I was rowing, crudely yanking the boat round to the west as we moved forward. Unfortunately, this intrepid defiance succeeded only in slowing the boat down. If the wind wanted to drive us north, we would go north, even if the front of the boat was pointing west.

Then I tried to row with all emphasis on my left oar, literally working to swing the boat towards Australia. This strategy frequently works on the park pond, but it had no impact at all amid the rampant winds and currents of the Pacific.

I eventually learned my lesson on 18 October, when I rowed throughout the day with my left arm, set the rudder to port and still drifted in a northerly direction. 'I have told myself not to fight the sea,' I groaned into the mini-disc player, my audio diary, 'but I spent the whole of today trying to fight the sea, and the sea won. I have to go with it. I am so tired. The longer this journey goes on, the more I feel it will last for ever.'

Calm down, I told myself, calm down; and the winds eventually pulled me back round to the west. The northern diversion had added another 1,500 miles to the trip but, by November, I was heading for Australia again.

And I rumbled again through December and January when, amid stifling humidity, the boat began travelling in circles, drifting backwards then forwards as it followed a corkscrew path to Australia. One afternoon, when the trip seemed to be dragging on interminably, I decided it was time for action. So I rose to my feet and started swearing at the ocean, effing and blinding. 'Maybe I am never going to reach Australia,' I told the mini-disc recorder. 'Maybe that's the whole ******* idea! I spend the rest of my life drifting around in ******* circles until I get fed up and then I will ******* jump off and find a ******* shark.'

Forty minutes later, the boat was still wandering aimlessly on the steaming millpond, and I was suffering from a seriously sore throat.

Calm down, I told myself, calm down; and the weather cooled and, mile by painstaking mile, we inched towards our destination.

These sporadic outbursts of rage and despair served a purpose insofar as they enabled me to let off steam in difficult times but, by and large, I managed to keep the lid on my strained relationship with the elements. Albeit with a huff and a puff, I grew to accept the reality of my own insignificance.

At stages, this newfound humility prompted me to behave with a greater degree of tolerance than I had ever imagined possible. My wife Jane would later observe that my voyage softened me as a person. She's usually on the money and, if so, it was these natural elements that started the process.

Even though I started to take the weather as it came, I remained obsessed with knowing at all times the speed and direction of the boat. It was no problem for me to glance at the plotter when I was rowing or cooking but I also wanted to track my progress from inside the cabin. So I found a spare compass, stuck it on the inner bulkhead, and then learned to interpret the noises emanating from the wind generator, and its blades, perched on the roof.

Was this the same man who had screamed and yelled at the ocean? Was this the same man who was now staying in bed, keeping an eye on the compass and sensitively listening to the sounds of the wind generator with all the calm and skill of a veteran tracker in the African bush listening to birds?

Silence was obviously disastrous because it meant there was no wind and the boat was going nowhere. A gentle, persistent, soft hum indicated there was a little motion, but the sweetest sound of all was a drumming whine that indicated whirling blades and powerful motion through the water. The whirr of the blades on the wind generator became part of my routine on the ocean, lulling me gently to sleep at night, and waking me softly in the morning.

Through this chapter so far, the natural elements have been portrayed as essentially hostile and malevolent, my opposition in the mind games, a menacing force for long periods of the voyage, and I have frequently repeated that I did not like the Pacific and ultimately could not wait to step off it.

This was all true. However, there were also a number of occasions when the elements charmed, thrilled and delighted me, and seemed to strengthen my spirits and psychological resolve to reach my destination. Such moments proved unforgettable and awe-inspiring, not least because they demonstrated what was possible when the elements acted with me, not against me.

I lost count of the number of times when I would be rowing hard into the evening and, for no particular reason, would be moved to stop, turn to look over my shoulder and survey the expansive majesty of a Pacific sunset, the scale of which I defy any camera to capture and faithfully reproduce.

It is even harder to convey the spectacle in words. The initial impression was of glorious golds, oranges and rampant reds gashed luxuriously across the western horizon, streaked extravagantly across a vast sky; and I would then sit and watch in silence and wonder, seeing the colours disperse and refract in an infinite, unfathomable variety of shadows, shafts and shades.

Before long, the weary sun would follow so many languid hours of edging across the sky by suddenly seeming to accelerate towards the horizon, dashing for cover and, in the blink of an eye, disappearing from view. And then the skies would change all over again, stepping out in elegant twilight shades of grey and deep blue, still tinged at the upper reaches in red and yellow.

Night would slowly, purposefully subdue the light and the stars would start to emerge, glittering against a charcoal sky; and there would not be just several of them, not just the relatively few stars that manage to break through the polluted skies of Europe. From my front row seat in the midst of the Pacific, I would survey literally millions of stars, spread deep and thick from horizon to horizon.

I had looked forward to such starry moments, and had even packed a CD that, if I typed in my geographical position, would produce a signposted simulation of the constellations visible in that part of the southern sky. Sadly, the computer had already expired when I wanted to indulge in astronomy. Even a dabble in astrology was also out of the question!

In truth, I had never been the sort of person to sit open-mouthed in awe of natural phenomena. I suppose it might be said that I had seen many roses in the world, but never found the time to stop and smell. However, this natural Philistine was converted by the scale and splendour of a Pacific sunset.

There was one other specific occasion during the voyage when the elements, often so inhospitable, conspired to give me an experience that only a few privileged people can ever have known . . . and, in the act, offered me the encouragement ultimately to survive the mind games.

Early morning on Saturday, 30 September 2000, was unfolding like many other mornings on the ocean. Feeling airless the night before, I had gambled and left the hatch slightly open to allow a draught through the cabin. Sometimes you win; sometimes you lose. I had lost, and a wave had rolled through the boat, soaking me into a new day, flooding my cabin, drenching everything.

So, soon after five o'clock in the morning, I found myself sitting quietly on the rowing seat with drying mattresses and sleeping bags draped over the front of the boat. I was savouring the half-light of an imminent dawn, vaguely looking around at the changing, chopping maritime landscape.

I suddenly noticed a solitary ten-foot wave rising out of the ocean behind me; this was not an especially unusual sight, but I kept watching, and the wave swelled to fifteen feet, then twenty feet. It was still heading directly for me, still gaining height. As it soared to twenty-five feet, I leaped to my feet and stood upright, now breathless, panting with excitement, and the wave started to crest at thirty feet.

This wall of water, equivalent in size to a three-storey building, was bearing down on my boat, and me, yet I felt absolutely no fear at all. I cannot explain why this should have been so, but the wave never threatened. I quickly sat down and anchored my feet in the straps, hoping to withstand the blow. The fifteen seconds or so that followed remain among the most sublime of my life.

Instead of crashing down upon us, this impressive mass of water seemed somehow to roll beneath the boat, to cradle us in its watery palm and effortlessly raise us thirty feet above the surrounding ocean. I felt as if I had been lifted out of a humdrum world and placed on an altogether different level.

Was this heaven? Was this a dream?

I stole a glance over the side of the boat. The top of the wave had started to break and froth, and I saw from the plotter that we were now moving in a westerly direction at twelve knots, six times our standard speed. Gazing for miles and miles in every direction, I felt consumed by joy and wonder.

As the wave eventually slid away to the fore, the boat returned gracefully to its familiar position, and I was left to reflect upon an experience, indeed a ride, more exhilarating and memorable than anything in any fairground. The fact was that we had been surfing on the crest of a thirty-foot wave, speeding across the Pacific, fleetingly feeling like the master of all we surveyed.

Later that morning, I sought out the mini-disc player to record my feelings in the wake of this extraordinary event. 'It was awesome,' I said. 'That's the only word that comes to my mind, but I am only three months into this adventure and something tells me it is too early to be using words like "awesome" because I can only imagine what lies ahead. For now, "awesome" will have to do.'

With hindsight, I only wish this scintillating, remarkable surfing experience could have happened more than once during the voyage. Maybe, in giving me a taste of the astonishing but denying me further opportunities, the elements were trying to lead me into a realm of frustration and despair.

Who knows?

I didn't mind. By the time I reached the coast of Australia, I felt as if I had withstood every mental challenge hurled upon me. I had fought arm-to-arm with the forces of loneliness, and kept my mind; I had accepted my insignificance on this heaving, grumpy ocean . . . and I had moved on.

And despite sporadic emotional fireworks, I had never once, not even for a moment, given the slightest consideration to opening a white plastic box strapped to the inside wall of my cabin. This was the EPIRB, my twenty-four-hour escape option and the ultimate maritime alarm that, by international law, would oblige the nearest vessel on the ocean to come and rescue me.

My resolution from the outset had been that I would only use the EPIRB in a life-threatening situation. I thought it would be downright irresponsible to summon assistance in any other circumstances. So far as I was concerned, and I say this with humility, an instructive measure of my success in surviving the mental battle could be the reality that the EPIRB never entered my thoughts, never featured in my dreams and never even entered the equation.

I had made a firm decision that, lonely or not, angry or calm, I was going to reach my destination in Australia. Possibly this was self-confidence; perhaps it was arrogance; maybe it was a combination. In any event, that grim resolve was dented now and then, but it remained intact throughout.

And it gave me the strength to win the mind games. And it gave me the resolve never to regard the EPIRB as an escape route from occasional bouts of hardship and discomfort . . . No, in fact, during my Pacific crossing of 2000/2001, the EPIRB served no more significant role than acting as a suitable perch for my parrot, bear and, from Christmas onwards, the fluffy, yellow, silent duck.

Mercifully, it served as a crutch for them, but not for me.

9
Alone among Friends

It is only accurate to say I crossed the Pacific alone in the sense that I travelled without the help or participation of other human beings, for the truth is that I was escorted most of the way by a school of yellow-fin tuna.

These affectionate, remarkable fish first appeared at the side of my boat perhaps 400 miles from Ilo and I saw them for the last time a few hours before I tumbled onto the beach at North Stradbroke Island, Australia. The experience of seeing these creatures every day for nearly eight months leads me to conclude I was not so much alone on the ocean as alone among friends.

Does that make me mad? I hope not.

The fish were my friends.

I recognise they were not able to hold much of a conversation, and neither were they able to help mend the water maker. Nonetheless, the prime purpose of a friend is surely to provide encouragement and support and, in many wonderful ways, the yellow-fin tuna did exactly this for me.

Known as 'Ahi to Hawaiians and *Thunnus albacares* to scientists, these rugby-ball-shaped predators roam the temperate and tropical oceans of the world in schools that range from dozens to hundreds. They are large fish, often weighing as much as ninety pounds and growing to seven feet, and they all appear to have a substantial passion for eating. It did not take long for me to realise the fastest way to a yellow-fin tuna's heart is through his, or her, stomach.

They are chunky, but they are also beautiful, with backs of a metallic deep blue and the most exquisite pearlescent sides of many subtle tones running from blue, green and silver to gold, set off by up to twenty nearly vertical broken lines along the body. I do not want to sound like an overexcited fashion expert at Royal Ascot, but I did gaze upon these fish hour upon hour, day upon day.

In fact, in my mind's eye, they resembled nothing so much as some breed of piscine double-decker buses with gaping Pacman mouths. They were comical and sympathetic, playful and loyal, friendly and mischievous, and they seemed to like me. They were, indeed, the ideal constant companions.

At first, I thought they could be sharks; then I thought they might be dolphins. Well, they did have two dorsal fins, the first spiny and the second soft-rayed followed by finlets, and they also had large, deeply forked tails. On reflection, I think it was their friendly nature rather than any marginal physical resemblance that led to the mistaken identity. At any rate, ignorance was bliss with nobody around to correct me and, for several days, I believed dolphins were escorting me.

Doubts eventually started to spawn in my mind. These 'dolphins' were not leaping around as they were supposed to. I had begun calling them 'dolphin-things' when, one afternoon, I happened to be browsing through a large book called *Atlas of the Oceans of the World* that I had covertly 'borrowed' from Sarah's bedroom and packed aboard the boat; and suddenly, there it was: a full-colour photograph of my fish! I was overjoyed.

'Yellow-fin tuna' read the caption.

I peered over the side, saw several of the dark shapes swimming a yard or so below the surface and could almost hear one of them say to another, 'The game's up. The old fool up there knows we're not dolphins.'

Now that we had been formally introduced, I started to wonder why these fish were following me for such a long time. Had they no families and jobs? How could they afford to take so much time off to follow one tour? Perhaps they were a tunny equivalent of the 'Barmy Army', those fanatical English cricket supporters who follow the team all over the world for months at a time.

Day after day, the yellow-fin tuna swam alongside my boat. When I surged forward at four knots, they also surged at four knots, although this was a snail's pace for fish that could move at speeds of up to thirty miles an hour. When I was becalmed, they seemed quite prepared to hang around and wait for me, even if it meant they had to perform their equivalent of running on the spot, swimming around in slow circles to keep the oxygen flowing through their gills. Even on the days when the current took me drifting back east, they backtracked as well.

Tuna are renowned for their constant motion, yet this troop was evidently happy to follow me, and my boat, to the ends of the earth.

Was this devotion? Was this love?

No, I suspect it was greed.

I stress that I am no expert, and these assumptions are made from what I witnessed with my own eyes rather than from any book, but it swiftly occurred to me that the splashing of my oars on the water surface attracted various forms of sea life, including the pitiable flying fish, to the vicinity of my boat.

As I have already noted, my friends appreciated their food. It didn't seem to matter what was on the menu, whether it was squid, mackerel or smaller fish and, if the motion of my oars attracted such tasty dishes, then the tuna seemed perfectly happy to remain in pole position near my boat, open their mouths and swallow whatever was borne on the current.

As time passed, I started to imagine that the tuna regarded my boat as a kind of fast-food restaurant where they would always be fed and never pay a bill. Like idle teenagers, they would hover around until I did all the hard work by starting to row and . . . Abracadabra! Seafood platter to go! No charge!

Increasingly, as we became more familiar with each other's habits, these ravenous souls were not even prepared to hover and wait.

I would be settling down for a quiet evening, reading a book or listening to the radio, generally minding my own business, when the tuna would start jumping and performing, thrashing their tails in the water, swimming to and fro, circling the boat, leaping into the air and landing with a belly-flop on the swell. These circus antics were frequently hilarious, rarely elegant, and they appeared to be an extravagant means of attracting my attention.

Within moments, I would see the tuna I had christened 'Big Fish' emerge from beneath the boat, swim to the surface of the water and somehow manage to float on her side so she could look at me with a big, round eye, as if to say: 'Jim! We're hungry down here. When will you start rowing?'

Big Fish was one of four tuna I had grown able to distinguish from the rest and instantly recognise on sight. She was larger than large with unique markings on her back, and her decisive behaviour earmarked her as a kind of leader of the school, maybe even the recognised headmistress.

Of course, I had no clear proof of this status. I couldn't even be certain if she was indeed a 'she', but instincts created this role for her and it was perfectly consistent with my assumption that it should be Big Fish who bravely shouldered the responsibility of rising to the surface and asking me to row.

How could I say no? Only with great difficulty. There would be blazing hot and humid days when I would ask Big Fish to be patient for another hour or so, and tell her I would row when the temperature began to fall. However, nine times out of ten, I would respond by mumbling an apology, shifting into position, taking up the oars and slowly beginning to row once again.

In truth, I would welcome her interventions. During my voyage across the Pacific, I found myself being hounded to row only by my conscience and by the hungry yellow-fin tuna; and, of these two incentives, there is no question the tuna proved the most difficult to ignore. One look with that large, round eye and I was reduced to pliable putty in Big Fish's dorsal fins.

In fairness, there were also many occasions when the yellow-fin appeared happy to take responsibility for preparing their own food, and I was impressed by the precision, clarity and ruthless efficiency of their plan.

Whenever the school was feeling peckish, and that could be at any time of the day, the tuna would fan out in two broad arcs, stretching 200 yards away on either side with my boat in the middle, creating a large crescent formation. The fish would hold this line for a few minutes, moving forward and trapping any flying fish that happened to be swimming within that 400-yard range.

Then, at a given moment, the feeding frenzy would begin. Amid a sudden burst of frenetic activity and splashing, the two arcs would wrap around towards the centre in a classic pincer movement. In this way, the tuna would encircle an area of sea now dense with food and gorge themselves to their hearts' content. My role in this hunt was simply to keep rowing on a line that ran from the edge towards the middle.

It was towards the frenzied end of one of these hunts that another of my recognisable fish, Big Dorado, leaped high out of the water to catch a flying fish and landed with a mighty wet slap on the deck of my boat. He gashed his back during the fall, but otherwise seemed fully conscious. Gazing at my friend in his full glory, I marvelled at his sheer size and muscular presence. Tuna might look like double-decker buses, but they have turbo engines.

'Hold on, I just want to take a picture,' I burbled.

Big Dorado was evidently not going anywhere in a hurry, but I detected a weary look of impatience as if to say: 'Oh all right, go on then.'

I swiftly produced the video camera and held it to my eye, but found it was impossible to fit his body inside the frame. I compromised by panning the camera from head to tail, and produced some excellent footage.

'Hold on,' I said. 'The stills camera has a wide lens, but it is packed away at the bottom of one of the hatches. Wait a minute for me.'

One glance at the now gasping Big Dorado told me he was not physically equipped to spend the remainder of the evening as a guest aboard my boat, so I quickly abandoned the portrait session and started to consider how I might most easily return him to his proper place beneath the waves.

Since my overriding concern was that he would slither out of my grasp and injure himself again, I decided I would use my last remaining tea towel to ensure a decent grip as I lifted this forty-five-pound hulk over the side.

Big Dorado appeared to trust me. He didn't move at all when I raised him in my arms but he did then flap his tail with excited enthusiasm as he arced back towards the water; and it was this powerful stroke that ensured my cherished tea towel also took flight, following him into the sea and borne away by the current.

Greater love hath no ocean rower than he who lays down his very last tea towel to save his friendly fish. At least, Big Dorado was OK. I watched his wound heal through the weeks that followed, leaving a dark brown scar that served as a frequent reminder of the three minutes we had spent together. He did not seem to be put off by the experience, and followed me to Australia.

When I related this incident to Pat Waggaman in Chile some months later, he insisted I had completely misunderstood the significance of events: it was his conviction that Big Dorado had drawn the short straw and been the chosen one to go up and take a closer look at the 'fish deity' and his home above the surface. Pat insists this is why Big Dorado lay so still – he was studying me in detail, so he could take a full report back under the waves.

I suppose we will never know the truth!

As the weeks passed, more of the tuna became progressively tame. Each morning, four or five of them would fearlessly approach the side of the boat when I was brushing my teeth.

Whenever I leaned over to spit into the water, it became standard practice for me to be confronted by a row of tunny mouths gaping at the surface, as if they were asking to borrow my toothbrush.

And our bond was strengthened by the reality that we both featured high on the menu of the most feared and powerful predators in the Pacific, the sharks who frequently arrived and seemed to have difficulty choosing between the fresh tuna and the slightly overcooked side of prime British beef.

An account of my own struggles with these sharks follows in Chapter Ten, but the tuna's self-preservation strategy seemed to be to swim as far as possible as quickly as possible. As a general rule, by the time I first noticed the approach of another ominous shark's fin, cutting through the water with evil intent, the tuna would long since have sensed danger and dashed for cover.

There were times when they didn't dash fast enough. I vividly recall an occasion when the steaming haze of another humid, hot afternoon was interrupted by one of my companion tuna leaping out of the water and into the air maybe twenty yards from my boat. My heart sank at the sight of the notorious fin in pursuit and, within fifteen seconds, the stirred waters suddenly fell deathly silent.

Even in the ocean, the good guys don't win all the time. I recall feeling upset for some time afterwards, and I was relieved to see Big Fish intact several hours later, again asking me to deliver the evening meal.

Shark attacks seemed to be an accepted part of tuna life, something like car accidents in the human world, and the frequent appearance of fresh cuts and wounds in tunny flesh provided vivid evidence of the threat. Of course, these were the lucky ones that lived to tell the tale.

As lives ended, so lives began. It was joyfully inevitable that my sustained, intimate encounter with tunny life in the ocean should sooner or later be regaled by the patter of tiny fins. Even for these nomads, swimming through thousands of miles of ocean, the circle of life would continue to turn; and I felt deeply honoured to be providing the maternity ward and delivery room.

The first signs of activity appeared as clusters of eggs laid both on the trip buoy attached to the sea anchor and on the hull, below the waterline. However, I quickly realised the tuna's favourite place for laying their eggs was the protected, enclosed gaps between the barnacles squatting on the hull. These shell-dwelling, robust sea creatures were unwelcome visitors underneath my boat, but they did partially redeem themselves by hosting the tuna spawn.

So far as I could see, the procedure began with a male and a female tuna splashing around together in the water, creating quite a disturbance; not long afterwards, the female would swim upside down beneath my boat, skilfully laying eggs between the barnacles. In due course, the newly born fish would peek their noses out from beneath the boat, seeking errant scraps of food from my plate or trying to eat from the inexhaustible supply of mini-jellyfish.

And they would appear as cigar-shaped fish, between six and eight inches in length, distinguished by white markings at either end of their body. And, with a little luck, they would grow and replenish the tuna population.

Now that I was spanning generations and starting to feel one of the family, I began to consider whether it would be possible to move my relationship with the tuna a step further and swim alongside them in the ocean. Simply visualising the image of a shark's fin slicing through the water had proved sufficient to dissolve this idyllic concept earlier in the trip, but I was beginning to grow more confident in assessing when the sharks were likely to threaten.

Following one particularly hot, clammy spell of weather, the prospect of a refreshing dip in the ocean had never seemed more attractive. We had not seen any sharks for at least a week, and I was starting to waver. At around two o'clock in the afternoon,

Big Fish appeared at the side of the boat and winked at me. I'm sure some highly qualified person is going to claim yellow-fin tuna are physically incapable of winking. They probably don't believe they have long eyelashes and sometimes wear mascara either! I don't mind what they say.

Big Fish winked at me, as if to say: 'Come on in, Jim.' And, in an instant, I had pulled on my goggles, snorkel and fins and flopped into the ocean. The rush of brisk water felt wonderful on my skin, and I proceeded to swim in what I hoped would be a secure area between the boat and my sea anchor. As a further safety measure, I had decided to keep my head underwater at all times, enabling me to keep my eyes wide open for any unfriendly arrivals.

I dived down to a depth of fifteen feet and, while I was relishing the colder layers of water more than eighteen inches below the surface, I became aware of Big Fish and three of her close friends swimming six feet away from me. This was the type of scene you see in the glossy Hollywood movies, but it was happening to me, a once-overweight management consultant from Middlesex.

Big Fish could hardly have been more friendly, but she clearly drew the line at physical contact. Whenever I reached out to touch her, she skipped away to maintain the six-foot distance between us; but if I pretended to ignore her, she would start to draw closer to me. We could have played like this for hours but I was not going to push my luck; and after ten unforgettable minutes, I clambered back into the boat, enriched by memories to last a lifetime.

A sustained series of shark assaults through the following week ruled out any chance of a repeat performance and, strange though it may seem, this would prove to be the only time I swam with the tuna. Perhaps I felt I should quit while I was ahead. Not even Big Fish's most appealing wink would once again persuade me to gamble with my life in this shark-infested ocean.

I hope the content and tone of this chapter so far explains why I reacted with incredulity when, at the completion of the voyage, I was repeatedly asked by interviewers why I had never actually eaten any tuna.

As I told Jay Leno on *The Tonight Show*: 'Well, you only eat your friends when you really have to, and I was never that desperate.'

He shot back: 'You'll go far in this town.'

Yet, the truth lies within the one-liners. Out on the Pacific, in a world where I greeted these tuna almost every morning and often wished them goodnight, the idea that I would sit down and eat one of them seemed as absolutely unthinkable as the idea on land that any dog-owner should devour their dog.

Having said that, I did not set out with the intention of being so friendly to the fishes. I had packed a fishing line and hooks aboard the boat and, at various stages during the voyage, actually practised my fishing skills, simply to reassure myself that, in a crisis, I would be able to gather food. However, there never was a sufficiently serious food crisis, and I remained content on a pre-packed diet.

If this school of yellow-fin tuna emerged as the undoubted superstars of my voyage, there was also a full cast of sea life that all played significant roles as the drama of my voyage ran, and ran, and ran across the Pacific.

The overpaid but underperforming celebrities in the production proved to be the dolphins and the whales. Their pre-launch publicity, distributed throughout the world in hundreds of films and documentaries, prompted wild expectations of profound relationships, nose-rubbing, cutesy squeaking and maybe even the odd dorsal ride through the surf. I was starting to believe my trip would be something between *Free Willy* and *Flipper*, but it didn't happen.

Maybe I was using the wrong agent.

In the end, I saw dolphins no more than five times during the trip and on each occasion, they left me with the impression of running late for a far more important appointment somewhere else. They appeared in pods of anything from twenty to forty, appeared to have a look, but then moved on, leaving me dismayed by their lack of interest and wondering if my bow wave was too small.

I had previously experienced the sight of dolphins playing in the bow wave of boats as they ploughed across the seas, weaving in and out of the swell, jumping and fooling around, and I had hoped they would stay with me. My sense of frustration was exacerbated by the fact that, even in the course of the briefest encounter, that famous dolphin magic was almost tangible.

They are truly magnificent creatures, combining remarkable athleticism with rare intelligence and an ostensibly sweet nature; I was most struck by their size, reaching lengths of ten feet, and the sheer presence of these fawned-upon, glamorous Bardots, Taylors and Lorens of the ocean. In my modest production, however, they would play no more than a walk-on part.

The whales also stuck around for only a few days' filming. Still harbouring vivid memories of the way David Jackson and I had been so royally entertained during the Atlantic race, I eagerly looked forward to more chance meetings with chronically exhibitionist whales. There are few more spectacular sights than one of these mighty beasts thrashing in and out of a rolling sea.

I thought I was in luck while I was having lunch on 31 July when I heard the familiar puffing sound maybe thirty yards away from my boat. I quickly turned, only to see an adult whale heading away, towards the horizon. There were other whale sightings at various stages of the trip, but none stayed long enough to warrant a special mention in the credits of this adventure.

At the opposite end of the salary scale, the volunteer extras were played by thousands upon thousands of flying fish, those bizarre creatures that looked like regular fish with wings and, from what I witnessed, were able to fly as far as 300 metres at a time before flopping back into the ocean.

Flying fish were unfortunately fated to be the favourite snack of yellow-fin tuna, which meant no clever flying fish would want to be seen in the vicinity of my boat as it edged across the ocean. Even more unfortunately, there seemed to be very few clever flying fish with the result that I often saw plenty of terrified fish flying around my boat, unremittingly pursued by voracious tuna.

Sometimes they were eaten, other times they got away, and far too many times their attempted flights to safety ended in a fatal miscalculation and a thud on the deck of my boat. I could accept their frustration at finding any solid vessel in the middle of the ocean – after all, it was hardly an everyday sight; but I battled to understand why they resisted my attempts to save them.

Early in the voyage, I had woken one morning to find five or six flying fish flapping around the deck. Immediately sympathetic, I scampered round the boat, trying to pick up these suffocating creatures with a cloth and throw then back to the waves. However, within a couple of weeks, I had decided to stop these regular dashes for mercy because they were manifestly futile.

In the first place, most of the fish were already dead; and, second, most of those that were still alive tended to battle and squirm so powerfully when I tried to put them back in the ocean that they often slipped from my grasp and damaged themselves for a second time as they fell against the boat. And, third, even if one did get back to the water, there was probably a tuna waiting for the supper to be delivered straight into his mouth.

This needless carnage continued on the deck of *Le Shark* until we reached Australia. One notably disastrous morning, I woke to discover no fewer than forty-three flying fish lying deceased in my boat. The average mortality rate on the boat eventually settled at around eight per day, ranging in size from three to fifteen inches. I suppose, for the flying fish, I had come to represent something of a traffic black spot.

Increasingly detached from their fate, I began feeding the corpses to the tuna; and this quickly became a game in itself because the tuna were clearly not prepared to eat dead fish, so my challenge became to attach a line to the expired mouth and drag the ex-flying fish through the water at such speed that the tuna would think they were alive, and swallow them whole.

Noteworthy supporting roles were played by a series of sleek, impressive swordfish that occasionally strayed across the stage. Dray-grey, slender, as much as seven feet long, they followed the classic formula of initially appearing to be hostile and threatening but ultimately turning out to be good guys. One morning, I was quickly inspecting the deck and was disappointed to find a baby swordfish, with a seven-inch body and nine-inch 'blade', stranded and already deceased.

Wilfredo Contreras, a member of the Club Nautico Ilo, had worked as a spotter for an international fishing fleet before becoming captain of a fishing boat himself, and he had told me to expect birds wherever there were fish. He said the quickest way of finding fish was to look for the birds.

He was right, and I reckon I saw at least one bird on every single day of the voyage. It remains a mystery to me how these beaked, web-footed creatures could have survived when we were often as far as 1,200 miles from the nearest piece of dry land, but they remained a constant presence, even if they generally acted more in the background than on centre stage.

There was one particular black seagull who showed the courage and presence to step forward and introduce herself to me. One bright morning towards the end of January 2001, I happened to notice this bird perched on the navigation light at the front of the boat, quietly minding her own business.

I was intrigued and took two steps towards her. Instead of flying away, she turned her head to look at me, gave me the beady eye and abruptly looked away, all the while remaining unmoved. This was evidently a seagull with attitude, akin to a gifted young actress who would take 'no nonsense from nobody'. She was to provide a focus of interest through the dying weeks of the trip.

By coincidence, only the previous day I had been following a programme on Radio New Zealand International on the subject of horse whispering, and one of the animal experts had been explaining how an important element in earning any creature's trust is to avoid looking it directly in the eye.

When it became clear that this seagull had found her preferred spot and was not going to move for anyone, I bore this useful advice in mind, only looking at the bird out of the corner of my eye and generally seeming as uninterested in her as possible. She stayed a week, and then another week.

I don't know why. The most likely explanation seemed to be that she was simply tired of flying across the ocean and wanted a lift to Australia. If I had been a seagull, I think I would have adopted the same tactics. In any case, she looked happy enough, if a little awkward perched on the radar reflector; in due course, she elected to move along the gunwale to bathe on the sun panel.

There was a downside to her presence, specifically the mess she tended to leave wherever she slept or spent an extended period of time, but I started to appreciate her company. At times when the boat was becalmed, I would look at my fellow passenger and conclude that if she could be so patient and wait for the next wind to blow, then I could certainly be patient as well.

The gull occasionally nipped off in search of food but she always returned and was evidently growing in confidence. One fine evening, she casually took a perch less than three feet from where I was rowing. She looked so relaxed that I decided to try my luck: dropping one oar, I reached across to stroke her feathers. The young gull turned towards me, but didn't take flight, or even walk away.

This turned out to be the highlight of our relationship and, as soon as she saw the coast of Australia, she was gone without even saying goodbye. I was not surprised because I always knew I was being taken for a ride.

An older, more established performer made an appearance scarcely two weeks before the end of the voyage. It is said turtles have remained essentially unchanged through many thousands of years, but I could not imagine what was causing the loud, persistent banging on the bottom of the boat. My first thought was that the rudder had broken and was hanging loose.

It was only when I squeezed through the back hatch and looked down to the lapping sea that I discovered an enormous turtle gnawing contentedly at the barnacles near and below the waterline. I had spotted a couple of turtles back in August 2000, but neither of them had looked as instantly endearing, friendly and gently benign as this old boy. Sustaining the movie metaphor, this was maybe a late walk-on part for a much-loved veteran like Sir John Mills.

His shell measured more than three feet in diameter and, considering how long this species had survived, I was surprised to see how vulnerable he looked when he stretched his scaly dinosaur head into the open.

The turtle gnawed happily through the afternoon and seemed content to play when he eventually moved around to chew the barnacles at the side of the boat. I would place the palm of my hand on his shell and, when I gently pushed him several inches under water, he bounced back to the surface.

As sunset approached, I unpacked the stills camera to record some film of this most civilised and welcome visitor in action.

However, no sooner had I raised the lens to my eye than I became aware of Big Fish and two of her closest friends jumping and thrashing around in the water barely five yards away from the boat. When I put the camera down by my side, their frantic and unruly behaviour stopped immediately. I raised the camera and they began splashing again. I dropped it, and they stopped.

This was a remarkable moment.

Nobody should ever try to tell me that fish don't have personalities and feelings. So far as I was concerned, it was patently clear that the yellow-fin tuna were turning green with jealousy because I was giving such close attention to the turtle. They were irritated with me, and they were letting me know.

'Calm down, Big Fish,' I shouted across the waves, grinning from ear to ear. After eight months together, I sensed she really cared.

So these were my friends on the ocean. I had no pretensions to becoming some kind of maritime Doctor Doolittle, but I had simply tried to interact with any living beings that crossed my path. The dolphins and whales might have ignored me, but I considered myself extremely fortunate to have crossed paths with Big Fish and her extraordinary school of yellow-fin tuna.

It would be inaccurate for me to declare here that I miss her and think of them all every day ... because I don't; but there is no doubt I will never forget how these special fish ushered and inspired me across the Pacific.

On one occasion, towards the end of a successful day when the boat had travelled thirty-five miles, I can remember putting Louis Armstrong's 'Special Party' CD into the machine, cranking up the volume and starting to dance.

Big Fish and more than twenty of the yellow-fin tuna were in close attendance and, for a blissful half-hour, the world seemed a perfect place.

'We're all in this together, and we're having a great time,' I recall shouting at my companions. They didn't reply. They never did, but it wasn't necessary. Through almost nine months, it had never been necessary.

10
Dealing with Danger

Danger and excitement are two sides of the same coin. If I was going to seek excitement by crossing the Pacific Ocean in a rowing boat, I realised an element of danger would be part of the package.

That is not what I told my family and, at stages, that is not what I tried to persuade myself. Yet it was always the reality. Of course, it was going to be dangerous. If the adventure was going to be worthwhile, I needed, almost by definition, to step as close to the edge of the abyss as I dared.

'It'll be fine,' I said repeatedly. 'It isn't such a big deal,' I added, without explaining why nobody had ever before crossed the Pacific in a rowing boat, unaided and alone. 'Everything is under control,' I stressed.

That was the point. I did feel everything *was* under control. I was not going to be reckless in any way, at any time.

If it were required that I put myself in hazardous situations, then I was determined to examine the precise nature of the threat, and take steps to pre-empt what could go wrong and minimise the risk.

This was my strategy: to ensure, through careful management and skilful planning, that the odds in any scenario would always be stacked as heavily as possible in my favour.

The 'eccentric Englishman' tag has tended to promote a view that I was generally casual in my approach to this voyage. That is not true. The odd lapse was inevitable in a venture of this nature, but my conviction is that I was extremely well prepared in the crucial areas of safety, communications, navigation, provisions and risk management.

I may have downplayed the potential dangers to shield my family from unnecessary concern, but I was never irresponsible; and, as the trip unfolded, while it was never possible to dismiss the possibility of a freakish accident, my safety procedures generally gave me peace of mind.

Furthermore, when peril did lurk somewhere beneath the waves, I grew to realise it was as important for me to remain psychologically strong and calm as it was for my physical infrastructure to be in order.

Was I ready for the sharks? Was I prepared to sit in my twenty-three-foot rowing boat and withstand the regular assaults of white pointers measuring up to twelve feet in length? You can prepare and plan the logistics as much as you like, but it is hard to simulate the danger and predict a response.

I didn't have to wait long. The sharks are the dominant predators in the ocean. I was rowing on their patch. They would be calling.

My pulse quickened, my heartbeat accelerated and I sensed a burst of adrenalin surge through my body . . . This was my first sighting of a dark dorsal fin scything through the swell with power and purpose.

It is difficult to communicate the full sense of foreboding, the chill in the air, the unnatural silence that fills those suspended seconds when an adult shark is preparing to attack. These brutes broadcast pure dread, and I found myself sitting in the boat, not quite sure what to expect, just starting to become a little bit anxious about the situation, feeling probably 70 per cent fear and 30 per cent excitement about the looming confrontation.

Oooouufff! The entire boat shuddered with the force of the white pointer battering for the first time against the hull. He had wheeled around behind me, gathered speed on the approach, crashed against the side, and now he was wheeling again.

Oooouufff! Another glancing blow rocked the boat. I felt like a small boy being pushed around the playground. I was being bullied by what appeared to be a solitary, grumpy shark. He wheeled around a third time.

Oooouufff! This bombardment was uncomfortable and irritating but, strangely, I did not feel in any real danger. It was true that a finely developed killing machine appeared to be angry with me for one reason or another, but my sense of relative security was founded on the knowledge that the white pointer was never going to reach his jaws around my boat. He could batter away all day, but his efforts were likely to be in vain.

After twenty minutes or so, the shark seemed to have reached the same conclusion and he disappeared into the depths from where he had sprung. I was breathing hard and fast, not sure whether to feel lucky to have survived or to relish the buzz of what had been an electrifying experience.

This incident marked the start of intermittent but regular attacks over a six-week period when a tribe of white pointers, numbering maybe five or six or more, declared open season on the sides of my boat. Day after day, they would arrive in the vicinity and launch their incessant pummelling routine. I don't know whether sharks suffer headaches but, if they do, these head bangers must have been overdosing on paracetamol after finishing with me.

A few days into this absolutely unprovoked onslaught, I took a decision that I would no longer sit submissively in my boat while the sharks attacked as and when they pleased. I resolved to hit back, and my initial tactic was to beat the aggressors around the head with an oar. However, it proved difficult to land a telling blow as they powered past, and, even when I did make contact, the shark seemed undeterred, wheeling round to charge again.

I clearly needed to take a harder line, so I started to look for a long pole and a sharp knife. This search eventually settled upon the twelve-foot handle of a handrail that had been broken earlier in the voyage when I was thrown against it by a sneaky wave, and a notably sinister fish-cleaning knife, equipped with a jagged six-inch blade. Nylon cord and the ubiquitous black duck tape served to strap and firmly bind the knife to one end of the oar. Before long, I was the proud owner of a home-made harpoon. Flexing my right arm like a javelin thrower, I braced myself for the battle to come.

'Good morning, Sharkie!' I muttered beneath my breath as the dark fin moved through the swell. Outside the water polo pool, I had always considered myself to be a gentle, peace-loving person whose first instinct is to shy away from confrontation, but these sharks were starting to bring out a dark and ruthless side that I had never known existed.

I tried to recall the cold-blooded ferocity of Charles Bronson in those movies of a few years ago, just to get in the right frame of mind, so that when the next grey mass reached the side of my boat, I lunged with all my might, digging the knife into his flesh and then snapping it back into my grasp.

Breathing hard, standing in the middle of a rowing boat in the midst of the Pacific, duelling with a furious ten-foot shark ... Well, it was better than filling out a VAT return. I was relishing the contest, and was thrilled to see the shark swing round and start his approach again. This time, my blade skidded harmlessly off the tough, slippery, grey skin.

Thus the battle lines were drawn, and so we continued through week upon week: white pointers charging endlessly through the waves, me thrusting my harpoon at the savage grey shapes as they passed. And, far from wilting under the pressure of this primitive confrontation that was centuries old, I found myself enthused by the challenge, eager, excited and invigorated.

There were brief moments of compassion, when I caught sight of the red, raw wounds that started to appear on the sharks' backs and around their heads, but such sympathy evaporated when I considered how red and raw I would look if any of them managed to get hold of me.

As we entered the sixth week of daily battle, the evil pointers' campaign against the inoffensive, peaceable, lone ocean rower began to founder on the aggressors' creeping realisation that they were getting nowhere. They might have been thick-skinned and bone-headed, but even they eventually saw the wisdom of seeking less obdurate prey elsewhere in the ocean.

Sharks continued to threaten sporadically through the remainder of the voyage, always employing the same battering ram strategy; and, each time, I would wield my harpoon in increasingly enthusiastic defence.

On the early evening of Saturday, 17 March 2001, two weeks from my destination, I happened be relaxing with the 'Greatest Hits of Johnny Cash' on CD when three large white pointers ominously started to circle fifty yards from the boat. The yellow-fin tuna efficiently evacuated the area, leaving me alone to prepare myself for another physical confrontation,

As the slightly incongruous classic Country music continued to play in the background, distributing mellow tones out across the waves, I positioned myself securely on the deck, legs astride, right arm braced, my harpoon at the ready, and I waited patiently for the opening exchanges.

Another threatening fin, another swift approach, another heavy thud on the side of the boat ... I lunged forward and plunged vigorously at a point just behind the shark's head, burying six inches of blade into the gristly flesh. The water beside my boat turned a deep, thick shade of red.

And Johnny Cash sang on, unwittingly providing an anthem for this fine and fleeting moment of triumph over an awesome opponent.

> I find it very, very easy to be true,
> I find myself alone when each day is through,
> Yes, I'll admit I'm a fool for you
> Because you're mine,
> I walk the line.

It is unlikely that the Country and Western legend was contemplating the act of harpooning sharks on the Pacific when he compiled his smash hit song 'I Walk the Line' but, as the shark swam away and I settled back contentedly into my seat, his lyrics seemed to suit the occasion.

Five days later, I managed to record another satisfying, though less bloody, success against a white pointer. In battering the side of my boat, the shark succeeded only in smearing his mouth against the bright red anti-fouling paint I had daubed on the underside. The next time he charged, he looked as though he had put on seductive red lipstick for the occasion.

Despite these lighter moments and very occasional triumphs, it would be wrong to create an impression that I ever became remotely complacent about the sharks that regularly pounded against my boat. I obviously gained in confidence as the weeks rolled by, but the sight of those fins protruding from the water never failed to send a frisson down my spine.

Less than an hour after laughing out loud at the shark with lipstick, I was taken aback to hear a report on the Australian radio news outlining how two men had been attacked by sharks barely thirty yards from shore. One was killed instantly, the other was seriously injured, and a breathless eyewitness reported the shark had been a white pointer.

I stopped laughing. Point taken. Perhaps the most vivid measure of my enduring respect for, and fear of, the sharks is that, even as somebody who swims regularly at home, in nine months at sea I only felt safe enough to swim in the Pacific on two brief, nervy occasions. Even in the most muggy, sweltering and uncomfortable conditions, I preferred to stay in the boat rather than run the risk of a chance encounter with a white pointer. The Pacific was, is and remains shark territory, and I never disputed that fact.

Through the months since my voyage, my attitude towards the sharks has unexpectedly blurred. On the ocean, I was unequivocal: I loathed them as an evil enemy trying to knock me out of the boat and eat me. However, sober reflection has raised the possibility in my mind that I might have judged these creatures harshly, that just possibly I could have allowed myself to be influenced and jaundiced by their uniquely malevolent reputation.

Is it remotely possible that these sharks were not attacking me so much as innocently trying to scratch an itch on the abrasive, barnacled sides of the boat? The suggestion has been made. Could it be feasible that my opponents in the ongoing wars were not murderous males but heavily pregnant females contemplating the underside of my boat as a suitable place to lay their eggs? Experts in this area insist sharks habitually lay their eggs at the bottom of the ocean, but there was generally 12,000 feet of water between my boat and the bottom. Perhaps my boat seemed an easier option.

I did notice four baby sharks swimming around the boat one day late in the voyage. Could it have been their mother that I so pitilessly stabbed when the sea ran red with blood? I don't know. Maybe it was. There again, maybe she was trying to knock me out of the boat all along; maybe she wanted to bite me in half and serve fresh ocean rower to the kids for tea.

I don't know the answer to any of these questions.

When I was young, it was generally easy to tell the good guys from the bad guys in the hoary, old Western movies because the good cowboys tended to wear white hats and the bad cowboys wore black hats. Maybe the lesson to be learned from my shark encounters on the Pacific is that, in the ocean as in the human world, it is not always so easy to tell good from bad and it is usually wrong to label one entire group under the same heading.

Can all sharks be wicked and hostile? Probably not. Perhaps I will have a chance to find out before my next adventure on the seas. Maybe, next time, they will ask before they come to scratch their backs. We'll see.

Another source of danger on the ocean prompted similarly conflicting emotions. Storms were obviously a major threat insofar as I could be hurled overboard or knocked unconscious by strong winds and high seas, but storms could also be fantastically dramatic and thrilling.

There were many occasions when I sat on the deck, transfixed by the spectacle of a storm system moving across the seascape. Like thoroughbred horses running free of restraint, exactly as nature intended, these storms seemed so pure and powerful, so unblemished and uncomplicated.

Thunder and lightning danced madly between sea and sky, at once illuminating and shattering, revealing and hiding, scaring and exciting. On this most perfect stage, these natural elements appeared liberated in the unbridled exposition of their power and wizardry. My instinct was to marvel at the sights and sounds of the Ocean Spectacular rather than fear the consequences; and yet, I realised grave danger lurked within the splendour.

'Capsize' was the word that sprang to mind. I had assured everyone who would listen that my boat had been designed in such a way that it simply would not be overturned in the water under almost any conditions and, even if it did, would not stay that way; that was at least what I hoped and why I had insisted on adding the two large fenders lashed to the cabin roof to provide extra righting moment in case the boat ever found itself upside down. Constructed for the Atlantic Rowing Race in 1997, it had served me well and had never given me any reason to doubt its remarkably solid credentials.

Never say never: I understood that.

Yet, even acknowledging the power of the wind, waves and rain, I did not believe my boat would capsize. This confidence was tested during a series of storms at the start of the voyage, never more thoroughly than on the wet, wild and windy evening of Wednesday, 12 July 2000.

I had watched the tempest rolling in towards me, and only retreated to the cabin when the first drops of rain splattered on the deck. However, by the time I had sealed the hatch, the downfall was becoming steady and the wind was brisk enough for white foam from the breaking waves to be blown in streaks approaching the boat from the rear on the port side. This, as all sailors know, indicates force seven on the Beaufort wind scale, around thirty knots. Within a further fifteen minutes, I felt as if I had boarded an extreme theme-park ride.

My boat was being tossed and turned on thirty-foot waves, frequently being tipped through angles of forty and fifty degrees, first to my left, then to my right. And as the boat rocked, so I would tumble, being flung against one side and then the other. I felt like clothes in a washing machine.

It was hectic, but everything appeared under control until one enormous wave thundered into the port side. I was splattered against one side with such force that I was fortunate not to break bones, and the boat tipped violently through sixty, seventy and eighty degrees. Loose items like books and bottles were flying around my head and I became aware that the wall had become floor. My boat was virtually lying on its side.

I caught my breath. Capsize would equal catastrophe. In this terrifying moment, the boat seemed to stay still, perfectly still, almost as though it was deciding which way to settle, top-up or bottom-up. Like the defendant before the jury, I waited impassive, powerless to influence the verdict.

My recollection of that instant when the boat righted itself remains as vivid today as if it had happened this morning. I was swamped by sheer relief and a sense that the fates, whoever or whatever they were, had been kind to me. I remained wide awake until the storm eventually abated at half past two in the morning, then climbed outside to check for damage.

The footwell was flooded and the loo bucket had been hurled across the deck, but the structure seemed to have survived intact. Occasional flashes of lightning away to my right signalled the storm's ongoing march across the sea and, feeling exhausted, I took time to sit calmly in the tranquil moonlight, watching the ocean as it settled back into a gentle swell.

It soon became clear that the only lasting damage of the evening had been inflicted upon my confidence that the boat would never capsize. That night, a long and precarious voyage seemed to stretch ahead.

What I know now, but I doubted then, was that my boat would triumph across the ocean, its inspired design withstanding everything the Pacific could throw at it and remaining the right way up all the way until its owner placed it in an impossible position 200 yards from an Australian beach.

My resistance routine to withstand storms developed to a point where situations that had at first seemed to threaten a major crisis started to appear relatively humdrum. I learned to react at the very first sign of turbulence, first checking everything was firmly battened down, even the loo, then clambering into the cabin.

Once inside, I proceeded to wedge myself into a position that would have looked bizarre to an outsider but which I knew, through trial and bruising error, would hold me secure in the washing machine. Lying flat on my back, I essentially used my four extending limbs to push equally and in opposite directions against the door, the left wall, the right wall and the ceiling.

I suppose this position must have felt awkward at first, but I am not 100 per cent sure because my memories are sweetly scented by the knowledge that, within a few days, various joints and muscles had adapted so well to the new shape and pressure points that this became my default sleeping position for most of the voyage. It may have looked odd, but it brought a welcome end to my days and nights in the washing machine.

Storms came and storms went. So the boat would rock and roll, so the loo would occasionally do the twist across the deck, so the footwell would be flooded. So what? Such events became part of the routine. However, nature held yet greater forces in store for me and my boat.

By February 2001, the voyage had started to drag slowly towards its conclusion. Denied any constant wind or current, the boat edged mile by mile through sweltering days of dense humidity and soaring temperatures, moving backwards one day, sideways the next . . . sometimes forwards.

My physical condition had improved steadily since leaving Peru, but I was starting to feel mentally exhausted. I had survived repeated shark attacks and storms, had mended fittings and repaired the water maker more times than I cared to remember. I had done all that and, to use a modern phrase, felt it was now time for me to get the T-shirt.

Midway through another languid afternoon, when it seemed far too hot to do anything but lie in the cabin and escape from the sun, certainly too hot to row, I was in my self-imposed state of semi-hibernation, casually listening to Radio New Zealand International as the music requests programme ebbed into the news. The presenter seized my attention by uttering one simple word . . . hurricane.

'We have received confirmation of a hurricane developing 220 kilometres (140 miles) north-west of Vanuatu,' she read. 'Reports indicate the hurricane is heading in a south-south-easterly direction at fifteen knots, and initial predictions are that it will continue moving in that direction.'

I would have been sitting bolt upright before she had finished the sentence if the cabin had been tall enough! It was not necessary for me to check the plotter to know that I was situated just west and south of Vanuatu, and it was not necessary for me to check anything to know that, just as I had been calmly contemplating its end, I was now being confronted by potentially the deepest crisis of the trip.

RNZI seemed alert to the gravity of the situation for all their listeners in the South Pacific, both on the islands and on the sea, and the station began providing hourly gale and then hurricane warnings, giving the position of the centre of the storm in miles relative to the nearest population centre. Each time I could pick up the broadcast over the next thirty-six hours, I would mentally note the figures as they were announced and hurry to check their impact by studying the plotter.

It was difficult to sleep under the circumstances, particularly when my situation was becoming graver and graver. Perhaps only somebody strapped to a railway track with a runaway train rumbling down the line can understand what it feels like to be an ocean rower helplessly stuck in the path of an approaching hurricane.

The facts were simple, and brutal. According to normal meteorological standards, a storm becomes a cyclone when the wind exceeds forty-five knots, and cyclones become hurricanes when the wind exceeds sixty-four knots. RNZI reported the hurricane that seemed to have an appointment with me enclosed winds gusting at 165 miles per hour. In all probability, such an awesome force would destroy both my boat and me.

At 18.00, on what was the second evening of this crisis, the RNZI bulletin gave the hurricane's latest position, and this enabled me to calculate that Hurricane Paula, as she had been christened, was now approximately 1,100 miles from my boat. If her speed and direction remained approximately the same, I would miss the eye of the storm by less than 100 miles but she would be wrapping me in her long arms in roughly two days.

I needed to be calm; I needed to be practical; and I needed to discuss the latest developments with my wife, so I telephoned Jane. She had been tracking the hurricane's progress on the Internet, and sounded extremely concerned about the most recent developments. I tried to reassure her that the situation was somehow still under control.

Jane asked: 'What about hitting the EPIRB?'

'There's no point,' I replied. 'It's too late.'

'Are you sure?'

It *was* too late.

In the first place, it was extremely unlikely that any boat would be able to reach me before the hurricane did; and, second, by summoning assistance, I would effectively be drawing someone else into the same danger that I was facing, and I was not prepared to be so callous.

As the minutes ticked away, I was becoming increasingly aware of my own fragile mortality. If this was going to be the end of everything, I hoped people would acknowledge it was bad luck rather than bad planning. There was no way anyone could have predicted a hurricane.

I banished negative thoughts, and once again implored myself to be calm and practical, and develop some kind of game plan. There was only one option. It was a fact that Paula was coming, and it was a fact that I was in her path: thus my only chance was to prepare the boat and myself to survive the onslaught of the hurricane. I had no idea whether this was possible and, to be honest, I did not care. However slight the chance of survival, it was my only chance and, as such, I was going to commit myself to the task.

I decided that I would literally tie myself down inside the cabin, with the intention of remaining anchored until Paula had passed by. If the hurricane was going to bounce my boat around the ocean like a tennis ball, my challenge seemed to be somehow to survive within that tennis ball.

A typical revolving tropical storm measures between 50 and 250 miles across. When one of the RNZI reports announced that Paula was travelling at around ten knots with winds gusting to 190 miles per hour (165 knots), it became quite clear to me that once the storm hit, I was likely to be in it for up to sixteen hours with some pretty rough weather around the edges! I resolved to prepare for up to three days in the cabin before it would be safe for me to emerge from my 'haven'.

That wasn't too bad, I told myself. Surely that was possible. So long as the boat was physically able to withstand the wind and the rains, then I would be able to survive by lying around and waiting. I managed to keep myself busy through most of the second day by preparing the cabin and shifting three days of basic food supplies into a position where I could reach them without moving from what amounted to a fixed, mummified position.

I also placed myself on a strict temporary diet of prunes and one litre of water per day, to ensure my bowels and bladder were as empty as possible at the moment when I finally closed the hatch behind me. By the time everything was fixed and ready, the RNZI weather forecast was placing the hurricane in a position only 450 miles away from me. On the Pacific, such distances equate to being 'just around the corner' on land. I felt calm.

Another hour passed, another set of statistics, another scamper to the plotter, another check . . . Hold on! How was that? It seemed as if the hurricane was veering to the south-east, away from me. I looked, but didn't say anything for fear of raising hopes only to discover I had made a mistake.

I checked the numbers again, checked the new position, and began to sense a dramatic eleventh-hour reprieve, but still I said nothing. An hour later, ear pressed to the radio, I took down another 'fix', positioned the cursor on the plotter and saw confirmation that, against all the odds and for no apparent reason, the hurricane was swinging eastwards.

Reprieved! I sat in the rowing seat, slumped forward, forehead resting on clasped hands, almost unable to believe what had happened. Yet again, I had been pulled back from the brink of the unknown, and possible disaster.

And, at that precise moment, I sensed the slightest of northern breezes caressing my face. 'Carry on, Jim,' Hurricane Paula seemed to whisper in my ear, 'but you know you were lucky this time.'

What represented salvation for me meant desperate news for Vanuatu and, to a lesser extent, for Fiji and Tonga, whose islands were battered by storms while I happily moved the three days of food supplies back from the sleeping cabin to the hold where they belonged. On reflection, I suppose Paula could easily have changed direction again but, at the time, it seemed as though the most nerve-racking crisis of the voyage had passed as suddenly as it had arrived.

I was beginning to appreciate that danger emerges in all shapes, sizes and speeds on the Pacific. A 190-mph hurricane might have threatened to end the voyage in what amounted to a high-speed collision, but other dangers had moved precisely nowhere in many thousands of years.

Mention the South Pacific, and most people conjure up images of idyllic paradise islands, sprinkled large and small across the deep blue ocean. Lush, mountainous, dotted with palm trees and populated by some of the friendliest locals, places like Fiji, Tonga and Tahiti have established themselves among the most popular holiday destinations in the world.

However, for solo Pacific Ocean rowers like me, these and many other islands assumed the status of immovable hazards blocking the route to our destination. Collision with an island could prove disastrous if the boat was run aground on a coral reef or stranded by an onshore wind. Given the ease with which an unhelpful wind and current could propel the boat exactly where you did not want to go, this remained a constant threat.

I looked forward to returning to visit these islands one day in the future, perhaps in a yacht when I had more time but, on this particular trip, the limit of my ambition was to pass every speck of land without alarm.

With fair winds and some luck, I managed to thread my way past most of these islands, only suffering a slight scare when I approached Ua Pou and a more serious fright near Grande Terre, New Caledonia.

On 29 October, I had recorded in my log: 'What excitement! First land since leaving Ilo.' This was the island of Ua Huka in the northern Cook Islands. My log entry at 20.40 the same day read: 'I am now quite concerned about getting south of Ua Pou' – even though I was still forty-eight miles away from it. I decided to wait until morning and hope that the wind would not blow me too far west.

At first light, I found myself less than twenty-two miles from

the island, and evidently on a collision course! I turned right
and started rowing hard to try to get far enough west before
we reached the northern tip of the island, managing to sneak
round the top of it and pass down its western side within a mile
of the beach! That might sound like a long way to swim, but it
is a hair's breadth in the context of the Pacific!

Ua Pou looked like an archetypal Pacific island, the sort of
place where you would expect to be greeted by Robinson Crusoe
or the Swiss Family Robinson bounding down onto the beach,
and I was excited to see signs of human life as we skirted past
it.

A boat was offloading goods at a small jetty and, while trying
to rouse someone on the VHF radio, I eavesdropped on snippets
of conversation about consignments of 'welding gas and beer'.
Gazing across the deep blue water, I could see through my
binoculars the barge carrying crates to the shore, and my mouth
ran dry as, even from a distance of two miles, I fancied I could
smell the beer.

Some of my more uncharitable friends will say I have always
been able to sniff out a beer from two miles away, and others
will say so many months of deprivation were playing tricks on
my mind. Well, they may say what they like. The truth is that
I could smell the beer and it was precisely for this reason that
I decided to stop trying to contact anyone on the radio. I was
scared they would invite me to join them ashore, and that, in
spite of my better judgement, the powerful lure of a beer or
three would prove too great.

Just as the best way of declining temptation is to avoid temptation, the best way of rowing unaided and alone is to avoid other
people.

The main island of New Caledonia is by far the largest in the
group, and I had recognised for some days that it could present
a serious problem because, as a large, cigar-shaped land mass
roughly 120 miles long, it seemed to be lying full square across
my preferred direct route to Australia. Even more incon-

veniently, close to the south-east coast lay the Ile des Pins, not to mention a swathe of other small islands and reefs which extended in a band fifty-three miles wide.

As we drifted closer and closer, I became progressively more desperate to pass the island on the south side and hurry on to my destination, but I could see we were being driven relentlessly north. The impact of passing on the north side of New Caledonia was going to be much greater than just adding 150 miles to the voyage, even if we made it up the eastern shore with a predominantly onshore wind blowing. Being forced north would mean we would be caught by winds and currents that would take us up towards New Guinea.

The extremities of eastern Australia would be receding at about the same angle as our approach and we would, if we were going to make landfall in Australia, have to navigate through the Great Barrier Reef! I studied the C-Map charts long and hard to find a viable route between what were shown as intertidal reefs. There were possibilities but without knowing where I could get to it was pointless deciding where I would like to go – the elements would send me where they pleased!

I had always set my heart on completing the crossing in Australia and, in a wholehearted attempt to remain on the right course, I hurled myself into three days of intensive rowing in sizzling temperatures, all the while working to swing the boat south and skip past the south-east corner of New Caledonia.

These efforts were spurred on by the emergence of a steady south-westerly wind, which helped my efforts towards the west but which was also taking me north at an uncomfortable rate. Using the wind to travel west and the oars to prevent too much northward drift, to my relief, my boat eventually edged forty-three miles south of the reefs and well clear of the shipping lanes into Noumea. It had been a perilously close shave.

So I had survived shark attacks, withstood raging storms, narrowly avoided a hurricane and even managed to dodge various islands in my path, yet probably the greatest danger throughout the voyage was the risk of being mown down by another vessel crossing the ocean.

I had developed genuine affection for my boat but I was not blind to the fact that, at twenty-three feet long, it was not ideally equipped for a physical collision on an ocean populated by large fishing boats and juggernaut tankers.

Indeed, at times, I felt like a resolute hedgehog trying to find his way across the M1 motorway at two o'clock in the morning. The plus points were that there was not likely to be too much traffic and there was plenty of space to make a safe crossing. On the other hand, I had to live with the constant knowledge that, if I was unlucky enough to be in the wrong place at the wrong time, any significant contact was likely to be fatal.

My situation was not helped by the realisation not long into the voyage that a hedgehog crawling across the fast lane would probably have had a far greater chance of being spotted by an M1 lorry driver than I seemed to have of being seen by the lookout of any large ship on the ocean.

The radar reflector seemed to be little better than useless. This piece of equipment was lashed on top of the navigation light at the front of the boat and had been intended to ensure my boat's position would be efficiently reflected on the radar screens of any ships or boats that happened to be nearby. In theory, if they could see me, these vessels would not collide with me.

However, in practice, the radar reflector was only going to function when the waves were sufficiently low for it to receive and return a signal. This problem could have been overcome if it were possible to fix the aerial twenty-five feet above the water, but there was no higher point on my boat than the top of the navigation light and that put the reflector approximately two metres above whatever level of water the boat was floating on at the time.

Thus, it transpired that the radar reflector would work if the swell was lower than five feet, but this appeared to be of limited use on the Pacific where the average swell seemed to be between six and nine feet. My astonishingly vulnerable status was complete whenever depleted power supplies meant it was necessary to switch off the navigation light at night.

By then, I had ceased to feel like a run-of-the-mill hedgehog crossing the M1 motorway and had started to assume the status of a magically invisible hedgehog wearing a blindfold and crossing the M1 motorway.

As we were a tiny speck on a vast ocean, the odds still seemed to be stacked in my favour that I would be able to complete a safe crossing, but what if . . . That was the point: what if I happened to be unlucky . . .

This precarious state of affairs was plainly demonstrated one fine and clear morning relatively early in the trip when I woke to find a large fishing boat travelling parallel to me, perhaps a mile away on the starboard side. I established VHF contact with the captain and, noticing the swell was rolling at barely three feet, casually and confidently asked him whether he had seen me with his own eyes from the bridge of his ship.

'No see you,' he replied blankly.

'Can you see me on your radar?' I enquired, becoming concerned.

'Hold on,' he said. 'Let me just go and switch it on.'

This was not an encouraging response, and I would soon discover that many ships on the Pacific rarely bothered to use their radar, at least during the daytime. In one way, this made me feel better about the state of my own radar reflector: even if it had been working perfectly, it would not have served much purpose.

'No, I no see you,' the captain replied in a thick South American accent. I imagined him to be broad, tanned, swarthy, resplendent with a bushy moustache and slightly perplexed by my line of questioning.

'You have the radar on now?'

'Yes, no see you.'

'OK,' I said, trying to sound calm. 'Can I give you my exact position, then you can check the radar one more time.' And I proceeded to read out the numbers indicated on my plotter.

'Hold on. I go check.'

After several more minutes, he returned on the line to declare: 'I have radar on maximum sensitivity. I have checked your position. I no see you at all. Nothing. *Nada*. Switch your radar reflector on.'

'It is on,' I protested.

'I see,' he said, voice filled with pity. 'Good luck.'

His two-word assessment of my situation was absolutely accurate. I would need to be unlucky to be hit, and even unluckier than I had hoped; I would even be lucky to avoid collisions when edging anxiously across the shipping lanes that run up and down the west coast of South America.

Other busy routes, such as the area lying between New Zealand, Vanuatu, Fiji and New Caledonia, and down the east coast of Australia, would present their own challenges later in the voyage, but my first task was to negotiate a path far from the South American aquatic highway.

Retiring to bed on 23 July 2000, I was starting to believe this task had been accomplished. In fact, I was approaching the fast lane.

It was just before two o'clock in the morning when I was woken by a deep, rumbling sound. I looked out of the hatch and saw the lights of a large fishing boat heading away 250 yards on the port side. We had passed in the night. I returned to bed, grateful yet again not to have been unlucky.

Thirty-six hours later, I was taking a midday snooze when I was woken by the sound of another intrusive engine, this time accompanied by shouting sailors, possibly from Bulgaria. I hurried on deck and immediately saw my luck was about to run out: a large fishing boat was bearing down upon me and, this time, some kind of collision was clearly inevitable.

Mercifully, the fishing boat managed to swing its bow to the left and a conceivably disastrous head-on collision was avoided by less than two yards. Yet, as the two boats passed each other and the gap between us narrowed with the approach of the fishing boat's wide belly, I counted six glancing blows, side against side.

Sitting in the middle, peering over the side, and carefully monitoring every moment of contact, I was relieved to see my boat emerge from this skirmish completely unscathed with body-work and paintwork intact. The same could not be said of the sailors, who by this time were shouting maniacally because they thought my boat would become tangled in their fishing lines. I gestured for them to stay calm, and managed to keep clear.

As the fishing boat motored away, I saw its name *Yalta X* across the stern, confirming my impression that the sailors came from south-east Europe, but I saw no point in trying to establish further contact by VHF radio. It was hard to tell whether they had seen me or not, but they had not seemed overly concerned by my situation. The message seemed clear: if you get in our way, you will have to accept the consequences.

I saw five more boats during the next three days before finally leaving the shipping lanes and reaching the open sea where I would travel for more than two months at a time without seeing any other vessel at all.

When I did come across a boat or ship, however, I found it hard to look upon it as anything other than a danger and an intrusion. At one stage, I took out my mini-disc recorder and complained: 'Why on earth can't these ships just leave me alone? This is an enormous ocean with more than enough room for everyone who wants to be here. Yet they try to run me over!'

I just wanted to be left in peace. Having said that, I should add there was one brief encounter on the Pacific Ocean that I cannot fairly describe either as a danger or an unwanted intrusion. I suppose it may have constituted a threat of sorts, but only in terms of being a sweet temptation.

It was the steamy first week of November, a time of perfect blue skies and a perfect blue ocean, but only ten degrees south of the equator, so very hot. I was indulging in another midday nap. I know this chapter is starting to create an impression that I was permanently asleep, but it just happened that danger crept up while I slept.

At any rate, I was once again dozing through the heat of the day when I was woken by the soft exclamation of a woman's voice. I thought I must be dreaming, but I soon realised this was the real thing and briefly contemplated how it made a welcome change from yelling Bulgarian sailors.

I poked my head out of the hatch to discover an image of perfection in the middle of the ocean. Here lay a brilliant white forty-foot catamaran yacht, dazzling against the blue sky and sea; and there, standing on the deck, were two beautifully bronzed young ladies, stunning in their bikinis.

As I blinked into the bright sunlight, they seemed to have interrupted their glamorous voyage to see if any inhabitants of this strange-looking boat required any kind of assistance. Having coasted their catamaran to within twenty yards of my bow, they looked kind, friendly and curious.

'Allo, 'ow are you?' said one of the ladies. She was evidently French, striking to look at and she was talking to me. The combination of these factors left me wanting to return to bed, close my eyes again, go back to sleep and slumber through to see the conclusion of this perfect dream. This could not be real.

'Fine,' I stammered, still waking up.

The French woman smiled. This was real. Wow!

'Where are you travelling to?' I asked, pulling myself together.

'We are sailing from Hawaii to Tahiti, just the four of us,' she replied in her lightly scented accent. The four of us? I squinted into the sun and peered behind the two women to see two French sailors hard at work.

'And you?' she added, smiling again.

'Oh, I am rowing to Australia.'

'I see,' she said, experiencing the momentary loss for words suffered by most people when they hear my plans. Perhaps she was debating whether to take me seriously or dismiss me as a mad old man of the sea. Charity took over as she smiled again, asking: 'Is there anything you need?'

'There are many things,' I said, by now wide awake and enjoying every minute of this sensational diversion from the daily grind. 'But, unfortunately, I am not able to accept any of them because my voyage is solo and unaided.' It was my teeth grinding now. 'Thank you,' I concluded.

'Are you sure? We have some fresh bread here.'

Oh, temptress! Croutons were fine, but real fresh French bread! Would it be such a disgrace if I abandoned my voyage? After all, nobody had done it before. It was supposed to be difficult. I could always try again. Displaying the same resolve that had carried me through the storms and past the hurricane, I looked the French woman in the eye, opened my mouth . . .

And said: 'No, *merci*.'

We bid each other farewell. Since the day was calm, the catamaran struggled to gain speed and it took longer than three hours for the beautiful people to disappear out of sight en route for Tahiti. The French woman had stood on the deck, waving an unforgettable farewell.

The common denominator linking the dangers outlined so far in this chapter is that they all threatened disaster, but ultimately allowed me to slip the noose and somehow continue on my way to Australia. The sharks started as if they wanted me for dinner, but eventually seemed content to pummel the boat; the storm had tipped the boat through ninety degrees but then permitted it to right itself; Hurricane Paula had scared me witless but had veered away; and New Caledonia had consented to my slipping past it to the south.

In each case, I was grateful, relieved and smiling.

However, there was another moment of extreme danger during the trip that left me disorientated and uncertain for many days afterwards, with a recurring nightmare that lasted for at least a week, and in modern parlance probably traumatised me!

I imagine that if I had been employed to row I would be entitled to compensation and early retirement for the mental anguish endured. At 03.23 during the night of Sunday, 23 February 2001, I stared the welded-steel, unambiguous certainty of death in the face . . .

But somehow survived.

I was sleeping again (well, it was nearly half past three in the morning!) when I was woken by what I thought was thunder immediately overhead. I woke instantly and wondered how I had not heard the storm approaching. The skies had seemed clear when I went to bed. This was strange. The thunder was continuous, louder and louder.

This was not thunder. This was louder, much louder. It was a big noise, the type of noise that fills your senses, fills your space, surrounds you, wraps you in fright, dominates you and overcomes you. The noise was everywhere . . . roaring, mechanical.

I crawled halfway out of the hatch and peered around the starboard bulkhead from where the noise came. I looked and I froze.

There was no sea, no sky and no stars. I saw nothing but metal, a vast wall of metal, shimmering in the moonlight and accelerating towards me, while everything was drowned by noise and metal, noise and metal, noise and metal. Within seconds, I was falling back into the cabin, losing control, losing focus, losing everything. Seconds passed like hours.

What was this? The last rites or the ultimate adrenalin rush? My life was about to end. I wanted to telephone Jane, but there was no time to start the satellite telephone. I wanted to hug my daughters one last time, but they were on the other side of the world. That was an oil tanker outside, heading straight for me. Ashes to ashes, dust to dust. The End.

I remember closing my eyes and waiting for impact. The tanker would crush us as an elephant crushes an ant. It would not even feel me, would not even know I was there. I waited, and waited.

Perhaps twenty seconds passed. I continued to sit perfectly motionless, but nothing seemed to happen and nothing seemed to move. Was this heaven? Where was I now? Had death been so quick and easy? I opened my eyes, turned to my right and saw the parrot, teddy bear and fluffy yellow duck still perched happily on the white plastic EPIRB case.

This was life, my life.

I scrambled to look outside the hatch once again, and saw metal rush by at speed, all brute power, no more than ten tiny yards from my boat. The tanker was flashing past. In a final moment of panic, I thought I was going to be chewed by the propellers, but these hurtled by as well.

And the ocean calmed and, within a minute, I was sitting stunned and silent in my boat, watching the spectacular super-structure at the back of the tanker, soaring into the sky and lit like a Christmas tree as it powered into the darkness. At last, the deafening rumbling of the engine began to subside and the pungent smell of diesel fumes swamped my nostrils.

I sat and watched, unable to take my eyes off this vast object that had come within a few yards of unwittingly ending my life. I glanced at my watch. It was 03.27, unbelievably only four minutes since I had been woken from my sleep. It had been the most terrifying four minutes of my life. I tried to stand, but my legs turned to jelly. I always thought that phrase was a vacuous cliché, but it isn't. At such times, one's legs do turn to jelly.

In a daze, I tried to contact the captain of the tanker on the radio. There was no response, and I could summon neither the energy nor the will to try again. Within ten minutes, the tanker had disappeared from view, moving towards the horizon at an estimated speed of twenty knots.

After an hour or so, I lurched back to bed and slept fitfully until dawn, suffering the first of many nightmares about oil tankers in the night, with the stench of diesel fumes and the deafening rumble of engines. I didn't really know how to feel or what to do. I didn't know whether I should be happy or sad,

217

jubilant or humbled. I didn't know. Nothing seemed simple any more.

The days that followed remain a blur and it was not until the following weekend that I finally began to accept what had happened, started to discuss my fortunate escape with Jane and the girls, and somehow moved on with the task of finishing the voyage and reaching Australia.

Looking back, I believe I was saved by the tanker's bow wave, which carried my boat sideways away from the tanker, miraculously easing it clear at the waterline, so ensuring metal never touched wood. Almost implausibly, I had been spirited away from within touching distance of disaster without a drop of water landing either anywhere on me or anywhere on my boat.

I had dealt with danger, and I suppose danger had dealt with me.

II

The End in Sight

My voyage appeared to have come full circle. I had started out from Ilo, Peru, with a strong mind and a wilting body. Nine months and a day later, I was approaching Australia with a strong body but a wilting mind.

During the planning stage of the trip, I had expressed the probably fond hope that, somewhere on the Pacific, I would find the elixir of eternal youth and emerge from this journey physically transformed. The management consultant struggling to contain his weight would disappear into the dark blue ocean and emerge many months later miraculously looking as though he had recaptured the lean, muscular shape of his early twenties.

That was the bold intention and now, with less than 500 miles out of more than 10,000 left to row, I examined myself and decided that, if I had not quite managed to rediscover my early twenties, my general state of health was certainly closer to what it had been in my early forties than it was before my departure.

The worn-down hip, which was due for a replacement operation before I left London, had eased remarkably during the voyage, and only started to ache if I happened to row too long. Otherwise, a variety of irritating aches and ailments had cleared up, and I was feeling extremely well. The gut had taken its leave to be replaced by a strong chest and legs.

'Ocean rowing cures everything,' I had said many times before the Pacific crossing and have repeated many times since. It really does and I would happily submit myself as the living proof.

Unexpectedly, my psychological state had started to become more and more fragile as I approached the final lap of my marathon adventure. Perhaps it was the realisation that I was actually going to complete the voyage. It was true that I had always been extremely confident of success, but absolute knowledge is several steps down the line from confidence, and the thought of being reunited with Jane and the girls, and of getting back home to England, was starting to overwhelm my senses.

There were times when I would not be thinking of anything particular, when I would maybe be cooking or rowing, and I would suddenly recall small things at home, tiny mannerisms or sayings that I had always taken for granted in various members of our family, but which I now missed so badly. And, involuntarily, I would find my eyes welling with tears and a lump appearing in my throat. I was becoming emotional!

Emotional? Unthinkable! Before crossing the Pacific, I would maybe have shed a tear during a really good movie, but crying tended to be something I didn't really do. That all changed.

One evening, I found myself in tears while listening to *Desert Island Discs* on the BBC World Service. My emotions, and tear ducts, seem to have been triggered when Sue Lawley's guest started choosing exactly the sort of music that my father used to enjoy so much; and, as the old songs rippled out from my radio across the ocean, my mind drifted back to childhood evenings when the entire family would gather in the living room and listen to *Family Favourites* on the radio.

So I sat and wept, thinking about my old man and his values. The ocean affords you time and space and, on this occasion, I was using both to wallow in happy memories that I had started to forget.

And even the natural elements, so often my rain-lashing, wind-pounding opponents, played along with my mood, providing one of the most stunning and beautiful evenings of the entire voyage. Thousands of stars shone down from a purple sky draped with the most extravagant vast cloud formations, reaching from horizon to horizon. The ocean lay still and content, perhaps enjoying the view. My incessantly hyperactive friends, the yellow-fin tuna, swam contentedly to and fro.

In this almost flawless place, I sat and listened to the music while my emotions unravelled. I felt wonderfully at peace, and there have been far too few moments in my life when I have been able to say that.

As ever, I was slipping effortlessly between the psychological plane and the hard, practical, logistical challenge, and Sue Lawley's gentle goodbye snapped me back to the increasingly tiresome task of getting my boat to Australia.

I had heard weather gurus on both Australian and New Zealand radio appearing on talk shows and admitting they had no coherent explanation for the astonishing lack of wind in the South Pacific during the first three months of 2001. There had never been such a hot, sweaty and sticky start to the year since records began. It was easy to imagine housewives in Double Bay and Auckland nodding their beaded brows in agreement but, to be honest, this freakish weather was starting to drive me to complete despair.

Around Christmas, I had looked at the plotter and confidently predicted I would finish at the end of January. Midway through January, I studied the plotter again and revised my time of arrival to the end of February. Up until the end of February, it had seemed inconceivable that I would miss Jane's birthday on 21 March, but that also became a reality. Now, it was the middle of March, and I was still some 400 miles away.

I had drifted both forwards and backwards, spending endless days in the cabin sheltering from a blistering sun and occasionally dashing out to check the plotter. If it indicated we were drifting east, I would spin out the sea anchor to reduce our pace back towards Peru. Thirty minutes later, I would take another look at the plotter, see we were now moving west and frantically pull the sea anchor back in so it would not affect our progress.

The sea anchor is essentially an underwater parachute, ten feet in diameter, dragged 150 yards behind the boat and primarily used to check movement in the wrong direction. During these long, hot summer days, the sea anchor had needed to be put out, then pulled in, then put out again, interminably. It was not uncommon for the wind and current to change direction every hour; and, I admit, it was not uncommon for me to lose my temper.

Just as I had become intensely frustrated during the opening two months of the voyage when grey, overcast and windless conditions prompted a severe lack of power, so the frustratingly windless conditions in the closing months were putting pressure on the solar panel to generate all the energy. Power had scarcely been an issue through the bulk of the trip, but it occupied my mind through the opening and closing stages.

I sensed everything was becoming complicated. I wanted the sun to shine because I needed the power but, if the sun did shine, then it was invariably too hot to row, and we would not make progress towards Australia. So every time I seemed to be winning, I was also losing. This irritating paradox summed up my general sense of exasperation.

And the sun did shine throughout the southern hemisphere summer but the constant lack of wind meant the power supplies were never better than fragile, and three or four successive days of grey, overcast conditions were all that was needed to prompt another power shortage.

Back at the start of the voyage, I had introduced power-saving measures such as hand-pumping the water maker and shutting down the Orbcomm satellite transceivers. Now those days had returned and I would once again find myself spending hours sitting and staring as the LEDs on the battery regulator, as the two batteries sagged towards the red light and 10.5 volts.

That was the bare minimum. When I reached 11 volts on the first battery, everything would shut down except the indispensable plotter. When it reached 10.5 volts even the plotter would switch itself off! My general strategy was always to keep one battery above 11.5 volts, enabling me to run down the other, safe in the knowledge that I had enough to make a telephone call in an emergency and keep the plotter running, or at least switch the plotter on whenever I wished to know my precise position and course.

I did not enjoy the sporadic power shortages, but they did serve as an indicator of how far I had progressed during the voyage. Perhaps it was inevitable that challenges that may have seemed daunting in July and August 2000 were beginning to appear manageable in February and March 2001, but I was encouraged by my increased capacity to solve problems.

When I first left Peru, a total loss of power had looked like a voyage-ending disaster but, towards the end, there was no doubt in my mind that we would be able to improvise without power and still reach Australia.

The most dangerous consequence of a complete power failure would be that the plotter ceased to function. Five of the six GPS satellite systems had already packed up by this late stage of the trip – some had never seemed particularly effective from the start, others had failed during the crossing – and this perilous state of affairs increased the pressure on the plotter.

If it did happen to fail, the danger was that I would be left drifting around the ocean with only a vague idea of in what direction and at what speed I was moving. In fact, even this extreme situation had been envisaged and I had put in place a Plan B to deal with a total electronics failure.

Two months before my departure, my sister Jan had noticed a magazine article about a Swedish man named Bris, who had invented a sextant so compact it could fit into a 35mm film container. Jan had taken the initiative of writing to this inventor, explaining what her brother was planning to do, and two weeks later one of these Bris sextants duly arrived in the post.

It was a remarkable piece of equipment, three pieces of plastic glued together forming a prism. In simple terms, the sextant enabled the user to calculate his or her longitude by holding the plastic prisms to the sun and timing the refracted suns dipping into the ocean. I managed to calibrate the Bris sextant but there was never any need to put it into the front line of my navigational artillery

And there was even a Plan C. If I couldn't get the sextant to work, I was confident of being able to reach Australia simply by using the magnetic compass to ensure I was constantly heading west. And, if the compass broke, there was even a Plan D: row towards the setting sun. Whatever happened, after almost nine months of trials and tribulations, I was going to reach Australia. I would not be denied.

If the lack of power was a nuisance, then it was no less frustrating to finish another long day's rowing by glancing at the plotter and discovering we had progressed only a few miles in a westerly direction. Day after day, I found myself virtually becalmed or, worse still, being driven back eastwards. It is hard to describe the frustration of being made to suffer such mind-numbing days of going nowhere after I had endured so much, when I so badly wanted to finish the trip, see my wife and children and get home to see my dog.

The result was more of the kind of dramatic mood swings that characterised earlier stages of the tour. If we were moving forwards at a reasonable pace, I would be animated and positive. If we were standing still, I would reach for my long-suffering confidant, the mini-disc recorder, and give vent to my innermost feelings and dissatisfaction.

'I am not looking forward to the next few weeks, but there is nothing to do but row,' I told the small machine on 10 March 2001, which turned out to be just twenty days away from Australia. 'I am going nowhere. I am not depressed, but I don't think I will ever get there. I have had no wind at all for three days, and I am now going backwards. If somebody somewhere thinks this is a big joke, I want them to know I don't think it is funny.'

Such despair was often soon blown away by a strong wind that would appear from nowhere and send the boat cresting westward.

On 12 March, I addressed the mini-disc recorder again: 'This is marvellous. At this rate, we will travel over eighty miles in a day. I could not ask for any more. The sea is huge and lumpy, and waves often break over the deck and drench me. Rowing is hard work, but I really don't mind because the plotter says we are now moving west at speeds of up to 4.2 knots and the battery indicator is moving into green! This makes me very happy.'

And, just as night followed day, despair followed joy. On 14 March, I pushed the record button on the recorder and let fly: 'I am as sick as a parrot,' I grumbled as the boat drifted east. 'I am totally, completely and utterly irritated. There are five different swells in the sea today, and the combined effect is that the water works like a corkscrew. We have been going in circles all day. I want to give up. I am going insane.'

Never mind. I need not have worried. There was always another day, 15 March to be precise, and I was back at the microphone, relating: 'I woke to discover a firm breeze moving me south-west. The cabin is soaking wet again, but I laid out the sleeping bag to dry with a smile on my face because we are making good progress. If I was offered steady winds in return for being drenched in the middle of every night, I would take the deal.'

Such swings and roundabouts proved mentally exhausting and I began to look for words of encouragement, just to keep me going in these last days, just to keep me pushing ever onwards to Australia.

The Magellan CSM100, which I had included as my 'emergency' communications and GPS system, incorporated a facility whereby it should have been able to send and receive short e-mails. The sending function worked for a reasonable period of time, but the brick-shaped piece of equipment managed to download only two messages during the entire voyage. These arrived freakishly one day in November when I happened to leave the Magellan out on deck in the hope of sending a couple of messages when the satellite passed overhead.

However, if I could have chosen to receive only two e-mails during nine months alone at sea, it would probably have been these two brief gems sent by Pat Waggaman, my new friend in Chile. I received them in November, but was still gaining courage from them four months later.

First, Pat wrote: 'The virtues and vices of land grow closer. Apparently you've hung onto enough sanity to appreciate them both. Keep fighting, you're pushing the Moitessier limits.' Second, he wrote: 'If Cape Horners are hunched over from pushing the barrow to transport their oversized balls, where in hell do we find the personal dump truck for you, my friend?'

Pat, of course, was a Cape Horner himself, having sailed around that notorious part of the world, and his compliment meant a great deal to me. Keep fighting, he had urged; that was my firm intention.

Ever since the day I decided I would cross the Pacific in a rowing boat, I have always been tremendously moved by any expression of support and encouragement. Perhaps this was because so many people thought I was mad. I don't know. But it just seemed to strike such a sweet chord when someone said something positive. Pat had written two positive messages in November, managed to get them through to me, and I am sure I will never forget them.

As this 'six-month' voyage moved into its ninth month, I became ever more grateful for my safety-first decision to take enough food for eight months at sea. In the event, some disciplined rationing towards the end meant I could have actually stretched these supplies for another three weeks if necessary.

Having paid myself that compliment, I have to confess that the quality of the menu aboard *Le Shark* did start to decline alarmingly.

I savoured my very last sip of Ribena on 6 February, first smelling the fragrance, then taking the final sip, splashing it against my palate and rolling it around my mouth as though it was the finest French wine. As the last hint of blackcurrant disappeared from my mouth, I courageously faced up to the prospect of almost eight weeks of drinking only water.

Eight days later, on 14 February, I bade an equally sad farewell to warm food as the third of the three petrol-fuelled stoves aboard finally packed up and shuffled off to the big kitchen in the sky. I was left with the miserable prospect of eating cold food until I reached Australia.

'Stay calm,' I told myself yet again, 'be practical.'

I took a quick stock check of the food compartment and discovered enough pre-cooked main meals to last until the middle of March, five more packets of powdered soup, one more packet of biscuits from Peru and what seemed a reasonable quantity of porridge.

Ever the optimist, I spent the next few days trying to persuade myself that, despite all evidence to the contrary, including sporadic retching, porridge oats mixed with water and then left for three hours in the warm summer sun is actually an acquired and substantially underrated taste.

Trying to be a pioneer by becoming the first man to cross the Pacific in a rowing boat, solo and unaided, was one thing. Having to become a culinary pioneer in the area of cold-water cooking was quite another. Yet there was no option if I wanted to keep eating, so I tried my best.

I had been sending brief messages for posting on my website at various stages of the voyage and I decided to use this method in an attempt to disseminate my discoveries to a wider global audience . . . of course, based on the assumption that a wider global audience was interested (I needed to stay motivated, and a lively imagination was often required).

'Tomato soup made with cold water is not like gazpacho but at least the croutons stay crunchy!' I wrote on 23 February. Later on the same day, I added: 'Pasta soaked in cold seawater for two hours is not too bad. If the same applies to noodles I could stay out here till Xmas!'

Of course, the pre-cooked meals were supplied on the basis

that they would be warmed before consumption. Following these instructions for eight months, I had enjoyed these meals tremendously; but now I would have to eat them cold and each dish would be a new experience.

Chicken tikka masala, of course, still tasted magnificent, but the same could not truthfully be said of the chicken and herb dumplings. Eaten cold, this normally delicious and filling dish managed to leave a nauseating coating of grease around the inside of my mouth. In fact, it is making me feel ill again just to mention it in print.

However, I was always going to be better fed than dead, and the two months of strict rationing towards the end of the journey played a significant role in enabling me to emerge from the surf with an impressive, slimmed-down, one hundred and ninety-three-pound frame. I was naturally delighted to attribute the cumulative forty-nine-pound weight loss during the trip to the result of hours and hours of rowing, but it also had something to do with the enforced diet.

My game efforts to make the cold-water cooking seem fun were only going to last so long and, by the end of February, my enthusiasm for this daily diet of stone-cold gruel and crunchy midnight feasts of dry spaghetti had started to fade. The only impetus for eating was to maintain my energy levels and I felt relieved if I could cobble together three meals that were not too large and could be swallowed quickly. Almost everything had started to assume the status of a vile, but necessary, medicine.

I was rescued from this progressively depressing daily ordeal by a series of unexpected discoveries, where I happened to stumble upon edible food in a long-forgotten and unchecked compartment. These timely boosts helped to sustain me through the last month of the voyage.

First, there was a consignment of additional breakfast meals, offering either baked beans and sausage, or baked beans and bacon. On hot days, I would put these meals and some porridge in the pressure cooker and leave it to warm in the sun. I won't say this process produced hot food but, at the very least, it made it easier to scrape all the food out of the packet.

For a week or so, I buzzed along on what seemed like a positively Cordon-Bleu diet of baked beans and bacon for breakfast, baked beans and sausages for lunch and a choice for dinner . . . either baked beans and bacon, or baked beans and sausage. This was the high life. Indeed, through this particular period of the voyage, it would probably have been true to observe there was more wind in the cabin than there was outside.

When the beans ran out, I was left for a couple of days with a staple diet of raw spaghetti. Now I had begun to believe this was an underrated snack for munching through the course of a rowing day, but it did lack a certain *je ne sais quoi* when served repeatedly as a main dish.

Relief arrived in the form of a large packet of Smash, accidentally discovered beneath a bundle of clothing. Rarely can a packet of processed and powdered potato have been greeted with such delight.

The Smash helped me through the last week, and saved me from having to rely upon the barely edible substance of last resort, the meal to be eaten when everything else was gone . . . powdered egg and onion.

My relative success in rationing the food persuaded me to try and save some money by cutting back on the number of satellite telephone calls home that I was making during the last weeks of the voyage. However, in this area, where it seemed so easy and initially painless (the bill came later) to speak to my family, my enthusiasm usually got the better of me.

In any case, I needed to be in contact to discuss the plans for Jane, Anna and Sarah to fly to Australia and meet me when I arrived. This was fast turning into a highly complex and anguished procedure because the unreliable winds made it impossible for me to predict my actual date of arrival, and both the girls were due to sit exams at Bristol University.

Jane and I had already reached a decision that, come what

may, the entire family would travel to Australia. Money was tight and, by the end of February, we had still not been able to confirm that anyone would pay for the flights, but we recognised this was going to be a one-off. So we made the commitment to travel, and then tried to confirm the pledge, tentatively offered by Le Shark, to pay for the family's flights and accommodation.

Anna, my daughter, decided to take a proactive approach to the issue, contacting a series of British media organisations to tell them how her father was crossing the Pacific in a rowing boat and offering them the inside track on the story in return for three airfares to Australia, four back and a week in a hotel for everybody. It seemed like a great deal to me.

However, the *Daily Express* alone responded and they only seemed to be interested in a brief story. Anna arranged to have lunch with the journalist, who would interview me by telephone during their meal.

We were getting nowhere, and we needed a break. It came through a pure coincidence when one of the girls' lacrosse team-mates happened to ask whether she was related to the Shekhdar who was rowing across the Pacific, because it transpired that her father had been asked to print T-shirts for the voyage. Not for the first time in our lives, we reaped a dividend from having one of the less common surnames in England.

That lacrosse father let me have the mobile number for Eddie Kohn, managing director of Le Shark, a big man with the kind of infectious enthusiasm to get anything done. I called Eddie from my boat on the Pacific and was delighted by his clear intention to follow through the pledge that had been tentatively made eight months before through a third party.

Eddie put together a generous sponsorship package in conjunction with British Home Stores, one of Le Shark's main retail outlets; the air tickets were purchased and hotel reservations made, not only for the three girls but also for my sister, Jan, and for Nigel Rutter, video editor extraordinaire. I was enormously grateful to Eddie, to Le Shark and to BHS, and relieved to have resolved an issue that was beginning to distract me from my task on the boat.

As the voyage drew to a successful conclusion, small pockets of media interest were starting to emerge and I hoped some of this attention would rub off positively on a charity to which I had made a commitment during the closing stages of the voyage. Saving Faces is an organisation run by Iain Hutchison, a former water polo team-mate turned consultant surgeon, which supports people who have endured major operations to their face or head. By establishing a clear association between my voyage and Saving Faces, I hoped to spread and propagate the benefits.

Eddie had enlisted a public relations company to stir up some interest and I started giving radio interviews from the boat, one to the ABC in Australia and one to BBC Radio Five Live at home. This hardly constituted a media stampede but it was a great improvement on the line of blank faces that had so depressed and discouraged me during the months before my departure.

In any case, I had long since accepted that my trip was never going to be a major attraction to anyone beyond my extended family and close friends. You can only knock on so many doors and be rejected before you start to think no one will ever support you. So I was not going to be remotely disheartened by media apathy upon the completion of my voyage, because I had already accepted it as a fact of life many months earlier.

One day, a week before I reached Australia, Radio Five Live telephoned me for a second interview. I eagerly agreed (only after checking my diary!), and the BBC person said he would phone back later. Well, I suppose some other more important news story broke that afternoon, and I understand that plans do change in live broadcasting, but the fact is that I spent three hours with the satellite phone switched on, soaking up valuable battery power, while I was waiting for the Five Live call that never came.

I didn't mind media apathy as a rule, but I was irritated by media apathy when it wasted so much precious power that I would not be able to switch on the navigation light for the remainder of that night.

But it didn't really matter. I was looking forward to finishing the voyage primarily because I wanted to be reunited with my family and friends. I had not the slightest inkling, expectation, or even hope, that there would be anything more than the most marginal media interest, maybe a paragraph on page 11 and a piece on the local TV news. The issue was dead.

I was far more interested in arranging a safe landing on an Australian beach or perhaps at a jetty on a river mouth. That old maxim – 'The hardest parts of crossing oceans are the start and the finish' – reverberated around my head. I had travelled so far and worked so hard that I was resolved to get the planning right for this last stage, to make no mistakes.

Nigel Clutterbuck, one of my oldest college friends, came strongly to the fore as a pillar of support and practical help during this crucial time.

First, he had helped Jane celebrate her birthday during March, going some way to filling the gap caused by my prolonged absence by meeting Jane and the girls for dinner at a restaurant in Bristol. Sarah had already secured permission to use my credit card for the occasion.

Then, he applied himself to the task of providing me with what I most needed during the last few miles of the voyage: some kind of protection from vessels powering up and down the busy shipping lanes running down the east coast of Australia. The memory of my night-time encounter with an oil tanker was still fresh in my mind and I suppose I had developed a serious paranoia about experiencing any more close shaves with ships. This hedgehog had had enough. He wanted a guarantee of safe passage.

Nigel used the Internet to establish contact with the headquarters of the Australian National Coastguard, based in Canberra, and was able to give me not only the telephone number but also the name of the person whom he had fully briefed and whom he was plying with regular e-mail, giving updates of my progress. He also contacted the Queensland Weather Bureau, which undertook to provide me with a rolling seven-day forecast, of which the first two days would be confidently forecast and the next five predicted. This information enabled me to calculate where and when I was likely to land.

Nigel's incredibly diligent legwork proved absolutely invaluable, and it was a tremendous bonus for me to be able to telephone the Australian Coastguard in Canberra and to be told by the voice on the other end of the line that they had been expecting my call for some time.

I was further amazed and encouraged when, after my call to them at about 16.30, at 18.45 the same day a fixed-wing coastguard plane appeared overhead in the failing light of dusk. He had been sent to check my position and condition.

'Hello, Jim Shekhdar?' It was the pilot, speaking on the radio as he circled above me for a second time.

'Hi! How did you know it was me? You found me pretty quick. These GPS things must work!'

'Jim, what are you wearing, mate?'

'The normal . . . sunhat and sunglasses.'

'Would you mind putting some clothes on because our regulations require us to film our contacts on these search missions?'

I was happy, no absolutely thrilled, to oblige. This first visible contact with Australian officialdom represented the beginning of the end. I was starting to get excited. It was all going to be over before too long.

In my first conversation with the coastguard, I had outlined my apprehension about crossing the shipping lanes. I now further explained I was essentially invisible because my radar reflector was effectively useless and my power reserves had become so low that I was unable to keep the navigation lights on at night.

The coastguard could not have been more sympathetic and

we agreed a daily routine whereby I would contact them at 18.00 every evening and give my exact position, course and speed. They would then issue an emergency bulletin to all shipping in the area, warning them to stay clear.

I felt tremendously grateful for this level of attention, and also a little self-conscious that such a slow-moving, invisible rowing boat should have become the centre of attention for so many merchant ships and coastguard stations along the coast of New South Wales and Queensland.

Without exception, the Australians on the other end of the telephone line could not have been more enthusiastic, supportive and capable. Indeed, if I could have chosen any country in the world as my destination for such a trip, I would have chosen Australia. The people are go-getters, up for anything and everything. It's as simple as that. They have tremendous spirit.

Nigel Clutterbuck was not finished. He had also gone to the trouble of contacting the three main television stations in Australia – Channel Seven, Channel Nine and Channel Ten – establishing contact people, bringing them up to date with the story so far and giving regular updates.

His efforts triggered a chase as the three channels competed to adorn their nightly news bulletin with the first video pictures of the 'mad Englishman' on the brink of completing his Pacific crossing. Their interest was surprising and tremendously encouraging. Nigel and Le Shark's PR company had evidently sparked some kind of media blaze. My long, long months of quiet solitude were coming to an end.

As soon as I came within flying range of the shore, I was several times caught unawares by the sudden arrival of a helicopter in the air above me. It was clearly time to start wearing clothes again.

By 27 March, three days before my eventual date of arrival, I seemed to be spending most of my time on the telephone. Media organisations, mostly from Australia, were calling me for progress reports and interviews; and I was calling coastguards and Brownie, the radio show host and coastal expert, for the best advice on how and where to execute a safe landing.

I was also telephoning Jane and the girls incessantly, finding out if they had arrived in Brisbane, checking their hotel was satisfactory, just letting them know I was all right and keeping them up to date with my progress. At times, I sensed they thought I was maybe calling just a little too often.

But I was excited. The last three months of the voyage had dragged on interminably, and I was exhilarated by the prospect of setting foot on dry land again. I was hardly sleeping at night. I didn't want to sit still. I wanted to row, to phone someone, call someone, do something, stay busy, do whatever I could to bring ever closer that moment when I could say: 'I did it.'

Immediately after arriving at Brisbane airport from London, Anna had eagerly accepted an invitation from Channel Seven to fly down the coast in their helicopter and then board Air-Sea Rescue's Sea King helicopter and come out to sea to find me, and maybe even talk on the VHF radio.

The Sea King was at the limit of its range but, during the five minutes they were able to hover over my boat, Anna and I waved, shouted and generally jumped around but we seemed unable to make radio contact. I was exhilarated to have seen my daughter again, albeit hanging out of the door of the Sea King, but was disappointed not to have spoken to her.

Then, as the Sea King headed back to shore, her voice suddenly came over the radio loud and clear. It transpired that I had been monitoring Channel 16, the usual VHF shipping frequency, but the helicopter had been monitoring Channel 6, normal for air-sea rescue. It was only the pilot's impulsive decision to try Channel 16 on the way home that enabled me to greet Anna and tell her everything was fine and that I couldn't wait to be there.

Jane, Sarah, and Anna were flown out to see me in a fixed-wing aircraft the next day. They flew for an hour, struggled to locate me and then spent approximately fifteen minutes circling overhead. I looked up and could see some faces in the windows of the plane but, in truth, it was hard to distinguish one person from another. We spoke on the radio.

'Keep rowing, Dad,' Sarah urged. 'Just keep rowing, Dad.'

After so long away from home, it was wonderful for me to sense them being so close. For no good reason other than that I was starting to feel very happy indeed, I started to sing out loud: 'Row, row, row your boat, gently to the shore. Merrily, merrily, merrily . . . life is but a dream.'

I was almost there. I was almost there. I had done it. I had done it. I was filling up inside. I had been so far, and now I was almost there.

Jane told me later how she and the girls had been absolutely horrified by how tiny my boat seemed in relation to the vast ocean. They had flown for an hour and then spent another fifteen minutes trying to find me. In spite of all our telephone conversations, they had had to see me rowing for themselves to appreciate the full scale of what I had undertaken.

As their airplane returned to Brisbane, I watched it become a speck in the blue sky and then disappear altogether. I was left on my own again and it felt strangely good. Obviously, I was desperate to complete the voyage, but I was also becoming concerned by what lay ahead.

Within the parameters of my emotional highs and lows, I had enjoyed nine months of solitude. I had led a simple life, without having to worry about any other person. Of course it had been an utterly selfish existence but, for long periods, it had suited me. Now I just wanted to be with my family, and I wanted to find the time and space to be alone with them. I worried whether this would be possible within the gathering media circus.

We would see. There was no turning back.

After extensive debate and constant reorganisation of plans, it had ultimately been agreed that I would land at North Stradbroke Island, an island separated by less than 100 yards of water from South Straddie, which was separated from the mainland by a further seventy-five yards of water. These were technicalities and the unanimous consensus of my soundings was that 'Straddie' counted as mainland Australia. This was important for me because I had set myself to row from continent to continent. I wanted to have done that.

The day when I would reach my destination, 30 March 2001, dawned slightly overcast. After managing to sleep for barely two hours, I woke and stood on the deck, thrilled, at last, to see the coast of Australia. There it was, my destination. Everything was happening so quickly.

My plotter, unbreakable and reliable to the last, showed I was still eleven miles from shore and I began to fret that the onshore current was not moving me swiftly enough to reach the beach in daylight. So I sat down in the rowing seat, slipped my feet into the straps one more time and started to pull at the oars, just to make sure I reached Straddie before dusk.

The circumstances of my arrival are described in Chapter One. Suffice it to add here that I still find it difficult to speak about the sheer, unadulterated joy of that moment when my family met me in the surf. I may be speaking at a function in front of several hundred people but, when I reach that stage of the story, something prevents the words coming out. I choke.

It is not easy for me to offer an explanation: part of the reason could lie in my sheer relief at having completed the voyage. For all the bravado that is part of my nature, I knew it had been a massive challenge and I realised I had come perilously close to the precipice several times.

But I had made it. I had made it, alone and unaided. In a sense, I had rolled the dice and won. Maybe it is the thought of what would have happened if I had gambled and lost that overwhelms me when I talk about those memorable scenes on the beach at 'Straddie' . . . that time when I staggered to the beach, Sarah under one arm, Anna under the other, Jane at my side.

We discovered a state of happy chaos on the beach. I recall

looking around and finding it hard to believe so many television crews, helicopters, four-wheel drive vehicles and journalists had come to see me arrive, quite apart from most of the inhabitants of North Stradbroke Island.

I tried to be as obliging as possible as I walked from one interview to the next, summing up the voyage with a broad smile and a bit of bluster.

'Oh, it was not too bad,' I told every microphone thrust in my direction. 'There were a few storms, shark attacks and a close encounter with a tanker but, apart from that, no real problems. It was a lot of fun.'

Officials from the customs department and the Ministry of Agriculture were on hand to inspect the boat, clear out any remaining food and stamp my passport, yet these were officials only in name. They could not have been more friendly and obliging. Like everybody else, including me, they seemed just happy to be part of an emphatically happy occasion.

The crowds eventually dispersed. It had been arranged that our family would be flown to the centre of Brisbane in the Channel Seven helicopter, but the helicopter had already left, rushing footage of my spectacular capsize and arrival to the studio so it could be broadcast on the *Six O'Clock News*. So we waited on the beach for the helicopter to return and collect us.

The adrenalin was still surging through my body, and I seemed quite talkative, wanting to hear all the news, just taking so much pleasure in looking into the faces of these people who meant so much to me.

After thirty minutes or so, the helicopter returned and we were whisked to a helipad at the Channel Seven studios. Upon arrival, I was asked if I would mind going straight in to be interviewed live on a prime-time current affairs TV programme. I instantly agreed because various representatives of Channel Seven had been so helpful to me and my family throughout.

More interviews followed, with people asking all the same

questions and me giving all the same answers, and, somehow, I kept going. If I sit down and watch the video footage now, I find it hard to believe I could have looked so bright and breezy when I was actually feeling so completely exhausted. I suppose that is the magical power of adrenalin.

It was almost half past eight at night, four hours after I landed, when we eventually arrived at the Brisbane Hilton. The hotel management had laid on a reception in the foyer, serving champagne and an ice cream sundae. Again, I was overwhelmed by everybody's kindness and enthusiasm.

I was genuinely gobsmacked. After so much apathy before and during the voyage, I was being swamped by good wishes.

Jane and I left after half an hour or so, and retreated to our hotel room. For the first time in several hours, I was able to sit down and think. Events had passed in a blur. I wanted to slow everything down, to appreciate things more, but that was not possible. You simply have to go with the flow.

My first shower in nine months felt magnificent. I had almost forgotten the sensation of warm water cascading on my head and down my back, and I stood there for at least fifteen minutes, relishing the smell of shampoo and soap, relishing the sensation of being completely clean again.

We returned downstairs for dinner and I completely failed in trying not to overdo the rich food. After six weeks of raw spaghetti and cold porridge, I was not going to hold back. Oysters arrived as a starter, followed by a huge steak with mushrooms and chips, with chocolate cake to finish. I drank a few beers and a bottle of wine, and thoroughly enjoyed the company of my family.

Jane and I finally got to bed at four o'clock in the morning and, so far as readers of the *News of the World* are aware, that is where the fun started. I suspect I was responsible for the newspaper's misunderstanding.

During an interview on the beach, I had flippantly remarked: 'Jane had better not have a headache tonight.' This joke had been taken literally, and the popular Sunday newspaper subsequently reported that I had returned to the Brisbane hotel to 'spend a passionate night with my wife'.

In fact, we were both exhausted. I was probably asleep before my head hit the pillow. I clearly recall the moment when I collapsed on that soft mattress. If felt wonderful. It didn't hurt my elbows. I didn't have to wedge one foot against the wall and the other against the door. There was no rocking motion.

I felt absolutely content, and slept soundly with, in the words of Winston Churchill, no need for cheering dreams. Facts are better than dreams.

12
Coping, Learning, Moving On

Within hours of emerging from the surf at North Stradbroke Island, I found myself transported into a world that I had never imagined.

In some senses, I felt like a lottery winner: an ordinary person who had been plucked from a familiar life and put on public display. I suppose it could be said the difference was that I had earned, not guessed, the winning numbers, but it did feel strange. All of a sudden, television programmes that you have sat and watched are suddenly on the telephone asking you to appear on them.

Through this dizzy whirl of appointments and appearances that began in Australia and continued when we got home to England, I found it hard to find the time and space I wanted to reflect on the voyage and what effect it had had on me, both as an individual and in the way I deal with others.

There would be time for this important analysis in due course but, through most of April and May 2001, I flitted across the public gaze. There were set-piece interviews, chat shows and appearances at awards functions; people would look at this white-haired man with the white beard and, I suppose, see some kind of eccentric Briton who had accomplished a rare feat.

In all this activity, there was an element of the freak show. It seemed to me that the media is challenged to entertain us, the people. They must fill acres of space in newspapers and magazines, and hours of time on literally hundreds of television and radio stations; and they not only need to fasten upon 'stories' like mine, but they also have to extract the 'story' in only a few minutes because we, the people, are busy and much prefer to be entertained in short, punchy, sometimes inevitably superficial packages.

So I found myself thrust aboard the conveyor belt: *businessman seeking excitement ... first man to cross the Pacific in a rowing boat ... why did you do it ... to get away from the wife* (ha ha) *... shark attacks ... forgot a can-opener ... what's happened since I have been away ... nearly run over by an oil tanker ... did you ever think you would not make it ... what's the next trip ...*

Each interview and each conversation seemed to follow the same route, casting me as a classic eccentric explorer in the British tradition. Everyone must fit in a box with a clearly marked label; and this was my label.

I did not mind and, in fact, many people were extremely kind throughout this process. With very few exceptions, I enjoyed myself tremendously, met many interesting people and, I think, generally survived.

This is Your Life was quick off the mark. I was in the middle of a thank you speech for a presentation by British Home Stores, one of my sponsors, when Michael Aspel crept up on me with the famous large red book. Jane and the girls had managed to keep the secret effectively, and I was amazed to be whisked to a television studio filled by many friends and acquaintances.

Michael Aspel could not have been more amiable, setting us all at ease, and I enjoyed the show. Mrs Jelfs, who had been so kind to me in my youth, emerged as the surprise appearance at the end of the programme, and she showed her mettle afterwards when she was, again, the last to leave the pub.

I was interested by the procedures of the show. One of my old university friends was brought from behind the screens, and he told a story that meant a lot to him and me, but not much to anyone else. So that element was simply cut and he did not appear in the broadcast of the final edited tape.

Perhaps Tim Sebastian, host of *Hard Talk*, a thirty-minute one-on-one interview broadcast on BBC World, provided the

most rigorous interview. He had evidently done his home-
work, with the result that I enjoyed our conversation and the
broadcast because there is so little editing and less chance of
distortion.

Richard and Judy, then on their ITV morning show, took a
more popular tone, and both seemed genuinely decent people
as they interviewed my daughter, Sarah, and me. They asked
what I smelled like when we hugged on the beach, and Sarah
replied: 'Not as good as the next day.'

I was pleased that my family were able to share in this experience, and I was particularly proud of the way Jane and the girls
handled themselves. We had been thrown into this goldfish bowl,
but we managed to swim.

My notoriety seemed to have reached far and wide, although
I was amazed when the people from *The Tonight Show* with
Jay Leno, one of the most popular television chat shows in the
United States, wanted to fly us across to Los Angeles for one
five-minute interview. It was an opportunity not to be missed,
so we boarded a plane and performed for America. The angle
was clear: 'Hey, look at this crazy Englishman!' but, once again,
Jay Leno could not have made us more comfortable, and I
enjoyed myself. People laughed. I laughed. It was fun.

There were many other interviews and experiences, all covering most of the same material, repeating the same questions,
but I managed to stay bright and cheerful, and started to bask
in all the attention.

This transient media fame presented other challenges, many
of them financial in nature and complex in substance. I was
suddenly surrounded by people telling me how I should translate
this profile into actual money that could help restore some health
and wealth to my flagging bank account. As I had been saying
almost since I came out of the waves, it's nice to be rich and
famous but the riches are still on their way!

I certainly needed to earn something . . . not because I wanted
to get rich, simply because I needed to try and break even after

an adventure that had cost me £75,000 plus twelve months' lost earnings.

So I needed an agent, somebody with the contacts and time to help me organise the process. As people bombarded me with offers of what they could do for me, I found myself in the awkward position of having to make firm decisions about issues of which I had no knowledge or experience.

Eddie Kohn, from Le Shark, had come out to Australia to meet me, and had a much better idea than I about what was going on and what was about to happen. He emerged as the first 'adviser', and he remains in the background not only as a sponsor, but also as a friend and supporter.

I don't think there is any easy way to deal with this situation, and people like me, who are plucked from obscurity and thrust into the spotlight, usually struggle to adjust to the brightness of our new surroundings. I felt fortunate to have hobnobbed with the glitterati at times through sport and business, and my experience of being a good salesman in one of my past lives equipped me for the glare of the spotlight. I have throughout my working career made quick intuitive judgements about people and situations, and have generally come out more right than wrong, working on the principle that it is better to trust people on sight but only allow them enough rope to do minor damage until I know them better.

So I decided the best way to handle the new situations that arose was to follow my gut instincts, particularly about people. In the past, that didn't mean I got everything 100 per cent right, but I rarely, if ever, got things 100 per cent wrong.

By the middle of May, I was still attending the odd function here and there, still being cast as the 'uniquely British eccentric' and still generally enjoying the opportunity to meet many interesting (and uninteresting) people belonging to the world of celebrities. It's not an original thing to say, but it is incredible how public profiles can be so completely different to the apparent reality.

Soon after arriving home, Eddie and I met Ken Bates, the chairman of Chelsea Football Club, and a man with the general reputation of being a bit of a bruiser. He had contacted me when he happened to hear on an interview in Australia that I was struggling to bring my boat back to England.

Over lunch at a quiet restaurant out of town, he emerged as a personable man with an admirably clear idea of what he wants and how he is going to get it. I liked him and we agreed that my boat, *Le Shark*, would be placed on permanent display as part of 'an exhibition of sporting excellence' at Chelsea Village, the new hotel and entertainment complex built around Chelsea Football Club. What I particularly liked about Ken was that once we reached agreement in principle, that was that. Even though subsequent negotiations dragged on for some time, there was never any doubt, in my mind, of the outcome . . . even without speaking again to 'the chairman'.

Le Shark would have pride of place in the new exhibition hall and I would have 'visiting rights' at any reasonable time. I find it quite natural for some sort of emotional bond to form between a person and an inanimate object in these circumstances, even if the emotions are obviously not reciprocated. However, it gives me great pleasure to know the boat is in a living, sporting environment rather than gathering dust in a museum.

Chelsea World of Sport is to be a living showcase of sporting achievement and challenge, an attraction to London visitors and probably a very busy site, a fitting resting place for that chunk of furniture ply that has served so well over the last five years.

Eventually, the pace of obligations began to settle and I was able to spend more time assessing the voyage and privately coming to terms with the nature of the achievement and the consequent impact on me. Jane was obviously going to be my partner in this challenging, maybe painful, process.

In six words, I was humbled by the Pacific. It was impossible to sit in such a small boat in the middle of such a vast ocean and not feel completely insignificant within the wider scheme of things. I didn't enjoy this feeling and often found myself singing that old Country and Western song out loud:

> Oh, Lord, it's hard to be humble,
> When you're perfect in every way . . .

That might sound arrogant. It wasn't meant to be arrogant. It just seemed the easiest way of convincing myself that I was still worth something, that I was significant. This sense of insignificance might have become a problem. Day after day, I sat there surrounded by waves on all sides, feeling tiny, helpless, at the mercy of the natural elements.

I knew I could withstand the wind because, in attacking me, the wind had only a limited surface to blow against; there again, I understood the wind could always beat me in the end because it could blow me backwards or, worse, onto an island. Equally, I knew a wave would not be able to harm me on its own; there again, I knew a series of waves could keep coming until they eventually capsized my boat and separated me from it.

My position was strangely uncomfortable. On the one hand, I knew I could survive on the Pacific; on the other hand, I understood that the elements had the power to overcome me, if they wanted. The ocean's power is not explosive like lightning, because it is accumulated and spent over a vast area.

Yet this power remains absolutely awesome in the truest sense of the word. Not a day passed when I did not stand in awe of the ocean, its depth, its tremendous power and its latent ability to overwhelm me.

I had expected that crossing the Atlantic in 1997 would change me as a person, but it didn't have much of an impact . . . perhaps because I returned to the same world I had left and didn't give the experience the chance to have an overt long-term effect. In any case, I had never been totally alone.

However, there is no doubt that the Pacific crossing and its aftermath have forced a bigger change on me. I had already spent time contemplating the future, getting back into a routine and changing my business focus, but I also wanted to try to be less abrasive with people close to me and altogether accepting of other people's values for themselves, not trying to impose on them what I thought was right for them. It seems to have made me more mellow, able to recognise another person's point of view even if it is not totally in line with my own, to be more tolerant, perhaps to get closer to people around me.

Jane says that before the voyage I used to walk around with my fists clenched up tight, scowling at the world, always ready to snap. This perception is, I think, a little extreme but I am sure that the spring is not wound so tight now. Perhaps there is no longer any need to prove myself, to myself or anybody else, at least for the time being. I still have a need to be successful in whatever I do, which inclines me to be intolerant of others.

The experience of being made to feel so small and insignificant for such an extended period of time has left me feeling less intense. I can see now that it is not important to win every discussion and always to prevail in every situation. If people are happy to be wrong, why shouldn't they be? In fact, even though their opinion is different to mine, it may have some validity!

I used to see the world in black and white; probably I still do, but now only as an easy starting place in a long process. My months on the Pacific taught me to appreciate the various shades of grey in every scene.

Just as I have learned to be more tolerant of imperfect situations, I have also learned to accept imperfect people and acknowledge that perhaps I am not perfect all the time! I still can't abide anyone who doesn't make a genuine effort either for themselves or for others, but it is easier to appreciate that not everyone is in a position to help themselves. They may need support.

In business, in fact in any walk of life, most people want to be big and feel successful. The Pacific impressed upon me that, whether you are the CEO or the cleaner, we are all tiny within the big picture, and that it is the small, everyday acts of generosity that tend to make the world of difference.

My experience also taught me the value of hard work. A few people reflected many times on what they perceived as the haphazard nature of my preparations, and apparently concluded I was lucky to make it across the Pacific.

Everybody is entitled to his or her view. Of course, there were moments when I enjoyed some good fortune, but there were many, many more occasions when I worked incredibly hard on that boat. In tough times it would have been much easier to despair, but I worked through and got by.

Gary Player, the great South African golfer, once chipped directly into the hole at the eighteenth green to win a tournament by one stroke. He was the fittest golfer around for many years and he worked as hard as anyone on the circuit, in the gym, on the driving range and on the practise green. When a journalist suggested to him afterwards that he had been lucky to take the championship, Player turned on him and said: 'You know, it's very strange. The harder I practise, the luckier I get.' I think I understand his point.

Second, it began to dawn on me that most human beings never realise their full potential because they never push themselves past the first of their limits. It would have been easy for me to sit back in my chair at home in Northwood and conclude that there was no way I could cross the Pacific Ocean in a rowing boat. Instead, I allowed myself to pursue the dream, gradually became committed and did it.

During the crossing, I heard Radio New Zealand International broadcast a story about the athlete Emil Zatopek that seems to illustrate the point. Zatopek had already emerged as a hero of the 1952 Olympic Games in Helsinki, winning the gold medal in the 5,000 yards and the 10,000 yards, but the Czech runner felt so strong that he decided to enter the marathon.

If anyone had asked him before the Games whether he would compete in the twenty-six-mile event, he would probably have laughed off the suggestion. Yet, as the Games unfolded, he started to believe he had miscalculated his limitations. He had won two events and still felt strong, so he decided to enter the marathon. Taking his place at the starting line, he approached an English runner, one of the favourites to win the race.

'I am going to run with you,' Zatopek said. 'I hope you don't mind.'

'If you can keep up, that's fine by me,' came the reply.

Still at the Englishman's side, in the lead at the twenty-mile mark, the Czech turned to his rival and asked if they were not running too slowly. The Englishman is said to have encouraged Zatopek to run faster, hoping he would go too early and blow himself out of contention. In fact, Zatopek proceeded to ease clear away, never looked back and won his third gold medal of the Games.

Only by pushing himself past what he thought was his limit did he start to understand just how much he could achieve.

Third, and lastly, I began to appreciate that age truly is a state of mind. Young people can get sick, just as old people can get sick. Physical illness and disability can prove as restrictive to eighteen-year-olds as for eighty-year-olds. The number of years that have passed since you were born might increase the probability of illness and disability but, in itself, one's age is absolutely irrelevant.

It seems to me that too many people pass their fiftieth birthday and start to behave as though they have been sent to the departure lounge. I was fifty-four when I crossed the Pacific in a rowing boat. My age made no difference. The challenge was the same for me as it would have been for anyone else.

Don Bradman, the revered Australian cricketer, died during the latter stages of my voyage and, among many excellent radio obituaries that I heard, one story referred to this issue of age and struck a chord with me.

Bradman was in discussion with a cricket journalist in Australia later in his life and the reporter asked: 'What do you think your average would have been if you were playing today'?

'Probably between seventy and eighty,' Bradman replied.

'Is that all?' the journalist asked. 'Your Test average was 99.9.'

'Yes,' said Bradman, 'but I'm seventy-two years old now.'

These were some of the tentative conclusions that I reached while crossing the Pacific in a rowing boat. It is human nature that we do tend to forget lessons as quickly as we learn them, but maybe something will stick.

Perhaps the one overriding answer that I would have liked to find out on the ocean remained frustratingly beyond my grasp.

I was baptised and confirmed in the Anglican faith. I attended Sunday school regularly when I was young but I am not a churchgoing Christian and, at this point, I am not able to say what or where I believe 'God' is. I am also not prepared to say I don't believe in God. I don't know. An agnostic was recently appointed to the head of BBC's religious services, and, according to many ordained clergy, he seems to be doing a good job.

I would like to be sure. I frequently think about the issue of faith and religion but all I can say with absolute certainty is that my ongoing internal argument has proved completely and absolutely inconclusive.

Of course, there were occasions out on the ocean when the thought crossed my mind that I should get down on my knees and pray for a fair wind or to be spared from a particularly rough adverse storm.

In those times of despair, when the wind and current were carrying me in the wrong direction, I began to think that there was nothing to lose in praying for relief. If God was there, then he might feel pity and oblige. If God was not there, well, then it was neither here nor there.

Even so, I didn't pray. What was the point? We are taught to believe God is omnipotent and has control of all the elements, so I can't understand why it would have made any difference if I had fallen to my knees and begged him. He knew what I needed. I didn't see the point in telling him something he already knew. If he had wanted to help me, he would surely have helped. Maybe he did help, but in ways and means that I did not recognise as his work.

This is the core of my difficulty with believing in God. The Bible teaches that he is an all-knowing and all-powerful God. If this is so, why doesn't he just kick out evil and allow everybody to be happy? Why does he allow there to be so much suffering in the world?

Above all, why does he allow so many atrocities to be carried out in his name? There have been many examples throughout history and in recent years, when religion has served to hold people together in times of hostility from their neighbours. Yet, these very neighbours are often attacking them in the name of their slightly different religion. Everyone claims to be following the same God, but they're killing each other in his name.

I don't know the answers.

I am not saying there is no God. I am simply asking why he has not taken control and rid this world of evil, pain and suffering.

I am not saying there is no God. It is just that I don't know how to reach him. Maybe that's why I row oceans, just in case he wants to find me. I would not say I go looking for him, but I am not exactly hiding either.

I know there is some kind of overwhelming power out there. I never saw the ocean or the wind as a force in themselves, but as powerful instruments in the hands of some other force. This was the force that, it seemed to me, had decided to allow me to cross the ocean but with the proviso that I should have to suffer now and then along the way. This 'force' seemed to be friendly on some occasions, and hostile at other times.

There were times at night when I was sitting in the middle of the boat and I considered I had found a form of paradise. The sky would be smeared with stars, a cool breeze would gently ripple the water, flying fish would occasionally launch themselves and splash down again, the yellow-fin tuna would be swimming from under the boat, flashing their pearlescent bodies and gaping up at me, and all would be well. And, in moments such as these, I would contemplate the presence of a friendly power, and wonder what more anybody could want . . . except, of course, someone with whom all this perfect peace could be shared.

The only problem was that such ideal conditions existed for only about fifteen minutes every month. Most of the time the ocean was messy and unfriendly, and the winds blew in every direction but the right one. In times like these, it was easy to regard the power as vindictive and malevolent.

Such experiences confirmed me as what I think can best be described as a neo-fatalist. I would define this as somebody who believes in fate. We can't change fate. However – and this is the important point – by our own actions, we can decide how fate will affect us.

For example, a close relative may die. That is fate and you can do nothing about it, but, in that situation, each of us can decide how we will react, whether we will slump into a depression or carry on living our own life, trying at the very least to be useful to others living theirs.

Equally there may be a forty-foot wave heading directly for the boat. There is nothing you can do about that, but you can decide whether to get in the cabin and give yourself the best possible chance of survival or you can do nothing, stay exactly where you are and probably be drowned. That is the choice. The wave is fateful, but you can decide how fate affects you.

Looking forward now, I am sure I will embark upon a new expedition. The experiences of crossing the Atlantic with David Jackson and crossing the Pacific alone encourage me to do more. There are still challenges out there that are achievable before my body and mind become too decrepit. I cannot stop now.

Jane thinks I will keep challenging the natural elements until they kill me, but I feel no compelling need to place myself in danger. If the odds of survival on a prospective trip are unacceptably low, then I simply won't do it. I have much too much to live for. What goads me on, I suppose, is the 'rush' or the 'fix' of finding out precisely what odds are surmountable.

My criteria for future projects are straightforward: I want to do something nobody else has done before. It must also be something worthwhile; I am not really interested in eating more peas than anyone else. It will be something real and meaningful, at least to me, and something that inspires me.

And it will almost certainly involve rowing. Although I would love to race ocean yachts or rally cars, rowing seems the most stimulating activity, because you have to play a role in propelling the boat forward. It seems a more primitive and muscular challenge.

There are drawbacks. When you are crossing an ocean in a rowing boat, you can never feel 100 per cent sure that you will be successful or know when you will finish. These factors will be decided at some point in the future: that's all you are allowed to know. Climbing mountains is altogether different because you are rarely completely alone, you are never too far from help and, if you do happen to get into trouble, the crisis is generally resolved within a few hours . . . or in a few split seconds, if it is resolved the wrong way.

Most projects incorporate various certainties, but when you row across the ocean, nothing seems certain. You simply do not know how far you will travel or in which direction you will travel on any given day. Conditions can change from hour to hour, let alone from day to day. Nothing can ever be taken for granted.

Weather forecasts are generally useless on the ocean because weather conditions can change so dramatically within the space of a few hundred yards in the middle of the ocean. The forecasts are only relevant when you are close to the coast, or when a hurricane is approaching.

During my Pacific voyage, I only listened to weather forecasts when I was leaving Peru, when I was nearing Australia and when Hurricane Paula was heading in my direction. Otherwise, I took no notice of them.

Finally, there have been two huge benefits from the Pacific trip.

I have started to receive letters and e-mail from people who have been inspired by what I have managed to do and who have gone out to do their own 'something'. No matter how small or how big, everybody has their own 'Everest'. It might only be walking 100 yards or it might be walking across Colombia: that doesn't matter. It is tremendously rewarding for me to know that, in some small, distant way, I have somehow inspired people to get out there and do it.

As a result of the publicity received, I have also been reunited with friends from as far back as primary school. I met my ex-next-door neighbour and his best friend from school, and then caught up with one of my first girlfriends.

I had not seen her for thirty-seven years and we met in Bath because that was the only place we could get together on her five-day visit from Canada. When I remarked on her still-lovely hair, she proceeded to lift it off and tell me she had just finished stem cell therapy for lymphatic cancer.

The thought did strike me that we too easily lose our sense of perspective in the modern world. It is these types of people, courageously battling against the odds, who are the true heroes . . . not people who deliberately put themselves in danger and, wittingly or unwittingly, put others at risk in the process.

Safely returned to a life of relative normality, I am now enjoying spending more time with Jane, Anna, Sarah and Munchkin; and I am focused on keeping my consultancy business on track in Eastern Europe, winning new contracts and expanding into new areas, trying to prevent our fantastic team being submerged in the quagmire of the ever-degenerative politicking of the European Union and their aid projects.

I have also formed a one-step-past-normal commercial adventure holidays company called Know Fear to provide the adrenalin rush for people who want it and can responsibly enter the arena. Next year, I hope to set up a thirty-six-hour event with a difference. We have almost decided to call it TEAM 36, standing for Testing Endurance and Mind – thirty-six hours of non-stop challenges, both mental and physical, something akin to existing 'iron man' events like the Eco-challenge and the coast-to-coast race in New Zealand.

Other business ideas have been formulated but I am afraid they won't see the light of day until the day has more than twenty-four hours; although, as Renata Prokova, my colleague at AJS Management in Bratislava, likes to say, 'The day has twenty-four hours and then, if necessary, there is the night.'

In conclusion, I am proud of what I achieved in crossing the Pacific, and, since completing the voyage, I have wearily grown to accept the label of being a 'British eccentric'. However, I wish there was more emphasis on the fact that I am British, and less on the subjective term 'eccentric'.

This voyage was a British 'first'.

It is not part of the national psyche to be boastful and brash, and I certainly do not want to appear either. However, I do sense that modern Britain has lost some energy and confidence, has become so politically correct that we far too easily tolerate, and sometimes even celebrate, losing. I don't understand why. Seinfeld, the American comedian, puts it as well as anybody when he describes coming second as being 'first loser'.

My abiding hope is that, in some small, humble and modest way, by successfully crossing the Pacific Ocean in a rowing boat, I will have inspired just a few of my compatriots to push themselves to the limit, and to show that, contrary to the modern consensus, this remains a winning nation.

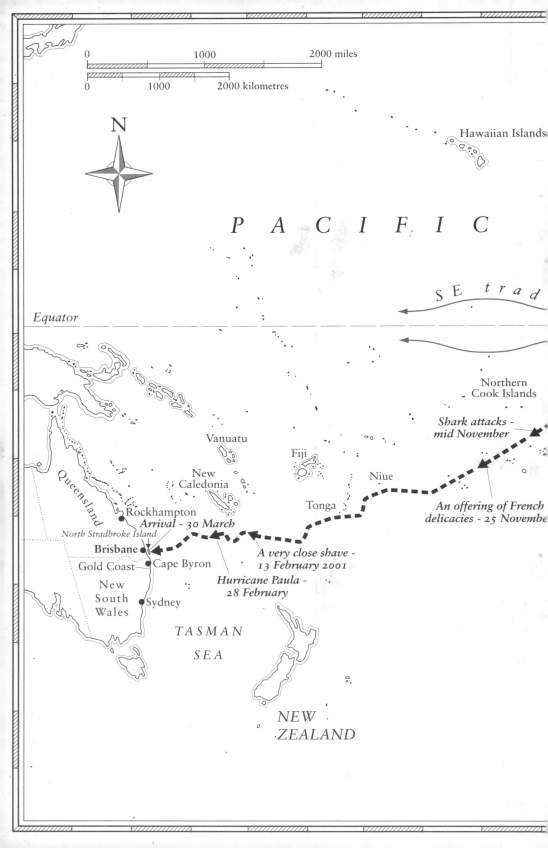